Genealogies of Political Modernity

Political Theologies

Edited by Ward Blanton (University of Kent), Arthur Bradley (Lancaster University), Michael Dillon (Lancaster University) and Yvonne Sherwood (University of Kent)

This series explores the past, present and future of political theology. Taking its cue from the ground-breaking work of such figures as Derrida, Agamben, Badiou and Žižek, it seeks to provide a forum for new research on the theologico-political nexus, including cutting-edge monographs, edited collections and translations of classic works. By privileging creative, interdisciplinary and experimental work that resists easy categorization, this series not only re-assets the timeliness of political theology in our epoch but also seeks to extend political theological reflection into new territory: law, economics, finance, technology, media, film and art. In *Bloomsbury Political Theologies*, we seek to reinvent the ancient problem of political theology for the twenty-first century.

International Advisory Board

Agata Bielik-Robson (University of Nottingham)
Howard Caygill (Kingston University)
Simon Critchley (New School of Social Research)
Roberto Esposito (Scuola Normale Superiore)
Elettra Stimilli (Sapienza University of Rome)
Miguel Vatter (University of New South Wales)

Titles in the series:

Massimo Cacciari, *The Withholding Power: An Essay on Political Theology*
Michel de Certeau, *The Weakness of Belief*
Charlie Gere, *Unnatural Theology*
Andrew Gibson, *Modernity and the Political Fix*
Elettra Stimilli, *Debt and Guilt*
Thomas Lynch, *Apocalyptic Political Theology*

Genealogies of Political Modernity

Antonio Cerella

BLOOMSBURY ACADEMIC
LONDON • NEW YORK • OXFORD • NEW DELHI • SYDNEY

BLOOMSBURY ACADEMIC
Bloomsbury Publishing Plc
50 Bedford Square, London, WC1B 3DP, UK
1385 Broadway, New York, NY 10018, USA
29 Earlsfort Terrace, Dublin 2, Ireland

BLOOMSBURY, BLOOMSBURY ACADEMIC and the Diana logo
are trademarks of Bloomsbury Publishing Plc

First published in Great Britain 2020
This paperback edition published in 2021

Copyright © Antonio Cerella, 2020

Antonio Cerella has asserted his right under the Copyright, Designs and
Patents Act, 1988, to be identified as Author of this work.

For legal purposes the Acknowledgements on p. ix constitute an
extension of this copyright page.

Cover design by Maria Rajka
Cover image: The Tree of Life, c.1310 (tempera on panel), Pacino di Buonaguida, (fl.1303–39) /
Galleria dell'Accademia & Museo degli Strumenti Musicali, Florence, Tuscany,
Italy / Photo © Raffaello Bencini / Bridgeman Images

All rights reserved. No part of this publication may be reproduced or
transmitted in any form or by any means, electronic or mechanical, including
photocopying, recording, or any information storage or retrieval system,
without prior permission in writing from the publishers.

Bloomsbury Publishing Plc does not have any control over, or responsibility for,
any third-party websites referred to or in this book. All internet addresses given
in this book were correct at the time of going to press. The author and publisher regret
any inconvenience caused if addresses have changed or sites have ceased
to exist, but can accept no responsibility for any such changes.

A catalogue record for this book is available from the British Library.

A catalog record for this book is available from the Library of Congress.

ISBN:	HB:	978-1-3500-7946-5
	PB:	978-1-3500-7947-2
	ePDF:	978-1-3500-7945-8
	eBook:	978-1-3500-7948-9

Series: Political Theologies

Typeset by Integra Software Services Pvt. Ltd.

To find out more about our authors and books visit www.bloomsbury.com
and sign up for our newsletters.

To the memory of my friend,
Massimiliano Caruso
(1980–2018)

Contents

List of Illustrations	viii
Acknowledgements	ix
Introduction: The Walking Tree	1

Part 1: On Sovereignty

1	*Rex Sacrorum*: On the Origins and Evolution of Sovereign Power	17
2	Space and Sovereignty: A Reverse Perspective	45

Part 2: Political Theologies

3	Encounters at the End of a World: Max Weber, Carl Schmitt and the Tyranny of Values	71
4	Until the End of the World: René Girard, Carl Schmitt, and the Origins of Violence	93
5	Religion and Political Form: Schmitt *contra* Habermas	117

Part 3: History and Archaeology

6	The Myth of Origin: Archaeology and History in the Work of Giorgio Agamben and René Girard	145
7	*Imago Mortis, Imago Dei*: An Archaeology of Political Sacrifice	169

Notes	192
Bibliography	241
Name Index	255
Subject Index	258

List of Illustrations

1   Funeral Effigy of Henry VII, 1509. (*Westminster Abbey, London. © Dean and Chapter of Westminster*)   25

2   Bronze Sestertius with a Portrait of Antoninus Pius (138–61). (*Musée des beaux-arts, Lyon. © Photo Alain Basset*)   29

3   Masaccio, Saints Jerome and John the Baptist, 1428/1429. (*The National Gallery, London. © The National Gallery*)   52

4   Masolino da Panicale, Pope Liberio Founding the Basilica di S. Maria ad Nives, 1423/1428. (*Museo di Capodimonte, Naples. © Photo Scala, Florence – courtesy of the Ministero Beni e Attività Culturali*)   53

5   Masolino da Panicale, Annunciation (detail), 1423/1424. (*Church of San Clemente, Rome. © Photo Scala, Florence*)   55

6   Brook Taylor, The Visual Pyramid from *New Principles of Linear Perspective*, 1719. (*The Max Planck Institute for the History of Science, Berlin. © The Max Planck Institute for the History of Science*)   62

7   Anthropogenesis: A Figurative Interpretation   165

8   Archaeological Regression: A Figurative Interpretation   166

9   Lodovico Cardi (called 'il Cigoli'), The Stoning of Stephen, 1597. (*Galleria Palatina, Palazzo Pitti, Florence. © Bridgeman Images*)   174

10   Martyrdom: A Theologico-Political Interpretation   177

11   The 'Dual Unity' of the Ancient World: A Figurative Interpretation   182

12   The 'Unitary Dualism' of Christianity: A Figurative Interpretation   183

13   Hobbes's System: A Figurative Interpretation   185

14   The Biopolitical Threshold: A Figurative Interpretation   189

Acknowledgements

There are many people to whom I owe a debt of gratitude for their generosity and assistance over the past few years of my English life. My thoughts go to the editors of this series for having supported the publication of the present volume. Special thanks, however, are due to Arthur Bradley and to the friends of the 'Fraternitas Academica Lancastriensis', Mick Dillon and Charlie Gere, from whom I learned much more than I can express here in words. I would also like to thank Riccardo Baldissone, Fred Dallmayr, Michael Marder and Thomas Sheehan who, through their work and their intellectual honesty, have been a constant source of motivation for my research.

As usually happens in life, 'disorientation' and 'distance' are the only dimensions that allow us to glimpse the authentic meaning of our existence, of its origins and future potentialities. Today, more than ever, the indissoluble bond with my old friends, with whom I have shared dreams and ideas, reveals itself to me in the form of an absence. I would like, therefore, to thank Alessandro Calboli, Germano Crociani, Carlo Di Cicco, Donato Di Fonzo, Luca Di Risio, Emanuele Felice, Francesco Marzella, Andrea Menna, Francesco Menna, Alessio Mucci, Flavio Rocchio, Antonio Sorgente, Ferdinando Tupone and Alfredo Varrati. *Maximum bonum est amicitia.*

Special thanks go to my wife, Giulia, who accompanied me around Europe for more than a decade, illuminating my path with her smile and silences. *Anche tu sei l'amore ...*

I dedicate this book to the memory of my dear friend Massimiliano: you taught me, through my pain, that presence is invisible and forgetfulness impossible ... *al panfilo ...*

PERMISSIONS

Acknowledgement is gratefully made to Palgrave Macmillan, Routledge, Sage, Cambridge University Press for the permission to reproduce, in an altered form and with corrections of a few *lapsus calami*, the essays which form the basis of Chapters 2, 3, 4 and 5.

Acknowledgements

Grateful acknowledgement is likewise made for the permission to reproduce extracts from the following works:

'Die Kunst und der Raum' by Martin Heidegger. In *Gesamtausgabe* Bd. 13: Aus der Erfahrung des Denkens, edited by H. Heidegger. Frankfurt am Main: Vittorio Klostermann, 1983, p. 207. Reprinted by permission of the publisher.

'Oktavheft G (II, 2, December 6, 1917)' by Franz Kafka. In *Nachgelassene Schriften und Fragmente II*, edited by J. Schillemeit. Frankfurt am Main: S. Fisher, 1992, p. 5. Reprinted by permission of the publisher.

'The Politics' by Aristotle. In *The Politics and the Constitution of Athens*, edited by S. Everson. Cambridge University Press, 1996, p. 31. Reprinted by permission of the publisher.

Hath your raising up of the earth into heaven, brought men to that confidence, that they build new towers or threaten God againe? Or do they out of this motion of the earth conclude, that there is no hell, or deny the punishment of sin?

John Donne, *Ignatius His Conclave* (1611)

Introduction: The Walking Tree

I

The Portuguese writer Fernando Pessoa once wrote that 'the village is larger than the city' because you can see 'more of the world from there' than you can from anywhere else. In this small world, the familiar and intermittent sounds of bells dictate the time of our childhood; a stroll through its worn alleys makes us imagine the echo of our ancestors' steps; the tired light coming from an old window suggests the lingering presence of lost loves. The village is larger than the city, and even than the modern metropolis, because, as Pessoa writes, in it 'I am the size of what I see, and not the size of my height.'[1] To be the size of what we see: there is an abyssal truth in these words. Within this form of life, the mantle of representation fits perfectly on the shoulders of existence. Here in the village, according to Pessoa, seeing and being coincide.

The contemporary world rests on a decisive reversal of these two experiences. Today the human is no longer the living being who has sight; if anything, she is the seeing creature who pictures life. Her historical existence has thus become a form of 'totalizing visualization'. This fracture that traverses our situational, corporeal and sensitive experience of space is what we call 'globalization'. When Heidegger, in some memorable pages of his *Contributions to Philosophy*, speaks of the emergence of the 'gigantic', he portrays in all its power this inversion between seeing and feeling, representation and experience:

> The gigantic is ... not something quantitative that commences when a relatively high number is attained ... The gigantic is grounded in the decisiveness and exceptionlessness of 'calculation' and is rooted in a reaching out of subjective representation to the whole of beings. ... [Thus] the gigantic manifests the greatness of the *subjectum* which is certain of itself

and which builds everything upon its own representing and producing. ... The gigantic brings about the completion of the basic metaphysical position of the human being, a position which proceeds to invert its form and to interpret all 'goals' and 'values' ('ideals' and 'ideas') as the 'expression' and offspring of mere 'eternal' 'life' in itself.[2]

The age of the gigantic or, as we commonly say today, of globalization is thus a form of representation shaped in the mould of modern metaphysics: to live is to be dragged on the surface of the world designed by the will to power; to see is to constantly represent oneself as this potency in act. It is no coincidence, then, that the ideal-typical figures of our age are the towers that dominate the skylines of global cities and from which the subject masters the uniform mass of her creations; or, perhaps even more, the drones that, flying over the earth's surface, project into the human eye the image of her newfound divinity. Height, Prometheus's cross, has become the most intimate dimension of the new global subject.

The essays gathered here can be read as tortuous pathways that lead from the global back to its historical roots: the crisis of modernity, of its political space and philosophical categories. Genealogies *of* thinking and *in* thinking, the forthcoming chapters provide interpretative hypotheses about the origins, evolution and crisis of modernity through the analysis of some of its fundamental categories: space and representation, sovereignty and sacrifice, archaeology and history. Before discussing their content, however, it is necessary to clarify the epistemological assumptions on which the present contributions rest.

II

In the preface to his *Genealogy of Morality* (1887), Nietzsche opposes an English or 'blue' genealogical hypothesis to a historically grounded or 'grey' one. The error that he imputes to his former friend Paul Rée, an advocate of the first position, is that of introducing into the genealogical inquiry tautological explanations such as this one: 'Since the human is an ethical animal, altruism and morality would be the origin and the purpose of her evolution.' For Nietzsche, this kind of analysis would be nothing but a type of

Introduction: *The Walking Tree*   3

historical metaphysics that essentializes the present, projecting it into the past and thus 'looking vainly into the distance as in the blue yonder'.[3] To explain something genealogically means, on the contrary, investigating the conditions of possibility that allow the emergence of phenomena, which is to say to study, as Nietzsche puts it, 'that which can be documented, which can actually be confirmed and has actually existed'.[4] But one wonders, what are the historical *conditions* that make a phenomenon *possible*?

Nietzsche clarifies his position in paragraph 12 of the second essay. Darwinists and other blue genealogists do bad genealogy because they tend to collapse the difference between *origin* and *purpose*: they usually turn the purpose of a phenomenon into the reason for its historical emergence. A heuristic assumption – namely the notion of teleological development – is thus superimposed onto the historical plane – that is on the origin of a phenomenon. But, for Nietzsche, who writes polemically against Darwinism, the function of an organ is unable to account for that organ's origin: 'No matter how perfectly you have understood the *usefulness* of any physiological organ ... you have not yet thereby grasped how it emerged.'[5] It is our logical apparatus that imputes an evolutionary direction to a phenomenon (be it an institution, an organ, or a tradition), thus linking the function it performs to its historical origin. However, the 'origin of the emergence of a thing and its ultimate usefulness, its practical application and incorporation into a system of ends' – Nietzsche concludes – 'are *toto coelo* separate'.[6] But what exactly is the gap that separates the origin of phenomena from their purpose?

What agitates the historical flow and the development of events is the fact that life, or the whole organic world, is a field of opposing tensions and forces, and everything that occurs in it consists of '*overpowering, dominating*, and in their turn, overpowering and dominating consist of re-interpretation, adjustment, in the process of which their former "meaning" [*Sinn*] and "purpose" must necessarily be obscured or completely obliterated'.[7] The meaning and the historical development of life forms are products of ever-changing tensions and power relations that cannot simply be traced back to our ideological position (as Paul Rée believes) or to our teleological perspective (i.e. as for Darwin, to the adaptive functions that life develops in relation to the changeability of the environment). And in fact, as we shall see, it is precisely the question of the *source* of historical change that Nietzsche problematizes.

4   *Genealogies of Political Modernity*

But if it is neither the original purpose nor its absolute absence (i.e. chance that forces life to live) that brings out a historical phenomenon, what explains its origin? What logic governs the disorder of things? This is how Nietzsche articulates his position:

> Every purpose and use is just a *sign* that the will to power has achieved mastery over something less powerful, and has impressed upon it its own idea [*Sinn*] of a use function; and the whole history of a 'thing', an organ, a tradition can to this extent be a continuous chain of signs, continually revealing new interpretations and adaptations, the causes of which need not be connected even amongst themselves, but rather sometimes just follow and replace one another at random. The 'development' of a thing, a tradition, an organ is therefore certainly not its *progressus* towards a goal, still less is it a logical *progressus* … instead it is a succession of more or less profound, more or less mutually independent processes of subjugation exacted on the thing, added to this the resistances encountered every time, the attempted transformations for the purpose of defence and reaction, and the results, too, of successful countermeasures.[8]

For Nietzsche, the origin and the evolution of phenomena are the result of an interpenetration of actions and reactions, transformations and resistances triggered by the will to power – life – that pervades its own manifestations – that is the multiple forms of life. From *our* historical perspective, then, these transformations can only appear to be *random* because, dazzled by metaphysical systems, we are not (yet) able to understand their 'logic'. But life is permeated by the will to power, and its 'purpose' is not ours. Preservation and adaptation are only some of its secondary processes. Species are born and die. The extinction of some forms of life is not merely caused by problems of adaptation – that is by a logic internal to the subject. Rather these changes are signs that the disappearance of particular entities favours the expansion of the will to power in the universe – that is according to a logic external to the subject. The 'purpose' of the will to power is continuous actualization – *eigentlichen Aktivität* ('actual activity'), Nietzsche calls it. It is the coexistence of adaptation and destruction for the sake of guaranteeing the actualization of a more potent and purer power: 'Even the partial *reduction in usefulness*, decay and degeneration, loss of meaning [*Sinn*] and functional purpose, in short death, make up the conditions of true *progressus*: always appearing, as it does, in the form of the will and way to *greater power* and always emerging victorious at the cost of countless smaller forces.'[9]

Despite their polemical intent, Nietzsche's theoretical assumptions end up replicating the logical structure of his intellectual adversaries. In fact his genealogical hypothesis rests on a functionalist logic, whose antimoralistic purpose escapes us nonetheless: life is power, which is the origin and purpose of its own development and vitality. Yet Nietzsche's historical-genealogical method fails to interpret life in its own terms but requires a heuristic crutch – the will to power – to understand its meaning (or the lack thereof). The origin of phenomena is thus interpreted through a hypothesis that remains (for now) unintelligible to the common person. In this tautology, which is reversed but symmetrical to that of the moralist Paul Rée, the will to power is what lies before and after the development of phenomena. In a certain sense, Nietzsche does nothing but reverse Darwin's doctrine of absolute chance and replace it with the idea of absolute potency; and this is the genealogical root of Foucault's notion of power, of Schmitt's concept of the political and of Agamben's idea of *archē* – in other words, of that mode of thinking that attributes the genesis of the *conditions of possibility* of historicity to an original energy – power, violence, language.

Although the notion of the will to power could be interpreted as a hypothesis – Nietzsche calls it a 'theory' (*Theorie*) – useful for liberating the historical course from ideological and teleological constructions, it still remains an unprovable assumption, which must be accepted a priori. This means that the historical operation always presupposes a purpose (teleology), a function (adaptation or preservation) or an arcanum (the will to power, the political, the power of language, etc.). The historical origin of phenomena thus remains unreachable without some kind of meta-historical presupposition. Without this heuristic prosthesis, genesis and genealogy, the historical event and its reconstruction would never fit together.

The genealogical approach used in the following pages, though it takes on board some Nietzschean epistemological suggestions, rests on a different strategy: to analyse the historical origin of some modern political phenomena through an intrinsically historical method. If we really want to reckon with the death of God – speaking more directly, if we want to interpret history in its absolute immanence – we must free the historical course from theological–

metaphysical residues but, at the same time, we need not flatten it on an image of the human construed as a tangle of biological instincts or utilitarian drives. To think the historical operation without the help of a meta-historical support, this is the challenge faced in the book (especially in Chapters 1, 2 and 7). This means, in the first place, renouncing the categories of 'purpose' and 'direction' as related to historical processes (besides, these notions had been already criticized by Nietzsche). But, even more importantly, it means denying the distinction between genesis and genealogy, or between the 'real', historical origin of phenomena and its artificial historiographic representation. Indeed, from my perspective, as we shall see, the historiographical openness of the past depends not only on the manner in which we interrogate it – that is on the method – but also, and even more, on the nature of the historical object.

History, it has been said many times and by many authors, is not only a mass of documents and monuments that, presenting themselves before us, require interpretation. The past is not simply a set of artefacts, texts and works, but a symbolic network of correspondences between these traces and their meanings. As Heidegger wrote in some of his most beautiful pages, what we call 'the past' is, essentially, something invisible: the web of meaningful relationships that gave life and significance to today's remains (objects, texts and monuments). Indeed, objects and artefacts might resist time, but their world, that is the totality of the involvement that animated them through symbolic relationships, 'is no longer'.[10] To reconstruct the past through its remains, then, means representing something invisible: 'What the historian is in search of' – Ernst Cassirer has written from a similar but opposite perspective to Heidegger's – 'is ... the materialization of the spirit of a former age'.[11]

Here, then, we encounter another sense of the historical operation according to which the imagined is nothing but the moving real, and the genesis of historical phenomena cannot but coincide with their historiographic representation. In the words of Benedetto Croce, historical judgement is always already the 'historicization of a fact', as much as history is, for this very reason, the 'determination of the character of a fact'.[12] In other words, the historical operation is a conscious act of self-positioning with respect to the past and of its *re*presentation; and the past is a network of significant and imaginative relationships through which a social group, a civilization, a nation, a village and so on had interpreted its existence in relation to its own world. From this perspective, then, history appears as an ontogenetic dynamic: historical self-representation is the human search for meaning, and the way of presenting the forms of representation of the past is our possibility to exist as a real community, to shed a new light on the present and on the future.

This historiographical approach is based on a specific ontological vision of the human, which is here conceived of as a representing being, an *ens repraesentans*. The American philosopher Arthur C. Danto is perhaps the one who, beyond all others, articulated in a very clear way this position, according to which not only history but also 'the entirety of philosophy is somehow connected with the concept of representation'. Humans are, according to him, *entia repraesentantia*,

> beings that represent the world ... our individual histories are the histories of our representations, and how they change in the course of our lives ... representations form systems that constitute our picture of the world ... human history is the story of how this system of representations changes over time ... the world and our system of representations are interdependent in that sometimes we change the world to fit our representations, and sometimes we change our representations to fit the world.[13]

In order not to fall into error, it is worth pointing out immediately that the notion of representation is not understood here in the strongly negative sense that critics of modernity, from Heidegger to Foucault, have attributed to it. Representation is here thought of in its semantic and etymological richness, as what makes present, brings to mind, symbolizes, reproduces, displays, represents, shows, sets in view and stages the drama of human existence. The representing operation is that which, through this range of possibilities, realizes the connection between the invisible and the visible, community and individual, past and present, history and historiography. To put it briefly, representation is our sensory mediation, through which we present ourselves in the world.

The second point to be clarified is that the 'systems' of representation should not be thought of as closed structures or bounded spheres but rather as *constellations of meanings*, always changing and stratified at various levels, which orbit around what Schmitt has called 'central domains' (*Zentralgebiete*), that is models of epochal self-representation (the 'theological', the 'metaphysical', the 'scientific', etc.) and within which other models of representation meet and collide.[14]

Nonetheless, the approach just presented runs the risk of reaffirming an essentialist ontology similar to that of biologism, but of an opposite sign. What is maintained here, however, is exactly the contrary: the human being has *no essence*, and this is so because she is constantly modelled and reshaped by her own representations. The human is therefore a creature *in fieri*, in the process of becoming, because she is exposed to the power of her visions and metaphysical creations. In the words of Hannah Arendt:

> Not the capabilities of man, but the constellation which orders their mutual relationships can and does change historically. Such changes can best be observed in the changing self-interpretations of man throughout history, which, though they may be quite irrelevant for the ultimate 'what' of human nature, are still the briefest and most succinct witnesses to the spirit of whole epochs.[15]

This reinterpretation of history seems to rest, at least in part, on the structure of Cassirer's philosophy of symbolic forms, namely on the premise that the human is a symbolic animal (*animal symbolicum*). My emphasis on the notion of representation, however, wants to highlight the *dynamic* and *immanent* aspects of the historical development. To recall Weber's powerful image, history is here thought of as 'the meaningless infinity of the world process'. Nevertheless, humans never tire of throwing new intellectual light on this process and of searching for new meanings. While the symbol can and has in fact been interpreted as an instrument of historical evasion and suspension (think of Eliade's concept of hierophany or of Jung's transhistorical archetypes), the notion of representation, on the contrary, presupposes a continuous self-crossing and historical self-rethinking. Faced with a real or imaginary construction, with a practical problem or a political challenge, humans question themselves by reimagining their position within the web of power relations that surround them. In this sense, representation, by necessity, never happens in a vacuum: it always calls another representation into question, reoccupying, overcoming or modifying the previous one. And this dynamic of occupations and reoccupations, inventions and restorations does not disappear even in the so-called age of technology. On the contrary, technology always requires an 'image-maker' (*eikonopoios*) – that is humans' imaginative participation to their own self-representation: we, too, *are* the eyes of the drone, to recall the figure discussed at the beginning of this introduction. The age of globalization or of 'the world picture', as Heidegger aptly called it, powerfully pushes us towards a very particular form of representation: deciding how to live it, occupy it and reimagine its future is the immense task that lies ahead of us.

III

The essays gathered here can be read as variations on the same theme – iridescent images of the same subject in the manner of Monet's water lilies – or as escape routes that, starting from the same origin, cross at certain points, then open themselves up towards the future. The guiding thread that runs through the chapters and unites them is precisely the notion of representation. In the two contributions to Part One (titled 'On Sovereignty'), this notion is addressed from a purely political perspective. The first chapter, in particular, analyses the historical and conceptual relationship between sovereign power and its representation. Generally, political representation is thought of as the activity of making citizens' opinions, interests and voices present in public arenas and in policy-making processes. And this activity is usually traced back to the formation of indirect democracies (also called 'representative'), following the logic of equating 'function' with 'origin' (as discussed before). By tracing the genealogy of the different interpretations and representations of power, the chapter demonstrates how the 'representative function' was originally the expression of a sacrificial economy. Royal doubles or representations – which (in physical form to begin with, metaphorically later) have characterized Western political history from ancient Rome until the late Christian Middle Ages – performed the function of protecting the body politic. They were in fact the sacrificeable images of power.

The second chapter explores the relationship between political space and its representation from a reversed perspective: that of the influence of art on political theory. The chapter highlights how Renaissance art, with its modern linear perspective, created the conditions of possibility for the modern political space to be conceived of in its geometric and isotropic purity.

Through a rereading of some key modern works and texts, from Masaccio's paintings to some lesser-known works by Thomas Hobbes such as *De corpore*, the chapter reconstructs the way in which the complex of references and reciprocal influences between art and political thought opened an ontological and epistemic space where the modern oculocentric paradigm realized itself.

The three essays that make up the Part Two (titled 'Political Theologies') focus on the conceptual nexus between transcendence and immanence, ethics and politics, that is on those theoretical perspectives that conceive of the polity as a community. The first of these essays, for instance, explores the relationship between the sphere of values and the sphere of the political through the work of two influential figures: Max Weber and Carl Schmitt. The chapter shows how the crisis of modernity – and of political mediation – forms the backdrop against which these two thinkers have shaped their concepts and ideas. In fact, for Weber as for Schmitt, the question of the foundation of values is not in itself ontological. Rather it is a historical problem, which translates into an ontological one when the process of rationalization–secularization has passed a certain critical threshold: that of modernity. Yet, as the chapter also argues, between the Weberian 'ethics of responsibility' and the Schmittian 'neutralization of values', there is an abyss crossed by an ideology: the political.

The next essay, Chapter 4, attempts to trace a theoretical genealogy of political violence – a history of its evolution and containment – by analysing the work of Schmitt and of another radical thinker René Girard. This exploration takes the form of a backward journey into the field of what we might call political theodicy, whereby the analysis mainly focuses on Schmitt's and Girard's conceptualization of political order, especially in relation to the problem of globalization and evil. In effect, the contemporary age can be *literally* described as 'apocalyptic', provided that one reverts to the ancient meaning of *apokalupsis* as a revealing or uncovering of all the contradictions that, having matured during modernity, have ended up exploding in the age of globality. The chapter also shows how the work of Schmitt and Girard might help us to reconceptualize the chaotic multitude and the social undifferentiation triggered by the dynamics of globalization.

The final contribution in this second part focuses on the concept of post-secularity. Made famous by the German philosopher Jürgen Habermas, this notion can be interpreted as a normative response to the phenomenon of the 'return of religion' to the public sphere, which sparked a new debate over the intricate nexus between transcendence and power. The chapter problematizes Habermas's analytical–normative proposal by seeking to frame the relation between the 'sacred' and the 'political' in the context of international politics. On this basis, the analysis also tries to overcome conceptually the dialectic of inclusion–exclusion that shaped the modern form of the state (by now hopelessly 'deformed' by the dynamics of globalization) and to suggest a few alternative lines of reflection on the role of religious and cultural pluralism in Western democracies.

Part Three (titled 'History and Archeology') consists of two chapters that present respectively two ways of interpreting and representing the past. Chapter 6 discusses the archaeological methods developed by Agamben and Girard. Although different in style and philosophical breath, the two thinkers are in divergent but tacit agreement as to the nature of the sacred and how to analyse the traces it has left in the Western political order. Girard's and Agamben's narratives are like two parallels that can never meet, or like the positive image and the negative image of the same philosophical film – one that seeks to capture the infinity of historical process in its foundational, paradigmatic moments. Nonetheless, despite their attempt to evade the problem of ontological anchoring through a demystification of the notion of origin, both Agamben and Girard end up conceptualizing 'history' as a quasi-deterministic and transcendental mechanism, a sort of emanation of their ontological and philosophical apparatus.

Chapter 7, which closes this last part of the volume, offers an archaeology of political sacrifice. It shows how the changing functions and shifting meanings of this practice are the fruit of a constant dynamic of semantic and metaphysical reoccupation carried out by political actors. In this sense, there is a close *structural* relationship between martyrdom and political power, that is between the act of self-sacrifice and the dominant political and metaphysical systems in which this act is inscribed. To understand the radical changes undertaken by the narratives and practices of martyrdom (e.g. from the sacrifice of one's life to the sacrifice for one's own country), it is, then, crucial to explore this dialectic between political power and the forms of exception that power allows, protects or generates and that constitutes the hidden matrix of these tremendous shifts of perspective.

12   *Genealogies of Political Modernity*

The example of martyrdom exemplifies the onto-epistemic vision discussed earlier: an event such as martyrdom can actualize, reinvent or illuminate a particular metaphysical conception. In this sense, the manifestation of a phenomenon is in the eye of the beholder; but the beholder, too, is the eye of a metaphysical worldview.

IV

The archetypal figure of genealogy is the tree. This plant is considered an image of power in movement, of the Whole that repeats itself within each significant fragment and of life that continuously branches out in its manifestations.[16] No wonder, then, that we encounter multiple variations of this mythical ideogram in many archaic cultures and religions. According to an ancient Indian tradition reported in the Atharva Veda, for example, the entire cosmos is an inverted giant tree whose roots penetrate the sky. Similarly, in the cabalistic tradition of the Zohar, the tree of life is described as a reversed plant illuminated by the sun, which extends from above downwards. We encounter a similar figure also in Norse mythology: Yggdrasil is an immense ash tree which is the centre of the cosmos and whose branches extend far into the heavens. And Mayan cosmology, too, envisaged an axis called *wacah chan* ('the world tree'), whose 'trunk went through the Middleworld; its roots plunged to the nadir in the watery Underworld region of the Otherworld, and its branches soared to the zenith in the highest layer of the heavenly region of the Otherworld'.[17]

In late antiquity, the Christian community was also represented as a 'tree of life', *arbor vitae*; its foundation and trunk consisted in the body of Christ, from whose sacrifice radiated the history of *christianitas* with its saints and demons, martyrs and hermits, churches and monasteries. This most powerful image, in which Christ is life and limbs, body and blood, lymph and foundation of the community of believers, served as a model for various historical genealogies: from the dynastic ones aimed at reconstructing parental relations and lineages to the more philosophically grounded genealogies that, through the study of linguistic, social and economic ties, have tried to determine the crucial offshoots of those historical junctures that have given shape to time and power.

Yet this archetypal image also presents some conceptual limitations. Taking up again the critical observations raised by Ernst Pulgram in the field of comparative linguistics, it could be argued that our view of the original purity of phenomena is in large measure due to 'the optical illusion foisted upon us by the genealogical-tree scheme'.[18] The image of the tree in fact presupposes – and imposes – the idea of an original event or root that determines both the direction (high > low or low > high) and the form (ramification) of the temporal development of our investigation. History and morphology thus remain conceptually caged in this archetypal form.

The image presented here is similar to this ideogram but at the same time different from it. To genealogy understood as an exclusively diachronic method is here juxtaposed another heuristic dimension: historical space. From my perspective, the tree of history grows not only in time – from the trunk upwards, to its branches – but also spatially. In the pages that follow the reader is therefore invited to imagine the historical flow as one of those 'walking trees' that can be encountered in the warm and tropical climates of the Pacific islands – one of those organisms that possess strength in the trunk but dynamism in the suspended roots, which, sinking into the ground, determine the organism's movement and continuously change its appearance and figure. The development of such trees is not determined simply by an original force that pushes them to grow upwards but also by the inevitable and unfathomable contingencies – wind, exposure to light, slope of the ground – that give them the power to take root in the four directions and that enable them to move, albeit slowly.

From this metaphor emerges a vision of history as an expression of a rooting in the past and in its conditions of possibility, which is, however, constantly agitated by the metaphysical and imaginative space that surrounds it and which also influences its direction, constantly transforming its appearance. Form and direction, morphology and history are not merely the result of the power of an original energy, which can be explored by retracing the various evolutionary and genealogical phases backwards. In time as well as in space, historical life is both rooted and self-uprooting; it is partly decided and partly undecidable, because its substance is living form in movement.

Thus we are rooted, yet unimagined. In this consists the beauty and tragedy of our human condition.

Part One

On Sovereignty

1

Rex Sacrorum: On the Origins and Evolution of Sovereign Power

Priscis ergo temporibus, antequam fasti a Cn. Flavio scriba invitis Patribus in omnium notitiam proderentur, pontifici minori haec provincia delegabatur, ut novae lunae primum observaret aspectum visamque regi sacrificulo nuntiaret.

Macrobius, *Saturnalia* i, 15.9[1]

In what has been defined as one of the more impenetrable pieces of prose in any modern language, namely the epistemo-critical prologue to his *Ursprung des deutschen Trauerspiel*, Walter Benjamin writes: 'The term origin [*Ursprung*] is not intended to describe the process by which the existent come into being, but rather to describe that which emerges from the process of becoming and disappearance.'[2] For Benjamin, original phenomena are endowed with a dual nature or 'rhythm'. As he explains, 'there takes place in every original phenomenon [*Ursprungsphänomen*] *a determination of the form in which the idea will constantly confront the historical world* ... This dialectic shows singularity and repetition [*Einmaligkeit und Wiederholung*] to be conditioned by one another in all essentials'.[3] Here the original moment is not understood simply as an absolute beginning but rather as a presence that lies latent in the phenomena that it originated. In this sense, 'origin is origination',[4] that is an energy that constantly forces the historical matter to reinvent its forms or, better said, the origin is itself the shapeless matter that gives life to historical forms through the drawing force that determines the always incomplete dialectic between original repetition and historical singularity. The origin is, in short, a sort of black hole that tends to reabsorb, though never completely, the historical energy that it produced. The task of the researcher, in Benjamin's view, should be that of revealing the 'innermost structure' of an original phenomenon, thus bringing to light its 'primordial essence'.

But how is it possible to decide on the originality of historical phenomena? In fact, as Benjamin points out, not all 'primitive facts' can and must be considered original. How can we discriminate, then, between primitive phenomena and original phenomena? According to the German scholar, the latter bear special signs of recognition, the marks of what he calls 'authenticity', for, as he puts it, 'every proof of origin must be prepared to face up to the question of its authenticity'.[5] For Benjamin, the authenticity of phenomena is their 'hallmark of origin', a sort of 'spark' ignited by the friction between the moment of emergence and its repetition – a revealing sign that the researcher should seek to trace. Authenticity is the beating heart of that 'maelstrom in the stream of becoming' of which Benjamin speaks in his magnum opus.

In this chapter, sovereignty is considered to be an original phenomenon in these Benjaminian terms. For sovereignty, as we shall see, can be understood as an original tension characterized by permanence and change, a tension that goes through the entire political history of the West. It bears in itself those marks of primordiality and authenticity that make it an ever present and yet transformative historical force, a future past, a power with two faces: one visible and one invisible. And it is the dark, 'nocturnal' side of sovereignty that this chapter seeks to explore.

It is surprising that Giorgio Agamben, one of the most acute and sensitive interpreters of Benjamin's work, has described sovereignty as a sort of ahistorical and ontological dispositive. As he writes in the first volume of the *Homo Sacer* project, 'the inclusion of bare life in the political realm constitutes the original – if concealed – nucleus of sovereign power. *It can even be said that the production of a biopolitical body is the original activity of sovereign power*'.[6] For Agamben, in other words, the sovereign gesture of inclusive exclusion of bare life in the polis would conceal the original nucleus of power, its 'arcane ontology'. In his genealogies, Agamben returned several times to the enigma of sovereign power. And, in the last volume of his project, he traced the structure of the exception back to 'first ontology' and to the 'event of language':

> In the course of the study, the structure of the exception that had been defined with respect to bare life has been revealed more generally to constitute in every sphere the structure of the *archē*, in the juridico-political tradition

as much as in ontology. In fact, one cannot understand the dialectic of the foundation that defines Western ontology, from Aristotle onward, if one does not understand that it functions as an exception ... The strategy is always the same: something is divided, excluded, and pushed to the bottom, and precisely through this exclusion, it is included as *archē* and foundation. It is possible, however, that the mechanism of the exception is constitutively connected to the event of language that coincides with anthropogenesis. ... That is to say, the *ex-ceptio*, the inclusive exclusion of the real from the *logos* and in the *logos* is the originary structure of the event of language.[7]

For Agamben, the logic of the exception is the reflection of an *appropriatio primaeva*, an 'initial appropriation': the event of language. As a sort of anthropogenetic Big Bang, this event reverberates in all spheres of human life and knowledge: from language to politics, from metaphysics to history, from ontology to law.

This chapter takes a different research direction. For I believe that it is fascinating, yet conceptually sterile, to think of an original ontology that determines, and operates in, multiple onto-epistemic domains.[8] No doubt the search for this theoretical Holy Grail, a sort of *archi-dispositif* ('ur-dispositive') capable of unveiling the dynamics of power in all its ramifications, is one of the most typical philosophical signatures of modernity.[9] But the assimilation or amalgamation of ontologically different phenomena (language, art, politics) into one and the same epistemic region seems particularly problematic, especially when one enters the territory of the political – which, as Schmitt himself pointed out, is a 'groundless ground', an *existential* intensity without *essential* scope.[10]

What follows can be read as a genealogical investigation of the autonomous origin of the political and of its representative form – sovereignty. The aim of this account is not to criticize previous genealogies, but rather to show that there is an intimate connection between modes of representation and forms of violence (specifically the political) and that changes in the ritualization of violence modify the modes of political representation. In Benjamin's terms, the 'sovereign constellation' is here understood to be as an energy that combines its regions and holds together and moves its boundaries. What changes historically is not the constellation itself, but rather the assembling of its matter. The present chapter tries to reconstruct the hidden and arcane plot –

20   *Genealogies of Political Modernity*

the mechanisms, if you wish – of those changes and permanences, singularities and repetitions, which represent the original force of sovereign power.

The representation of power

Representation is a fundamental – if not decisive – aspect of power. It is no coincidence that Carl Schmitt devoted the densest pages of his academically more sophisticated work, *Verfassungslehre* (1928), to the problem of *repraesentatio*. According to the German jurist, representation is the determining principle of a political unity; indeed, it is possible, Schmitt writes, 'that the political unity is first brought about through the representation itself'.[11] This principle is therefore thought of as a pillar of the immanent order. It gives life to the body politic, integrates its parts and makes them transparent to themselves as a whole. 'Every political unity', Schmitt points out, 'must somehow be integrated because such unity is not by nature present ... and genuine representation is an essential factor of the process of integration'.[12] There is no state without representation; and 'there can be no representation without the public and no public without the people'. By concretizing the spiritual principle of political existence, representation constitutes the people as a higher unity.[13]

But what is the relationship between the principle of representation, which is a morphogenetic mechanism, and the governing function, which is instead a dynamic force? By distinguishing between *Repräsentation* and *Vertretung*, Schmitt establishes an indissoluble nexus between representation and government: in the act of representing, in his view, there is something 'that exceeds every commission and every function. Consequently, not just any "organ" is representative. Only he who *rules* takes part in representation'.[14] Here Schmitt resumes and radicalizes Thomas Hobbes's personalistic doctrine of representation. In order to create a body politic by means of representation, one needs a 'special being' – a *person* – that literally *embodies* the political unity and is capable of mediating between representation and power, rulers and ruled, totality and multitude. In Hobbes's words, *[e]tiam plurium hominum fit una Persona, quando repraesentatur ab uno, qui habet a Singulis Authoritatem. Non enim Repraesentati, sed Repraesentantis Unitas est, quae Personam facit esse Unam; neque Unitas alio modo in Multitudine intelligi potest* ('one single person can be made even out of several people, when it is represented by a single one who has authority from each. For the oneness [= the principle of unity] that makes a person be a single one belongs not to the represented but to the one who represents; and there is no other way to understand oneness among a multitude').[15]

To support his own vision, then, Schmitt relies on Hobbes's without, however, explaining the validity of the doctrine of representation elaborated by the English philosopher. Some commentators have in fact argued that Hobbes's conception of political representation is incomplete, merely formal and nominalist – devoid of a detailed treatment of the relationship between the governed and their representatives – and, moreover, ideologically close to absolutism.[16] But, although Hobbes's conception is heavily abstract and personalistic and lacks an explicit discussion of the dynamics of democratic representation, this weakness should not be read as a theoretical lacuna but rather as a strategic choice on his part, for Hobbes considers the principle of representation to be as something much more original and radical than an institutional mechanism.

The problem Hobbes poses is that of theoretically framing the genetic event of the creation of a political unity (the leviathan), and not that of explaining the institutional dynamics or other forms of representation that, as he polemically points out in chapter 16 of his masterpiece, cannot exist 'before there be some state of Civil Government'.[17] Indeed, *authoritatem dederunt Civitates*: 'the state bestowed authority', or authority emanates from the state. For Hobbes, too, representation is the moment in which the great person, *magnus homo*, comes to life; it is the spark that makes the body of the leviathan alive: 'A *Commonwealth* is said to be *Instituted*, when a *Multitude* of men do Agree, and *Covenant, every one, with every one*, that to whatsoever *Man*, or *Assembly of Men*, shall be given by the major part, the *Right* to *Present* the Person of them all, (that is to say, to be their *Representative*).'[18]

Despite some ahistorical undertones, the Hobbesian doctrine cannot be considered merely as formal. For therein lies a substantial problem that reflects the crisis of the foundations of modernity.[19] The question that occupies Hobbes's reflection is this: How is it possible to create a detheologized and secular political unity out of a multitude, which is now fragmented by the lack of the unifying power of transcendence? How can a disparate assemblage of faiths and beliefs be turned into a new unity without resting on a sacral axis? In short, how is it possible to transform immanence into a new form of transcendence from below?

The explosive problematic that permeates Hobbes's thought comes here to light – namely his attempt to create a social physics that no longer relies on God or on a transcendent notion of sovereignty, but rather rests on the individual, understood as fulcrum and axis, reality and representation, body and image of the new political order. As Émile Durkheim rightly observed in his sharp comments on the English philosopher's work, by focusing on the individual, Hobbes could not but construe another individual, abstract and gigantic, concrete and artificial, plural and unitary, in equal measure:

> In principle, it is from the individual that the collective reality derives. But how does it happen that the collective reality can overcome the individual to this extent? This is the origin of the solution of continuity that permeates the frame of [Hobbes's] reasonings and the double aspect of his doctrine: liberal and authoritarian, democratic and monarchical, artificial and naturalistic.[20]

In sum, behind the Hobbesian doctrine of representation hides the complex relationship between self-transcendence, representation and political order, to which we shall return later. This problematic reflects the crisis of foundations opened up by modernity – a profound crisis that secretly crosses a good part of the philosophical, sociological and anthropological literature between the eighteenth and twentieth centuries. It is enough to mention Durkheim's notion of totem, conceived of as a symbol that materializes the social unity by making it palpable (*totum ex parte*),[21] or Rousseau's idea of law, based on the assumption that 'the great problem of Politics, which can be compared to that of squaring the circle in Geometry', is to '*find a form of Government that might place the law above man*'[22] – or any attempt to create *endogenously* an exogenous point capable of transcending the relativity of the particular and of shaping a collectively shared political order.

However, as is often the case in modernity, problems of a substantially political nature take on formal and epistemological garments.[23] For, if in Durkheim's work the enigma of representation was still addressed as the problem of the origin of the 'social fact',[24] in the liberal tradition from Rousseau to Kelsen the law is reduced to a formal or pure foundation of Right, to a sort of logical autopoiesis or rational presupposition (*Grundnorm*).[25] In this way, the old political syntax is concealed under the novel positivist morphology.

Lévi-Strauss has the merit of having recalled the attention of scholars to the complex nexus between self-transcendence and immanence, political order and social unity. In his critical assessment of the theories of totemism, he returns to the heart of the matter:

> In order that social order shall be maintained (and if it were not there would be no problem, since the society considered would disappear or would change into a different society), it is necessary to assure the permanence and solidarity of the clans which compose the society. This permanence and solidarity can be based only on individual sentiments, and these, in order to be expressed efficaciously, *demand a collective expression which has to be fixed on concrete objects*: individual sentiments of attachment > ritualized collective conduct > object representing the group. This explains the place assigned to symbols such as flags, kings, presidents, etc. in contemporary society.[26]

Representation is therefore a political metamorphosis, a sort of social crystal through which a group becomes visible to itself as a symbolic totality, thus transforming its parts (the individuals) into a political unity (the community). And these reflections bring us back to Schmitt.

As we have seen, the German jurist understands representation in a personalistic way precisely because, in his view, only when embodied in one person is sovereignty capable of concretizing power's invisibility by means of a political autopoiesis or vertical self-projection. For Schmitt, in fact, a multitude *qua* multitude is incapable of representing itself, except as a sort of chaotic and Babelish unity. As he writes in some cryptic pages of his *Glossarium*, Sieyès's idea of *plenitudo potestatis immediatae in omnes et singulos* (the fullness of non-mediated power in all and each one) is an unorganizable principle of organization. The immediacy of the crowd is not capable of unity and representation but needs to be symbolically and constantly mediated. The relationship between rulers and ruled, between power and its representation, requires therefore a vertical projection 'through which the government represents the political unity'.[27] As Hobbes puts it, the body politic is united in the person of the sovereign.

It goes without saying that by describing representative sovereignty in monarchical and conservative terms, Schmitt shows here the most 'reactionary' side of his thinking. There is, however, something much deeper and arcane in his analysis. For, unlike many of the nineteenth-century sociological and anthropological enquiries, Schmitt raises in his work a radical historical matter. As he traces back, genealogically, political forms of representation from parliamentary to monarchical ones, from legality to legitimacy, he finds himself before a conceptual vacuum, an original abyss, a suspended question. What is the *origin* of the principle that *originates* or initiates political unity? He writes:

> Representation is part of the sphere of the political. Hence, *it is essentially something existential.* One cannot grasp it by subsuming it under general norms. The nineteenth-century monarchy sought to adhere, theoretically and ideally, to the principle of legitimacy, thereby retaining an essentially normative foundation while surrendering its representative character. Legitimacy and representation are completely different concepts. Legitimacy alone establishes neither authority nor *potestas* nor representation. In the period of its most intensive political existence, the monarchy called itself *absolute*. That means *legibus solutus*, or simply the renunciation of legitimacy. … What was still historically vibrant in the monarchy's principle of form did not lie in legitimacy. … A monarchy that is nothing other than 'legitimate' is already politically and historically dead.[28]

But what is hidden behind the power of representation that, as Schmitt emphasizes, precedes both the legal norm and the royal legitimacy? What is the origin of the founding principle of political unity, if it cannot be derived from a general norm, from prestige, from personal charisma, from political office or directly from the power that it represents? And from whence the power of *re-praesentare* ('re-presenting') the existential unity of a political group spring? Schmitt gives us a clue about this when he speaks of the existential nature of representation. He then adds:

> To represent means to make an invisible being visible and present through a publicly present one. The dialectic of the concept is that the invisible is presupposed as absent and nevertheless is simultaneously made present. That is not possible with just any type of being. Indeed, it presupposes a special type being. *Something dead, something inferior or valueless, something lowly cannot be represented.*[29]

Once again, Schmitt seems to touch upon a conceptual limit here, thus presaging an arcanum of power: for what invisible being is represented in its political double? What is the relationship between the visible and the invisible within the political sphere created by the representation? And in what sense is it said that something that is dead cannot be represented? In sum, wherefrom does the power of representing originate?

***

In truth, one of the first explicit uses of the notion of representation was in relation to the dialectic of visibility and invisibility as described by Schmitt. In 1327, in London, at the death of Edward II, it was decided to call a craftsman to make *quandam ymaginem de ligno ad similitudinem dicti domini Regis* ('a certain wooden image in the shape of the said master and king').[30] This seems to be the first documented case of the tradition of making and displaying 'doubles' of monarchs during their funerals – the famous funeral effigies, also called *representationes* – which lasted until the seventeenth century both in England and in France (see Figure 1).[31] But why were the effigies crafted and exhibited during royal funerals? What were the function and the meaning of these forms of representation?

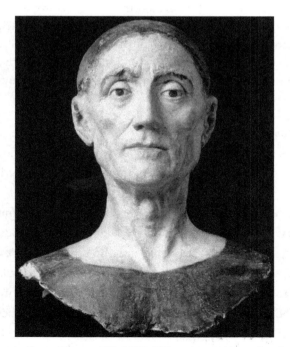

Figure 1 Funeral effigy of Henry VII, 1509. (*Westminster Abbey, London. © Dean and Chapter of Westminster*).

26 *Genealogies of Political Modernity*

Ernst Kantorowicz related the funeral effigies of sovereigns with the juridical doctrine of the king's two bodies. According to the German historian, the corpse of the king represented his natural body, or the perishable and transitory aspect of power, while the funeral effigies symbolized the political body, or the immortal and eternal soul of sovereignty. As he argues, 'enclosed in the coffin of lead ... there rested the corpse of the king, his mortal and normally visible – though now invisible – body natural; whereas his normally invisible body politic was on this occasion visibly displayed by the effigy in its pompous regalia: a *persona ficta* – the effigy – impersonating a *persona ficta* – the *Dignitas*'.[32]

As Kantorowicz repeatedly stresses, the doctrine of the king's two bodies and its visual transposition in the effigies therefore hide a problem of *continuity*. Thanks to its double, sovereign power can be conceived of as an infinite reserve of charisma; it is a sort of phoenix that constantly arises from its own ashes, in a dynamics of perpetual renewal that guarantees the immortality of power:

> The funerary procession itself demonstrated very clearly the concurrence of two heterogeneous ideas: the triumph of Death and the triumph over Death. There was the ecclesiastical ritual of the exequies and the general care attached to the dead king's body and soul; and there was the triumphal state ceremonial attached to the sempiternal glory symbolized by the effigy.[33]

Thus, through this use of representation, what is not alive – the effigy – becomes a guarantor of the continuity of political order; the representation literally stages the glory and eternity of power. Thanks to his double, the king never dies – as the traditional formula 'the king is dead, long live the king!' witnesses'.[34]

But if, as we have seen, *dignitas* represented the continuative, public and immortal aspect of power while the king's natural body represented the transient, private and perishable one, how come that the sovereigns' mannequins were introduced precisely during funeral rituals? What was the Charonian function, so to speak, of these effigies?[35] According to Carlo Ginzburg, who takes up Robert Hertz's and Elias Bickerman's theses, the use of royal effigies should be analysed within the long-lasting historical development of the complex relationship between biological death and social body.

As a matter of fact, communities have always experienced death as a critical event. Collective rituals would serve, then, to alleviate the drama of those disappearances brought about by time and to mend the social fabric torn by physical absence. Biological death must be transmuted into a sociopolitical event through a collective and cathartic process of assimilation. That would explain the purpose of representation, which is to visualize the dead in order to soothe the pain of her absence, to make disappearance less distant by presenting the dead again. For Ginzburg, the Egyptian rituals of mummification as well as the corpses of Peruvian kings exhibited in solemn circumstances carried out this function of mediating between death and life, between the decaying corpses and the living collectivity.

The analogies between these archaic rites and the apotheosis of the Roman emperors, or the public ritual of *consecratio*, are too obvious to escape notice. As is known, in Rome under the Antonines a deceased emperor could be proclaimed 'divine' (*divus*) by his successor, with support from the Senate. During this rite, a wax figure of the dead emperor was adorned, celebrated and then burnt on a pyre; thus it was made to ascend to the Gods through a *funus imaginarium*, 'funeral of the image'. In this case, too, the image performed an eternalizing and ritualistic function. Through this transhistorical journey, Ginzburg has been led to conclude that 'waxen imperial images and royal effigies, through which the rulers' deaths as a social process came to a conclusion, were equivalents *on another level* to mummies or skeletons'.[36] But, if it is true that the representation of power is a ritual that serves to heal a 'social trauma', what kind of trauma are we analysing here?

Following the genealogical path opened by Ginzburg and radicalizing the use of historical analogy, Agamben argued that behind the 'category of the double' lies a true political arcanum. For him, too, the use of images and representations (funeral effigies, wax statues, colossus, etc.) must be read as a form of mediation between the realm of the living and the realm of the dead. The double or the colossus, in his view, would represent 'analogously to the corpse, but in a more immediate and general way – that part of the person that is consecrated to death and that, insofar as it occupies the threshold between the two worlds, must be separated from the normal context of the living'.[37] Unlike Ginzburg, however, and contrary to what has been argued by Kantorowicz and his pupil Giesey, who found the analogies between

28 *Genealogies of Political Modernity*

the funeral effigies of English and French sovereigns and the pagan rituals provocative but hazardous,[38] Agamben stressed the elements of continuity that would characterize the dialectic of the power's two bodies, the visible and the invisible; and he traces these elements back to the archaic paradigm of *sacertas*.

For it is in this light that he rethinks the process of apotheosis in ancient Rome. The ritual of *consecratio*, in Agamben's view, would serve to free up the excess of the emperor's sacred life, which is nothing but 'the cipher of the absolute and inhuman character of sovereignty'.[39] In this sense, biological death would release the deposit of sacredness, the double life – absolute, transcendent, yet incarnated – of the emperor who, through *funus*, can finally 'ascend to the heavens and be deified'.[40] This double life of the sovereign – eternal and transient – would be the symmetrical, although reversed, figure of *homo sacer*, the paradigm of bare life that constitutes the arcanum of Western politics.

Yet what surprises in Agamben's analysis is the ease with which a *formal* analogy (the ritual use of images, the category of the double) is assumed to be a transepochal and metaphysical paradigm. As Ginzburg himself had warned, transepochal similarities should be used if we want to understand the specificity of historical phenomena.[41] This is because the morphological approach cannot exhaust the historical investigation of the *political function* of representations (imperial doubles and royal effigies). In fact a more careful reading of funeral rituals, pagan and medieval, suggests a different interpretative path.

For instance, in the ritual of deification (*consecratio* in Latin, ἀποθέωσις in Greek), it is not *power* itself that is eternalized. Rather it is the *person* of the emperor – his metaphysical image – that is made to ascend among the Gods (ἀποθεωθῆναι), thus attracting the epithet *divus* to the name (see Figure 2). It was Caesar's personal charisma that, after his death, was exalted and used to reinforce the structure of imperial power and that, later on, would have given rise to a true cult of personality.[42] The emperor's historical figure, in other words, is used to legitimize his office and to enhance his succession. What is at stake in the process of apotheosis is the transmutation of the personal charisma of *some* emperors into a public force operating in the city. And this becomes evident if one thinks of the symmetrical but opposite procedure of *damnatio memoriae*. That procedure allowed the Roman Senate to condemn *post mortem* to oblivion any imperial figures that had endangered public safety. Possessing imperial powers was therefore not enough to guarantee the title of *divus* or to trigger the public procedure of deification. In principle, the historical charisma of Roman emperors was not endowed with any transcendent force but was exposed to fate, depended on deeds and was subject to public scrutiny in the Eternal City. As we read in the *Historia Augusta*, the memory and statues of 'impure' figures such as Caligula or Commodus were wiped away (*memoria aboleatur, statuae detrahantur*).[43]

The ritual structure of medieval royal funerals is wholly different from that of the apotheosis of Roman emperors. In England and France, it was not the historical figure of the sovereign that ascended to eternity and it was not his person that was deified; these things happened to the supplement of power that was deposited on their body like a second skin and that manifested its original immortality through funeral rituals. It is this superindividual body, as Kantorowicz described it – a body that is always already eternal, yet incarnate – that separates itself from the sovereign at the moment of his

Figure 2 Bronze sestertius with a portrait of Antoninus Pius (138–61). (*Musée des beaux-arts, Lyon. © Photo Alain Basset*).

passing. Here eternity does not need to be sought for, but only celebrated, for it is ontologically inherent in the immortal body of power.

If Kantorowicz and Giesey never wanted to acknowledge a continuity between the medieval doctrine of the king's two bodies and its pagan 'precedents', this is not due to the Christian roots of the Kantorowiczian interpretation, as it has been written,[44] but rather to the historical and conceptual hiatus that separates the two rituals. In memorable pages that illuminate our argument, the German historian has shown how the metaphysical conception of duality that informed the pagan world is diametrically opposed to that of medieval times:

> The *genius* or *numen* of an emperor, though an object of public worship, was not separated from the individual but was still an immanent component of the individual human being. It would, therefore, be difficult to maintain that the emperor became the *instrumentum numinis* or *genii* in the sense in which the late-mediaeval Prince became the *instrumentum Dignitatis* and the incarnation of his immortal office.[45]

To understand, then, the historical peculiarity of the English and French royal funeral ceremonies within the transepochal problematic of the sovereign representation, it is necessary to analyse the specific function that these rites performed. Royal doubles or representations were in fact used in a specific 'dead time', in a very special ceremonial space: the period preceding the coronation of the new king, when power was physically vacant – a period that Giesey has appropriately called 'ceremonial interregnum'.[46] It is as if there were a specular symmetry between the *suspension* of power that takes place on the death of the king and opens the interregnum and the 'birth' of his double, which stages the *perpetuity* of sovereign power. In my opinion, here lies the key to understanding the concrete political function of the legal fiction (*fictio iuris*) according to which the king – that is the crown, or government – never dies (*rex nunquam moritur*).

The hypothesis developed in the next pages is that the double of the king, his representation, serves to fill an abyss of power, an original peril: the fear of interregnum. For it is known that the periods of royal succession were particularly delicate from the standpoint of the sociopolitical body and its stability. As Kantorowicz pointed out, 'interregna, whether long or short, had been a danger even in earlier times; they fitted badly into an age which had developed a relatively complicated machinery of state administration, as was the case in the later Middle Ages'.[47] But what kind of danger was lurking in the interregnum that the king's representation was meant to reduce?

In his *Calvin's Case* (1609), Sir Edward Coke vehemently tells us of seditious doctrines that developed around the sixteenth century – doctrines according to which 'the king before his coronation "was no complete and absolute king" and that therefore ("observe their damnable and damned consequent") one might commit any act of violence against an as yet uncrowned king without being charged for treason'. This 'heretical' position, politically dangerous for the survival of the kingdom (*regnum*), was an echo of more ancient doctrines and ideas. In England, for example, in 1135, people 'were said to have indulged in robberies and other disturbances because allegedly on the king's death the king's peace ceased to exist'. And more than a century earlier, in 1024, in northern Italy, 'people of Pavia ... on the death of Emperor Henry II, destroyed the imperial castle because they claimed that there was no longer an emperor who owned it'.[48] The death of the sovereign literally creates a vacuum of power.

The interregnum that opens up at the physical disappearance of the king is, in other words, a dead time that must be revitalized; otherwise we could witness the entropic dissolution of the dynastic power and of the political order as a result of riots, looting or violent conflicts. This means that the *perpetua necessitas* personified by royal doubles is, first and foremost, a figure of order, an automatism through which the gap opened by the death of the *person-king* is covered by the mantle of *kingship*. And it is no coincidence that, over time, the interregnal period will become shorter and shorter until 'on the death – or burial – of the ruling monarch the son or legitimate heir became king automatically'. Here is the link between the sovereign's representation and the perpetuity of power:

> The continuity of the king 'body natural' was secured, when the two Western monarchies did away not only with the 'little interregnum' between accession and coronation, but also eliminated, once and for all, the possibility of a 'great interregnum' which might occur between the death of a king and the election of his successor. 'Time runneth not against the King' – it did not run against the dynasty either.[49]

As it happens, at times when the social and political crisis is most acute, there is also the moment of utmost theoretical visibility. Thus the reader will not be surprised to find in the work of Thomas Hobbes the most precise and clear description of the fundamental connection between political continuity and the suspension of sovereign power. Summarizing centuries of medieval doctrines and speculation, Hobbes writes:

> For the death of him that hath the Sovereign power in propriety, leaves the Multitude without any Sovereign at all; that is *without any Representative in whom they should be united*, and be capable of doing any one action at all: and therefore they are incapable of Election of any new Monarch; every man having equal right to submit himself to such as he thinks best able to protect him; or if he can, protect himself by his own sword; *which is a return to Confusion, and to the condition of a War of every man against every man, contrary to the end for which Monarchy had its first Institution*. Therefore it is manifest, that by the Institution of Monarchy, the disposing of the Successor, is alwaies left to the Judgment and Will of the present Possessor.[50]

It is as if the death of the king left the leviathan headless, and this beheading risks causing the death of the entire body politic, which might atomically decompose into its parts (i.e. *bellum omnium contra omnes* or civil war). The artificial man – the leviathan state – needs then a prosthesis to keep himself alive: this prosthesis is the *representation of the representation* – the double of the king. In other words, if one wants to keep alive the artifice of the sovereign representation, if one wants to avoid 'the return into the condition of War', it is necessary to create a further artifice to maintain the *homo artificialis* in existence. 'This Artificiall Eternity' – Hobbes writes with usual undertones of magical realism – 'is that which men call the Right of Succession'.[51]

Power cannot and must not allow solutions of continuity. The interregnum is a dangerous abyss that must be filled at any cost; otherwise we can expect the return to *stasis*, the 'war of all against all'. At this level, then, one wonders what force hides behind the physical interruption of power that calls into question the sovereign's artificial double. In other words, what lies behind the space of the exception that was opened by the suspension of power and is veiled behind the two prostheses of *repraesentatio* and direct succession? What unites the two parts of sovereign's body, the real and the represented? As we shall see, it is precisely in the double of power – in its sacral reflection – that something like an arcanum of politics must be sought.

The power of representation

The Romans had no single word to express what we mean by 'power'. They used three words that, though interrelated, indicated distinct social and political functions: *imperium*, which referred to the sacral, transcendental and foundational source of power; *auctoritas*, which expressed social wisdom, or a socially recognized vision of truth; and *potestas*, which designated force, or the concrete expression of a socially acknowledged power.[52]

The triangular relationship between these dimensions gave life and dynamism to the political order of the ancient Roman Republic. So it was that, when the consulate became vacant for voluntary or involuntary causes (abdication or death of the consuls), *imperium* returned to *patres*, that is to that small group of senators who were the custodians of sacral wisdom (*auctoritas*) and who had the duty to preserve the political order during the interregnum; this would explain the obscure and controversial dictum *auspicia ad patres redeunt* ('the auspices return to the patrician senators').[53] If *renovatio auspiciorum* ('the renewal of auspices') was the cornerstone of the Roman political and legal system, this was due to the fact that *patres* were invested with the transcendent power (*imperium*) that bound them both symbolically and directly to the founding act of the city: Jupiter's blessing. Re-election was therefore an act of *re*foundation that lent continuity to the political order: Jupiter's power is eternal and transcendent, yet continually 'reincarnated' in its historical and sapiential forms. As André Magdelain observed, 'Rome constituted itself as a sort of continually renewable reserve of providential men'.[54] By means of this articulation, the problem of the foundation, actualization and above all continuity of power found its proper rhythm.[55]

However, the power attributed to *patres*, the reigning senators, was not unlimited; indeed, it was strictly regulated. For example, during the 'dead' or 'suspended' time of the interregnum, the senators, in view of the election of the new magistrates, were required to hold power individually and in rotation for a maximum of *five days*.[56] It has been convincingly argued that the use of the number five in this context was not casual, as this figure was endowed with a strong symbolism related to the ancient Roman kingdom, to its rituals and calendar.[57]

34 *Genealogies of Political Modernity*

In *De lingua latina* (vi, 13), for example, Varro speaks of five intercalary days that were added at the end of the year, on the last day of the last month, which means on 23 February (*duodecimus enim mensis fuit Februarius et cum intercalatur inferiores quinque dies duodecimo demuntur mense*, 'the twelfth month was February, and when the extra month is inserted the last five days are taken off the twelfth month').[58] They fell exactly after the festival of the Terminalia, just before the beginning of the new calendar year, 'on the sixth day before the calends of March' (*ante diem sextum kalendas Martias*). These five supernumerary days, otherwise referred to as epagomenal, which mirror the length of the senatorial interregnum, are not a Roman peculiarity. We encounter a similar use of five additional days in many other ancient calendars, from Egypt to Mexico.[59] Despite the historical and cultural differences of these celebratory rituals, the period leading to the 'dead time' between the end of the old year and the beginning of the new one is characterized everywhere by 'a system of periodic purifications (purges, fasting, confessions of sins, etc.) and of a periodic regeneration of time', that is to say, by 'rituals that guarantee *the continuity of the life of the community in its entirety*'.[60]

In this respect, the Roman system is no exception. As we have seen, ancient sources testify that the five intercalary days began exactly at the end of the festivities of Terminalia, an important celebration that marked the end of the year through various purification rituals[61] (even February, Varro reminds us, took its name from a similar practice: 'for *februm* is the name which the Sabines give to a purification, and this word is not unknown in our sacrifices').[62]

It is this symmetry between the suspension of time and of the calendar (*extremo anno*), the suspension of the political order (*interregnum*) and the suspension and regeneration of the order of things (*ordo rerum*) that caught Magdelain's attention and that requires further investigation. Indeed, the French historian has shown that the five-day interregnum of the republican period is a political mould of the cyclical suspension of power that took place at the end of the year in the ancient Roman kingdom.[63] More important for my argument is the fact that the first of these days of suspension opened with a special ceremony: the Regifugium or flight of the king.

In the ancient Roman kingdom, the suspension of the year coincided with a suspension of power and with a periodic vacancy of the royal office. The five-day interregnum must, then, be understood as carrying the 'memory' of a much more archaic and mysterious procedure, which is linked to the problem of holding, renewing and representing power. In the republican period this rite of passage between the two times or 'states'[64] of the year was celebrated by an enigmatic figure: *rex sacrorum*.

***

Rex sacrorum ('the king of the sacred') is among the most mysterious and fascinating figures of ancient Rome.[65] The origin of this title is highly disputed. According to Arnaldo Momigliano, for example, this senatorial priesthood would have been instituted in the republican era to perform functions that the drastic end of the monarchy, marked by the exile of Tarquinius Superbus, had handed down.[66] For others, the title would be much older, as evidenced by the Etruscan and Italic inscriptions in which explicit reference is made to this figure.[67] But perhaps the darkest mystery remains that of its function and rank. According to Festus, for instance, in the ranking of the highest Roman priests (*ordo sacerdotum*), *rex sacrorum* was the highest-ranking Roman priesthood, being followed by that of the three *flamines maiores* (*flamen dialis, flamen martialis, flamen quirinalis*) and by the *pontifex maximus*.[68] Yet this prestigious title was not accompanied by any political power; indeed, as Livy tells us, its bearer was barred from having a political and military career.[69] In sum, this 'mannequin of the king', as Magdelain calls him, was an archaic and paradoxical figure within the complex Roman political and juridical world.

But how are we to explain that *rex sacrorum* was the most prestigious and at the same time the least politicized figure of the Republic? The thesis that the formal nature of this title was the result of a compromise between the abolition of monarchy and the continued relevance of its sacral functions is not convincing.[70] As a matter of fact, the sacral and religious duties could be performed by the *pontifex maximus* who in fact went on to occupy the most eminent position in the Roman religion. The idea that *rex sacrorum* is a fallen king, analogous to the *archōn basileus* in the Greek world – a sovereign stripped of the supreme political and military power and who can only perform *sacra*, religious rituals – does not shed much light on the functions he performed. Moreover, such a thesis is unable to explain why, despite his totally apolitical role, this king-priest officiated a profoundly political and arcane ritual, which must have had roots in the archaic royal period: the festivity called Regifugium, the flight of the king (*regifugium* = *regis fuga*).

According to Plutarch, who describes this ritual in his *Quaestiones Romanae*, every year, on 24 February, the king-priest was allowed to appear in the Comitium – the main public meeting space, forbidden to him during the rest of the year. He went there in order to perform certain sacrifices, after which he withdrew in haste.[71] This symbolical flight is said to have been called Regifugium. The explanation advanced by Ovid, who sees this practice as a commemoration of the flight of Tarquinius Superbus, the legendary seventh and last king of Rome, can only be a retrospective projection of a ritual of which even the memory had been lost in his day.[72] For why would the king have to officiate such a re-enactment on one of the most important days of the year? And what was the meaning of his flight from the popular assembly in the first of the five epagomenal days?

To André Magdelain belongs the merit of having demonstrated the conceptual and symbolic symmetry between the ritual of the Regifugium and the five-day interregnum. Both occur in a dead, suspended time – in a hiatus. And here is the key to understanding their function. Regifugium, in fact, falls precisely on the first of the five-day suspension of time that concludes the annual cycle.[73] In the archaic period, the eclipse of the calendar was thus followed by a royal eclipse: what the king fled from was precisely the 'dead time' between the end of the old year and the beginning of a new one. As Magdelain has argued, the noxiousness of the epagomenal days

> is well known in the ancient calendar of Mexico, Egypt, and Persia. Supernumerary time is dangerous. Faced with it, in Rome, the king disappears; his reign is suspended during these inauspicious five days. The study of compared religion provides several examples of these royal retreats … the king withdraws in front of a recurring danger or a bad presage. Regifugium is the Roman version of these retreats that occur at a critical phase of the year: the dead time between its end and its recommencement.[74]

Thus the flight of the king re-enacted the suspension of the annual cycle. But then one wonders: Why does the king have to escape? What is so dangerous, so nefarious about this period of time in the annual cycle? In *The Myth of the Eternal Return*, Mircea Eliade has shown how, in many archaic societies, 'the expulsion of demons, diseases and sins coincides ... with the Festival of the New Year'. For at that time, 'on the occasion of the division of time into independent units, "years", we witness not only the effectual cessation of a certain temporal interval and the beginning of another, but also *the abolition of the past year and the past time*'.[75] In this sense, the rituals of purification that are carried out in the period leading up to the beginning of the new year (e.g. Terminalia) should be considered a practice by which ancient communities seek 'to restore – if only momentarily – mythical and primordial time, "pure" time, the time of the instant of the Creation'.[76] It is from this cosmogonic moment, from this passage 'from chaos to cosmos', that the king flees; and he does so because *he is exposed to the regenerating forces of the sociopolitical order.*

It has been argued, for example, that in many archaic societies the rituals of regenerating the order of things (*ordo rerum*) involved the sacrifice of the ruler.[77] This was due to the fact that the sovereign – *rex* – represented the point of connection between heaven and earth, necessity and contingency, order and disorder, sacrifice and renewal. It was precisely because the sovereign 'was responsible for the regularity of the rhythms of nature and for the good estate of the entire society' that 'upon him fell the duty of regenerating time'.[78] As Frazer has shown amply in his multivolume *The Golden Bough*, in some archaic cultures *renovatio mundi*, the world's renewal, was believed to be effective only through the sacrifice of the apex, the representation of the community in its entirety: the body of the sovereign.[79] Following this analytical path, Elmer T. Merrill was led to the conclusion that, originally, Regifugium was a ritual sacrifice of this kind. It is worth reading in full his analysis of Frazer's thesis:

> The King ran away at the end of the rites of the Regifugium. But why should he run? ... Sir James G. Frazer has offered ... a most illuminating and convincing conjecture regarding the origin and nature of the name and rites of the Regifugium. He suggests that we have in them a survival ... of a custom that he shows by sufficient examples existed, or in some form still exists, among many primitive tribes, and even among Indo-European peoples. In some such communities ... there was a man who was regarded as the incarnation of the mysterious spirit of all vegetation. On his strength and vitality depended the success of the farmer's labors. He was therefore regarded as divine. He bore the title of 'King', and was free from all control and restraint during his reign. But that reign was brief. It lasted but a single

year, ending shortly before the approach of seedtime. He was then put to death as a sacrificial victim, or forced to immolate himself, and a successor took his place. For it was deemed necessary that the King's physical powers should never be permitted to pass into decline. That would bring ruin upon the crops, and perhaps also sterility upon flocks and herds, or even upon the human race. At what we may presume to be a later time, instead of being sacrificed, the King was permitted to prove, if he could, the retention of his pre-eminent strength by a duel to the death with an opponent, who, if successful, became King in his stead for the following year. The flight of the King perhaps marks a later stage yet in the history of the ordeal, and may indicate that if he could demonstrate his continued vigor by successful escape from his would-be executioner and successor, he might be permitted to prolong his reign for another year without further molestation. So by gradual stages the annual test becomes a mere form, and the King reigns for the term of his life.[80]

According to Merrill and Frazer, the regeneration of the sociopolitical order would follow the seasonal cycle and the latter, in turn, to renew itself productively, would require the sacrifice of the holder of power. In short, to preserve itself, a political order *must return to the beginning*: it must establish itself through the ritual sacrifice and the constant replacement of its own representative. It is suggested here that in some archaic societies the sovereign was not an inviolable entity, as is customary to believe. On the contrary, he was inexorably exposed to the power of contingency and to the forces of the natural world: through the sacrifice of his own life, the sovereign moulded the sociopolitical order. In a sense, then, the king possessed a double body, which was constantly crossed by the forces of nature (the vital cycles, the seasons) and by the forces of culture (rivalries, violence). He was a 'god on earth', a mediator between the unpredictability of nature and *renovatio ordinis*, the renewal of order – that is between contingency and necessity – and came 'to a violent end in that capacity'.[81]

It is in this light that one should analyse the figure of *rex sacrorum* – the 'king's ghost'. This figure, too, is functionally located within the complex and violent relationship between order and contingency, cosmos and chaos, cyclic eternity and periodic killing of the ruler. The thesis advanced in these pages is that the king's flight has nothing to do with a gradual process of formalization of an annual trial to which the king was subjected, as suggested by Frazer and

Merrill. On the contrary, this ritual originally staged the moment in which power hides from itself, from its own cosmogonic-sacrificial functions, through its double or representation.

It is known that, in many different ancient cultures, during the most nefarious moments of the year – or during periods when the royal office is vacant – a king's substitute took control in order to ensure the continuity of power and, by doing this, exposed himself to the very risk from which the actual king had extricated himself. Examples of this practice of royal substitution are attested in ancient Babylon, in India (Bastar) and in Cambodia.[82] It is in this light that we should examine the figure of *rex sacrorum*.

This enigmatic priest was not a depoliticized descendant of the king, a fallen royal figure stripped of political powers; he was the king's sacrificial double, a disposable interrex, a royal scapegoat – the pulsating and violent heart of political representation.[83] As we have seen, in order to guarantee the continuity of power, it was believed to be necessary to bridge a gap in time: the cosmogonic vortex of regeneration. From this perspective, then, *rex sacrorum* must be considered the royal double or 'mannequin' that guarantees both continuity, by closing the gap between two times or 'years', and the renewal of political order, by exposing his own body to the regenerating forces of the social order. 'The king' – Henri Frankfort has written – 'was a divine pledge in the hands of man'.[84] And in those hands his body was shaped and traversed by the uncontrollable forces of nature and history. It is not inappropriate, therefore, to claim that political representation was, originally, the expression of a sacrificial economy. But, perhaps even more than that, it was a protective shield – the sacrificeable image of power.

Power and its double

At this point in my discussion it is possible to advance a general hypothesis on the relationship between sacrificial violence and sovereignty, and on how this relationship has shaped the problem of political representation.[85]

As we have seen, in many archaic civilizations (Balylon, Greece, India, etc.), the sovereign is conceived of as the holder of the order of things. He is a mediator – a physical point of intersection – between culture and nature, necessity and contingency, order and chaos. For this reason it was believed that he was capable of regulating the weather by performing 'ceremonies which were deemed necessary to ensure the fertility of the earth and the multiplication of animals'.[86] He had the power to cultivate and distribute the goods of the earth: indeed, his justice caused 'the clouds to gather, the thunder to peal, and the rain to descend in due season, that the field might bear fruit and the pastures be covered with luxuriant herbage'.[87] The government of these archaic worlds constitutes itself as a form of control of the cyclical – but not entirely predictable and therefore contingent – forces of nature. As Arthur M. Hocart has powerfully argued, 'the invention of man who did no work with his hands, but merely existed and acted on his environment at a distance, like the sun, was one of the most momentous in the history of man; *it was nothing less than the invention of government*'.[88]

In ancient times, then, the sacred and the political were merged in one sovereign point upon which the whole community depended: the king, whose life was constantly exposed to the risks of holding this power. Thus, the role of the sovereign was constantly affected by the impossibility of establishing a certain and definitive order – an order sheltered from the cyclic instability of the vital and natural forces: 'for if the course of nature is dependent on the man-god's life, what catastrophes may not be expected from the gradual enfeeblement of his powers and their final extinction in death?'[89] No matter whether the king was sacrificed periodically, in accordance with the seasonal cycle, or as soon as he showed the first signs of weakening and decadence, or when his power did not match slavishly the natural rhythms, but gave bad omens, the purpose of the royal sacrifice was always the same: to reconstruct the nexus between rebirth and order – between killing and renewal – or to transform the chaos of contingency into a new order of necessity. The sacrificial gesture is therefore always archetypal, as it seeks to regenerate 'the world and life through repetition of the cosmogony'.[90] In its originary form, sovereignty is not an exception that captures the bare life of its subjects but rather an absolute power constantly exposed to itself, to its own incommensurability – a body that is traversed and crucified by the forces of chance and time.

If it is plausible that the expulsion of the contingency from the order of things took place through a sovereign sacrifice, the meaning of the king's substitution becomes more intelligible: 'when kings were bound to suffer death ... it was natural that they should seek to delegate the painful duty, along with some of the privileges of sovereignty, to a substitute who should suffer vicariously in their stead.'[91] The representation of power – the king's double – is literally a veil of Maya, a screen invented by the sovereign to protect himself. It is as if the king created safeguards for himself by redirecting the risk of violence against surrogates and doubles in order to guarantee the renewal and continuity of the kingdom without risking being slain. This implies that the process of desacralization and division of powers is driven by violence – or it would be better to say by the diversion of sacrificial violence towards representative forms (royal doubles and substitutes). In fact the origin and transformation of political representation and the dynamic of the separation of powers cannot merely reflect the evolution of society in its complexity, as has often been argued,[92] they are also the product of a *sacrificial economy*. The sacrificial mechanism is anything that allows the ancient metaphysics of order to regenerate itself constantly. In a certain sense, the political mystery par excellence is that of the original, and perhaps ontological, nexus between ritual sacrifice and political order.

From this perspective, then, it is difficult to support the theses of those who claimed – like Frazer, following Dionysius of Halicarnassus – that the sacred royal functions 'were instituted after the abolition of the monarchy in order to offer the sacrifices and to discharge the religious duties which had formerly fallen within the province of the real king.'[93] The differentiation of power between *sacra* and *imperium* would thus be reduced to a question of political economy. But why should the king, the consuls or the representatives give up their most important and significant celebratory functions, if these did not involve exposure to an archetypal risk (the ontological sacrifice), of which I have spoken extensively?

The thesis presented here is much less reassuring: it was the sacrificial mechanism that generated a first form of political representation and then the various doubles of power (substitutes, delegates, representatives, etc.). For the transformation and ritualization of sacrifice generated constant protection for and, at the same time, dislocation of the forms of power (and of its representations). Let's repeat it: in ancient times, governing meant controlling the cosmic and natural cycles, adapting human life to them. In this sense, the archaic notion of order involved the elimination of contingency, the ritualization of exceptions. When this was not possible, royal representation – the sovereign's substitute or double – saved the king by giving himself up as sacrificial object. Representation is, in this very particular sense, the first political artifice that stages the control of what is not directly controllable: the contingency of nature.

The relationship of co-belonging that unites and at the same time divides life and death, power and its representation, order and contingency, manifests itself in all evidence in the figure of *rex sacrorum*: he is a piece of 'nature' within culture, a residue of disorder inserted within the social order. Perhaps even more, his body can be thought of as a threshold constantly open to and agitated by contingency – a body that must be sacrificed to ensure the world's renewal (*renovatio mundi*). The royal representation is, in this sense, the first fiction, the original political technology, which will give life to other abstractions and images of power. In fact, in the process of doubling the king (as a concrete person) in his office (as royalty), the 'royal mannequin' is the one who plays a decisive role. For the representation, while saving the sovereign from self-sacrifice, also establishes the principle according to which his role can be played by someone who is not *physically* the sovereign but can assume the royal functions and his sovereign office, even if only for a short period. Thus is created the notion of kingship – a place of power detached from the body of the sovereign.

However, under the pressure of unavoidable social changes, the sacrificial paradigm will transform itself, moving from the concrete dialectic of sovereign versus double to more abstract forms of representation. This secret dual relationship between representation and political order is fundamental for understanding the evolution of Western political history. In fact, over time, power will increasingly find shelter behind its doubles and monopolize the use of (sacrificial) violence. Nature and culture, contingency and necessity, will reverse their polar positions.

The modern age is the acme of this evolution. For in modernity the so-called state of nature is no longer conceived as nature per se, but rather as the *nature of culture*, or the politicization of the earth carried out through human forces. At this juncture, it is no longer nature that bears the signs of contingency, but rather the human who acts within it. In other words, as humans gain greater control over the forces and resources of nature, they introject the problem of contingency and political order, just as Hobbes puts it: 'The force therefore of the law of nature is not *in foro externo*, till there be security for men to obey it; but it is always *in foro interno*, wherein the action of obedience being unsafe, the will and readiness to perform is taken for the performance.'[94] It is the human who, as an absolute agent, needs to be controlled at any cost. In fact there is nothing more dangerous than human nature ('the naturall right of Preservation which we all receive from the uncontroulable Dictates of Necessity, will not admit it to be a Vice, though it confesse it to be an Unhappinesse').[95] It is at this historical juncture that the biopolitical threshold emerges: to the naturalization of culture symmetrically corresponds the culturalization of nature, and control over nature and its resources coincides with growing practices of social and political control. Human life thus becomes the political problem par excellence, which requires a further screen or artifice to be nourished and protected.

And, indeed, with the advent of modernity, the fiction of representation is taken to its extreme consequences. Hobbes's *Leviathan* is perhaps the most iconic example. In this masterpiece of paradox, representative power is embodied by an artificial man: the state, the mortal God. In the new leviathanic machine and, in a more evident way, from the French Revolution onwards, what is to be protected through the sacrifice of one's own life is power as such – a power imagined as personal but endowed with a collective body, individual but without a recognizable face; a power that is conceived of as mere, absolute (baroque, according to Schmitt) representation: an enlarged and abstract reflection of the individual who looks herself into her own illusory image. The leviathan is, in other words, a cage that the power has built for itself through this new modern, absolute and abstract form of representation.[96] Hence the state is a giant double, an 'oversized man' (*makros anthrōpos*), whose sacrificeable body belongs to its people, while its empty soul is nothing but the refuge of power: an empty chair – an imperishable and insacrifiable office, in fact.

From the analysis of abstract images of power to the figure of its living and sacrificial double, this genealogy has allowed me to cast some light on fundamental transformations that have characterized the Western conception of sovereignty and its arcane mechanisms: from the medieval proclamation 'The King is dead, long live the King' to the modern sacrificial principle 'The people is dead, long live the people'.

2

Space and Sovereignty: A Reverse Perspective

A Multitude of men, are made One Person, when they are by one man, or one Person, Represented; so that it be done with the consent of every one of that Multitude in particular. For it is the Unity of the Representer, not the unity of the Represented, that maketh the Person One. And it is the Representer that beareth the Person, and but one Person: And Unity, cannot otherwise be understood in Multitude.

Thomas Hobbes, *Leviathan*, chapter 16

Räumen ist Freigabe von Orten. [Making space is the release of places.]

Martin Heidegger, *Die Kunst und der Raum*

In his several 'archaeologies', Michel Foucault never clarified the theoretical basis of art history and its relevance to our understanding of what he called *epistemai*, that is 'those configurations within the *space* of knowledge which have given rise to diverse forms of empirical science'.[1] Yet his books abound in descriptions and interpretations of works of art and literature. It may suffice to mention here the opening chapter of one of his best known works, *Les Mots et les choses* (1966), in which Velázquez's masterpiece *Las Meninas* (1656) is reinterpreted as marking the transition to a new epistemological era: the age of the sovereign gaze, in which the subject is both master and slave of his own perspective. Already before, in *Madness and Civilization* (1961), Foucault had endowed the works of Antonin Artaud and Vincent van Gogh with the hermeneutic power to operate as 'black boxes' for the modern collective consciousness: in these works, he claimed, 'art opens a void, a moment of silence, a question without answer, provokes a breach without reconciliation where the world is forced to question itself'.[2]

46 Genealogies of Political Modernity

In one of his most accomplished works, *L'Archéologie du savoir* (1969), Foucault indeed attempted to explain the 'archaeological potential' of art, understood as an epistemological means to explore a deeper dimension of power. In discussing the various possibilities of his method of inquiry, he writes:

> In analyzing a painting, one can reconstitute the latent discourse of the painter; one can try to recapture the murmur of his intentions, which are not transcribed into words, but into lines, surfaces, and colors; one can try to uncover the implicit philosophy that is supposed to form his view of the world. It is also possible to question science, or at least the opinions of the period, and to try to recognize to what extent they appear in the painter's work. Archaeological analysis would have another aim: it would try to discover whether space, distance, depth, color, light, proportions, volumes, and contours were not, at the period in question, considered, named, enunciated, and conceptualized in a discursive practice; and whether the knowledge that this discursive practice gives rise to was not embodied perhaps in theories and speculations, in forms of teaching and codes of practice, but also in processes, techniques, and even in the very gesture of the painter ... It would try to show that, at least in one of its dimensions, it is discursive practice that is embodied in techniques and effects. In this sense, the painting is not a pure vision that must then be transcribed into the materiality of space; nor is it a naked gesture whose silent and eternally empty meanings must be freed from subsequent interpretations. It is shot through – and independently of scientific knowledge (*connaissance*) and philosophical themes – with a positivity of a knowledge (*savoir*).[3]

In its complexity, this passage illuminates the epistemic status of art and of the artistic gesture, both being understood as pathways towards revealing a more profound level of the order of discourse (and of its historical, political and scientific significance).

The present chapter aims to explore this relation between the epistemo-political background and the artistic gesture, which is both concealed and revealed therein. In the wake of Foucault's investigation, my attempt consists in analysing the relation between the work of art, the space it occupies and represents, the political space into which it is forced and that, perhaps, it aims to set free. This kind of enquiry should be seen as a provisional outline of a research programme that has not yet been sufficiently developed. In effect,

Space and Sovereignty · 47

although there are notable exceptions,[4] the complex relationship between art and politics, in the various theoretical genealogies of politics, has usually occupied a modest place. The study of systems of thought – and of conceptual and ideational histories, which are of course relevant and necessary – has been usually preferred and, at times, elevated to the rank of history *tout court*. It has been considered possible, for example, to discover the ethico-political meaning of an entire age in the mind of a Thomas Hobbes or a Duns Scotus.[5]

The strategy developed here, although partly equivalent to the one just mentioned, provides a twofold advantage. First, art – and in particular visual art –represents a threshold, an articulation between the said and the unsaid, the 'real' and the imagined, the represented (the object) and the act of representing (the subject). On the one hand, therefore, art carries and preserves within itself, as it were, a structural nature. 'The work of art' – the Russian philosopher Pavel Florensky has argued – 'is the center of an entire cluster of conditions, which alone make possible its existence as something artistic; outside of its constitutive conditions it simply does not exist as art.'[6] In this sense, conceptual archaeology should try to reconstruct, through the remains, the discoloured fresco, the 'empty tomb', those 'signs of life' in a lost unity, and not merely consider works of art 'as self-sufficient objects, severed from the living spirit, [and] outside of their functional relationship to the whole.'[7] In other words, the work of art is at the heart of a complex unity, a field of tensions and forces in constant relation with one another. In its turn, this 'unity', I argue, presupposes an operation on the subject; and, in their mutual influence, 'unity' and the 'artistic gesture' give rise to a functional metamorphosis of the systems of knowledge that Foucault has called 'discursive formations'.

Second, unlike Foucault, this approach places a greater emphasis on individual artistic perception, in the belief that, if 'art is a historical step in the evolution of the spatial awareness, real artists are those who see people and things better and more accurately than the rest, more accurately in regard to the historical reality of their age.'[8] This implies that, if it is true that there is an epistemic plane through which artists look at the world and filter it, it is also true that there are artists who look better and further than others, anticipating, moving, and modifying the conceptual and unconscious boundaries of their *episteme*. It goes without saying that, as pointed out by Foucault, the elements of a discursive regime are stronger and more *rigid* than subjective forces, and that, in Carl Gustav Jung's words, even the genius 'has to bear the brunt of an outsize psychic complex'[9] and cannot distance herself from her times. Nonetheless, within the semi-rigid grid of sociopolitical and discursive restrains, there remains a *time* in which it is still possible to 'establish relational tactics (a struggle for life), artistic creations (an aesthetics), and autonomous initiatives (an ethic)'.[10] There remains, in other words, the possibility of reoccupying, although not permanently, a discursive or epistemic space by means of one's own actions in time: the artistic gesture is one of these actions. These constant cross-references, mutual influences, and exchanges between the *represented*, the *representable*, and the *representer* open a space, a cognitive window within which the formation, evolution, and dispersion of specific artistic phenomena can be investigated.

In what follows I explore this complex relationship between art, space and sovereignty by analysing exactly how it has taken concrete form and 'crystallized' in a crucial historical moment: that of the emergence of linear perspective, which inaugurated the modern conception of humanism. As we shall see, art and the 'natural sciences' were closely interwoven and their relationship cemented into the Cartesian–Hobbesian representation of the modern sovereign state. Looking at the artistic space therefore means exploring a multidimensional window, a liminal category, a crossroad where the 'gaze' and the 'sovereign' intersect and reflect themselves into the aesthetic field, designing (and imposing) a specific vision of modernity and of its epistemo-political discourse.

The space of art: Sovereignty of perspective and materialization of the gaze

The relationship between Masaccio (1401–28) – usually considered, along with Donatello and Brunelleschi, one of the 'founders' of 'modern' Renaissance art[11] – and the enigmatic artist Masolino da Panicale[12] (1383/4–1440) has long been shrouded in mystery. Once thought to have been Masaccio's teacher,[13] Masolino had his own work largely obscured and almost dragged into oblivion by the image of the *meraviglioso* ('marvellous') – a younger pupil who became 'the most important painter of the early quattrocento'.[14] This generated a paradoxical exchange of roles between teacher and student whereby the student becomes the teacher and the teacher follows the style of his student; and the exchange has given rise to a proper riddle, if it is true that 'in the unclear distinction of their works, the figures of the two artists have lost their identity; for many years, critics have labored in vain to distinguish their profiles, and yet the most industrious demonstrations have so far led to no agreement on the exact solution of the problem' – as Pietro Toesca wrote in 1908.[15]

This enigma has persisted in contemporary debates. In fact, due to the historical importance of the two artists, 'the division of the work between Masaccio and Masolino has been the subject of more intense analysis and controversy than any other collaboration.'[16] Scholars today are fairly certain that there was a genuinely mutual collaboration (and not merely a master–apprentice relation) between the two artists, the most sublime and mature outcomes of which are the frescoes in the Brancacci Chapel in Florence (1424–28).[17] Nonetheless, the confusion between the works and lives of Masolino and Masaccio cannot be attributed solely to the spatial and temporal distance that separates us from the original sources. Indeed, Giorgio Vasari, in his second edition of *Le Vite* (1568), had already misidentified the works of the two artists, attributing to Masaccio the frescoes of the Chapel of St Catherine in the Church of San Clemente in Rome.[18] What is important to highlight here, however, is not the erroneous attribution per se, but rather the reasons behind this initial misunderstanding.[19] Given the strong 'naturalness' of the frescoes and their powerful perspectival effects, this work was ingenuously attributed to the man who, as Vasari put it, 'purged the art of painting of its harshness, imperfections, and difficulties, and … paved the way toward more beautiful expressions, gestures, boldness, and vitality, achieving a certain relief in his figures which was truly *appropriate* and *natural*'.[20]

At this juncture, then, the stylistic and comparative method used by Vasari – and indeed the source of the confusion – should be clear. For, if Masaccio's genius consists in having 'realized that painting is nothing other than the art of imitating all the living things of Nature … just as Nature produced them', then only the one who 'fully follows Nature should be considered a splendid artisan'.[21] In this way naturalism, which is 'lifelike, true and natural',[22] is transformed into a new analytical paradigm, a prism through which one can distinguish the good from the bad, the artistic from the nonartistic, the agreeable from the disagreeable. For Vasari, the capacity of representing or reproducing nature becomes an ontology of the real, the fulcrum upon which the aesthetic world rests, the watershed where the 'true' and the 'beautiful' meet and tend to overlap:

> The most excellent Masaccio ... gave birth to that modern style which has been followed from those times down to our own day by all our artists ... a more highly expressive depiction of feelings and physical gestures combined with an attempt to make their designs *reflect the reality of natural phenomena*; and *facial expressions which perfectly resemble men* as they were known by the artists who painted them. In this way, these artists attempted to *produce what they saw in Nature and no more*; in this way, their works came to be more highly regarded and better understood; and this gave them the courage to establish rules for perspective and to make their foreshortenings exactly like the proper forms of natural relief, while proceeding to observe shadow, light, shading, and other difficult details, and to compose their scenes with *greater similitude*; and they tried to make their landscapes more similar to reality, as well as their trees, grass, flowers, skies, clouds, and other natural phenomena.[23]

For these reasons, Vasari attributed those works in which naturalism is more pronounced and the perspective more precise to the painter of the *splendido* ('gorgeous') fresco of *The Trinity*, which, through its exaggerated realism, seems to open a hole in the wall.[24] For Vasari, it was unthinkable that Masolino should reach the same expressive level as his pupil. This naturalistic–perspectivist ideologeme was erected, for a long time, as a paradigm of artistic analysis. Even in 1898, more than three centuries after Vasari published his book, Giovanni Battista Cavalcaselle, singling out the weakness of the perspective and separating it from the general strength of the painting, attributed *The Crucifixion* to the young Masaccio who, under the influence of his 'master Masolino', had not yet fully developed his art.[25] In short, linear perspective had become the epistemological background through which the success and the authorship of a work of art could be assessed.[26]

Perhaps the most obvious example of this 'perspectivist paradigm' is the controversial debate around the Colonna Altarpiece. Probably commissioned by Pope Martin V (1369–1431) for the renewal of the Church of Santa Maria Maggiore in Rome, the work consists of three panels painted on both sides, which form a double triptych. According to Vasari, who attributed the entire polyptych to Masaccio, the panels were placed 'in the church of Santa Maria Maggiore inside a small chapel near the sacristy and contained four well-executed saints, painted as if they are in relief, with Our Lady of the Snows in the middle.'[27] The attribution of the work has been the subject of a long dispute and, to date, there are at least four different positions and interpretations of the altarpiece.[28]

The difficulty in dating the six panels stems mainly from the diversity and distinctiveness of styles that characterize the painting. For example, in the panel *Saints Jerome and John the Baptist* (Figure 3), attributed to Masaccio, 'the two saints are different from any of Masaccio's other known works.'[29] In this regard, the art historian Paul Joannides has argued that, although the work was probably painted in Rome (it is known that Masaccio died there in 1428), the panel should not be classified among the artist's later work, because 'in no sense' does the painting follow 'a *logical development*'. Although 'the intelligence is distinctively Masaccesque', the 'somewhat *Byzantine features* suggest an artist who has not yet fully worked out his own characterization.'[30] In the figure of John, for instance, the centre of gravity is 'such that he appears to be stationary, not an error that Masaccio would have made after the Brancacci Chapel.'[31]

'To explain a date of *c.* 1428' – Joannides continues – 'it must be argued that Masaccio was developing a new manner, *retrogressive in figural grandeur, but demonstrating great refinement in illumination.*'[32] Joannides here touches upon an important point. For what if the spiritual strength that the painting exudes was the result of a conscious choice and not of mere 'figurative decadence'? What if the interpretative key of the painting lay in its suspension of linear perspective and in its somewhat 'iconographic asymmetry'? As Joannides sensed, the unique qualities of the figures might be the 'result of *their function*' and not of Masaccio's development as figurative artist.[33]

The same uncertainty, problematic and perspectival, characterizes the centrepiece of the composition: *The Founding of the Basilica of S. Maria Maggiore* by Masolino (Figure 4). This work represents the miraculous event of the foundation of the basilica of Santa Maria Maggiore in Rome. According to legend, during the hot August of 358, a prodigious snowfall traced or described the perimeter of a church on one of the hills of Rome. To commemorate the importance of this extraordinary event, the then Pope,

Figure 3 Masaccio, Saints Jerome and John the Baptist, 1428/1429. (*The National Gallery, London. © The National Gallery*).

Figure 4 Masolino da Panicale, Pope Liberio Founding the Basilica di S. Maria ad Nives, 1423/1428. (*Museo di Capodimonte, Naples. © Photo Scala, Florence – courtesy of the Ministero Beni e Attività Culturali*).

Liberius, decided to found a basilica (in the painting, the pope is dressed in the triple tiara and portrayed tracing with a hoe the foundations of the church). It has been said that the painting is 'weak' by comparison to other works by Masolino, because perspective 'seems here not fully understood'.[34] More specifically, the attention of critics has been drawn to the 'simplicity' of the perspectival lines created by the clouds, which attempt to give depth to a composition whose figures nevertheless 'have slender and poorly balanced proportions' and that, moreover, lacks the 'liveliness and skill seen in the paintings of San Clemente'.[35] Yet the painting possesses great expressive power and, as Vasari noted, after having examined the altarpiece in the company of the 'most divine' Michelangelo, even he 'praised it very highly'.[36]

What, then, if these deviations from linear perspective were the result of conscious artistic choice, and not of poor execution? What if the artists had taken a step back from 'naturalism', given the content of the panel? What if, behind the suspension of linear perspective, there was an awareness of another perspective? What message can be concealed behind this return to the spiritual to the detriment of perspectivism and naturalism? A closer look at Masolino's panel may perhaps open an alternative interpretative path.

The panel (Figure 4) is divided into two sections by a large cloud, which of course is anything but naturalistic as serves to mark, symbolically, a threshold between two horizons or worlds: transcendence and immanence. In the transcendent world (the upper part of the painting) are represented, in a nonperspectival but iconographic way, Christ and the Virgin Mary inside a circle of glory. This is a timeless world, or rather one in which time and space are fused together. And this is why linear perspective cannot be used to 'pierce' eternity. Contrariwise, in the lower part of the painting flows the secular time of the human creature in which space takes on a quasi-naturalistic and worldly form. Masolino stresses here the temporality of the human world by means of a perspectival spatiality precisely in order to emphasize the difference between these two planes or horizons of sense. The clouds, in fact, design such strong vanishing points that the contrast between the 'low' and the 'high' world strikes the observer. The painting, in short, is dominated by two principles: the perspectival and the nonperspectival, the temporal and the spiritual, the human and the divine. Nonetheless, these principles do not play against each other: on the contrary, they coexist, enter into dialogue and give life to the central motif of the painting, which is miracle. For the eternal breaks into the temporal, Masolino emphasizes this 'interference' by painting the hand of Christ coming out of the circle of glory (which is in fact a symbol of perfection). A simple comparison with two of Masolino's later works may suffice to confirm the intention of the artist.

Both in the paintings of Castiglione Olona and in those of San Clemente in Rome (Figure 5) the Eternal Father is in fact represented inside a circle that is never crossed. In the two frescoes, the eternal is iconographically suspended over history. In *The Founding*, however, the miracle is accomplished: the 'divine snow' enters time, settles on the earthly land and conveys the heavenly message. A time-space short circuit has happened: the two worlds, even if only for a moment, have come into contact.

The painting, in short, is endowed with a twofold principle of representation based on a *reverse perspective*. The upper part of the painting, the one most distant (physically and conceptually) from the observer, should in fact present smaller figures; but Masolino increases the size of the Christ and the Madonna in proportion to their elevation in the fresco, in reverse proportion to their

Figure 5 Masolino da Panicale, Annunciation (detail), 1423/1424. (*Church of San Clemente, Rome. © Photo Scala, Florence*).

distance from the observer. 'This is a characteristic of that *other*, spiritual space: the further away something is, the bigger it is; the closer it is, the smaller.'[37] In the painting there are therefore *ontologically* heterogeneous spaces, which require a different conception of representation. For this reason, the panel presents a perspectival polycentrism. It is a metaphysical reason, which 'bends' linear perspective to the needs of the painting and of representation.

The same logic applies to Masaccio's panel (Figure 3). The strongly iconographic, 'Byzantine' representation gives strength to the painting, which breaks the lines of perspective in favour of a spiritual polycentrism where objects seem to have a reality of their own, thus communicating a peculiar symbolism.[38] In this artistic choice lies the nontrivial gesture of the artist to free himself from the forced historicization of two figures – St Jerome and John the Baptist – who lived in completely different times and places. Would it be artistically sound to set the transhistorical encounter between the two saints against the naturalistic background of a Rome or a Florence? To convey a spiritual meaning, Masaccio's choice falls upon the *timeless* force of the icon. His atemporal message, in fact, might be betrayed by the 'naturalness' of linear perspective.

What I am suggesting, then, is that the two artists, in this extremely important work,[39] consciously disregard (or force) the 'laws' of perspective in order to communicate a more honest spiritual experience (which is certainly related to the theme of the altarpiece). Placed on the threshold of modernity, Masaccio's and Masolino's work relied on a twofold mode of representation: perspectival naturalism and polycentric iconography. These two forms or modalities (in the sense of Italian *maniere*) of representing reality respond to different intentions, perceptions and conceptions of the world. Having lived in an age of transition, both artists mastered this dual sensibility, which was based on different ontologies, and it would be simplistic to evaluate that merely by means of the 'iron law' of linear perspective. In discussing the historical transition – and the ontological difference – between the Middle Ages and the Renaissance, Pavel Florensky has powerfully argued:

> When the religious stability of a *Weltanschauung* disintegrates and the sacred metaphysics of the general popular consciousness is eroded by the individual judgment of a single person with his single point of view, and moreover with a single point of view precisely at this specific moment –

then there also appears a perspective, which is characteristic of a fragmented consciousness. But besides, this initially happens not in pure art, which is essentially always more or less metaphysical, but in *applied* art, as an element of decoration, which has as its task *not the true essence of being, but verisimilitude to appearance* ... As the religious *Weltanschauung* of the Middle Ages became more secular, pure religious ritual reinvented itself as the semi-theatrical mystery plays, while the icon became so-called religious painting, in which the religious subject increasingly became just an excuse for depicting the body and the landscape.[40]

It is within this process of the secularization of the gaze that the 'dictatorship of the True' takes centre stage.[41] The medieval conception – according to which 'space itself is not merely a uniform structureless place ... but is in itself a distinctive reality, organized throughout, everywhere differentiated' – is gradually replaced by an ahistorical ontology which conceives space as 'qualitatively homogeneous, infinite and boundless, a space that is, so to speak, formless and devoid of individuality'.[42] The ancient multiperspectival ontology – based on several, living and autonomous centres of reality – is therefore replaced by a novel monocentric ontology, which is conceived as valid, natural and, most important, subjective.[43] Nonetheless, as Florensky observes with acuity, this form of subjectivism is, paradoxically, impersonal and 'unreal', as it projects its transcendental ego over a depersonalized, abstract, geometric reality where objects have meaning only within a homogeneous space: the subject could, theoretically, occupy any space within the geometric field whatsoever. Perspective thus becomes '*a method that of necessity results from a Weltanschauung in which the real basis for half-real things-notions is admitted to be a certain kind of subjectivity*, which is itself devoid of reality'.[44]

But what lies behind this de-personalization of the individual and materialization of her gaze? What epistemic politics is concealed behind the only perspectival point from which the lines of force of this new worldview ultimately radiate? If it is true that Masolino and Masaccio show, through their genius, the different possibilities of the representing gaze, what does it mean 'to see' in an age in which everything has become perspectival and single-centred? A look at the other, political side of modernity might help us to clarify the transition to this 'new space' and to the subjectivity that occupies and interprets it.

The space of sovereignty: Immanence of power and violence of the gaze

In *Verfassungslehre* (1928), which many consider to be his *magnum opus*, Carl Schmitt discusses two political principles through which 'every political unity receives its concrete form': identity and representation.[45] Although different, these principles are not mutually exclusive but represent 'only two opposing points for the concrete formation of the political unity'.[46] According to Schmitt, in fact, 'there is no state without representation' – but at the same time 'there is no state without structural elements of the principle of identity'.[47] This means that political unity does not exist in nature but needs to be created and established on two pillars: the people, in other words, its living substance; and representation, that is the principle by which the people become conscious of themselves as a whole, as a public and political community. It goes without saying that, without the body politic (the people), there would be no representation. But, assuming that a certain community aspires to unity, the principle of representation is, for Schmitt, 'an essential factor of the process of integration'. In fact 'it is possible that the political unity is first brought about through representation itself'.[48]

The principle of representation rests, however, on a paradoxical logic. As Schmitt puts it, 'to represent means to make an invisible being visible and present through a publicly present one.'[49] Political unity, therefore, is not created through an algebraic addition (by which the parts are assembled into a whole), but rather through a symbolic representation that makes visible to the parties the significance of their existential community. 'The dialectic of the concept' – Schmitt continues – 'is that the invisible is presupposed as absent and nevertheless is simultaneously made present'.[50] Once more, for the German jurist (political) representation is an *existential* matter, and this implies that to represent is 'not possible just with any type of being ... something dead, something inferior and valueless, something lowly cannot be represented. It lacks the enhanced type of being that is capable of an *existence*, of raising into the public being.'[51]

Although Schmitt is never explicit about the kind of 'special being' that would be capable of giving life to the dialectic of representation and, consequently, to the political unity of a living community, there are traces of a Hobbesian vision scattered throughout his work. 'The personal quality of the state lies' – he writes – 'in representation and not in the concept of the state'.[52] In other words, political unity must be, literally, *embodied* if it is to become actualized and effective. And to strengthen the argument, Schmitt explicitly refers to Thomas Hobbes and his doctrine of representation: 'The multitude ... united in *one person* is called a COMMON-WEALTH, in Latine CIVITAS.'[53] The 'great leviathan state' is made alive through this embodiment of the political multitude in the exclusive authority of the sovereign.

This understanding of sovereignty – and of its space and representation – has been so influential that it has not only determined the modern, Western conception of the state but also thrown a long shadow upon the contemporary age. It is therefore crucial to take a closer look at how this vision has taken form in the English philosopher's thought, if we wish to understand the epistemic symmetries that Hobbes's idea of sovereignty shares with the Renaissance conception of space.

It is well known that Hobbes's philosophy was strongly influenced by the 'exact sciences' and their epistemologies, and in particular by geometry. We know, for example, that he was an admirer of Galileo, whom he met in Florence. However, it was in Paris, between 1629 and 1631, that Hobbes made an acquaintance that proved to be crucial to his intellectual development: Euclid's geometry.[54] In the dedicatory epistle to his treatise *Concerning Government and Society*, he forcefully states, addressing the second Earl of Devonshire, William Cavendish: 'Whatsoever things they are in which this present age doth differ from the rude simpleness of antiquity, we must acknowledge to be a debt which we owe to geometry.'[55] For Hobbes, this science is so fundamental and illuminating that, 'were nature of human actions as distinctly known as the nature of *quantity* in geometrical figures, the strength of *avarice* and *ambition* ... would presently faint and languish; and mankind should enjoy such an immortal peace.'[56]

With this conviction in mind, Hobbes ventures to develop a philosophical system based precisely on a 'geometry of man' and his *space* in the world. More than a political theory, therefore, Hobbes's philosophy is a vision of humankind and its relation to the physical space of the world. In *De corpore* (1655), a work devoted to foundational matters, Hobbes openly writes: 'The *subject* of Philosophy, or the matter it treats of, is every body of which we can conceive any generation, and which we may, by any consideration thereof, compare to other bodies, or which is capable of composition and resolution; that is to say, every body of whose generation or property we can have any knowledge.'[57] Philosophy, in other words, deals only with those *effects* and *appearances* that are properties of bodies and that, by manifesting themselves, 'make us distinguish them from one another'.[58] In this sense, human beings are nothing but *bodies* distinguishable from other bodies only by means of their distinct movement and rationality. As Hobbes has it, 'put together ... *body, animated, rational*, are in speech compounded into this one name ... *man*.'[59]

Given that, for Hobbes, everything is ultimately related to body and matter, the category of space becomes the ontological background of his philosophical vision. In effect, 'a body' – Hobbes writes – 'is that, which having not dependence upon our thought, is coincident or coextended with some part of the space'.[60] This idea is reminiscent of the Aristotelian doctrine of place. As Martin Heidegger has acutely argued:

> Despite all the differences in the manner of thinking between Greek and modern thought, space is conceived of in the *same* way, that is, from the body. Space is three-dimensional extension, *extensio*. In it, the body and its movements have their orbit, their stadium, their time intervals and paths in which they move around [*herumspazieren*], as it were.[61]

In effect, Hobbes includes *extensio* among the universal accidents – that is the ways in which bodies give themselves to reason and perception – 'for no body can be conceived to be without extension'.[62] Nonetheless, this seemingly objectivist theory of space is characterized by strongly subjectivist undertones. Indeed, if, for Hobbes, on the one hand, there is a 'real space' in which bodies manifest themselves through their extension, on the other hand bodies are also '*subjected* to imaginary space' – in other words they 'might be understood by reason, as well as perceived by sense'.[63] This implies that space is the result of a complex interaction between the objectivity of the world and the filtering perception of the knowing subject. Only in this way can we appreciate Hobbes's cryptic definition of space: 'SPACE *is the phantasm of a thing existing without the mind simply*; that is to say, that phantasm, in which we consider no other accident, but only that it appears without us.'[64] Presumably what Hobbes means here is that space, although 'objective', reveals itself only when, by 'encountering' us, it creates in our mind an image of its 'objectivity'. The object becomes *spatialized* only when the subject's perception being 'hit' by the body-symbol projects her mind upon it, thus imagining the 'object'.

It goes without saying that objects exist without the 'subject', but at the same time we can know bodies only because we experience them, only because they 'encounter' us. In other words, what Hobbes calls the 'phantasm' is the result of a short circuit that occurs between the objectivity of the world and the human way of sensing and representing it:

> The phantasm, which is made by hearing, is sound; by smell, odour; by taste, savour; and by touch, hardness and softness, heat and cold, wetness, oiliness, and many more, which are easier to be distinguished by sense than words … For seeing in all sense of external things there is a mutual action and reaction, that is, two endeavours opposing one another, it is manifest that the motion of both of them together will be continued every way.[65]

This conception, which 'has a remarkably Kantian flavour',[66] is indeed a *perspectival image of the world*. The 'ghost', which is an *imago*, is in fact the reflection of the 'perspectival encounter' between the human being and the world of objects.[67] For Hobbes, to see an object means that, through its movement, 'notwithstanding any distance', that object will encounter 'the foremost part of the eye', which

> will be pressed; and by the pressure of that part, the motion will be propagated to the innermost part of the organ of sight, namely, to the heart; and from the reaction of the heart, there will proceed an endeavour back by the same way, ending in the endeavour outwards of the coat of the eye, called the *retina*. But this endeavour outwards … is the thing which is called light, of the phantasm of a lucid body. For it is by reason of this phantasm that an object is called lucid.[68]

This dialectic between external and internal reproduces very closely the perspectival conceptions of Brunelleschi and Alberti, whereby rays from the object that converge into the eye are subsequently re-projected from the eye onto a plane of representation (Figure 6). The picture that emerges is precisely a representation or the perspectival image of the object. In short, *Hobbes's phantasm is the world as seen through the visual cone of the modern subject.*

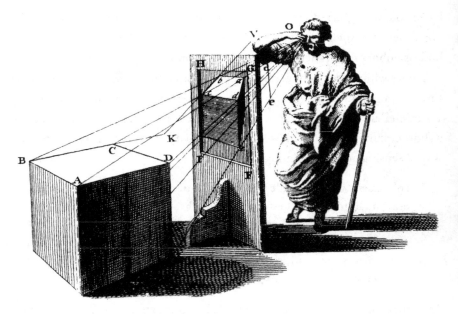

Figure 6 Brook Taylor, The Visual Pyramid from *New Principles of Linear Perspective*, 1719. (*The Max Planck Institute for the History of Science, Berlin. © The Max Planck Institute for the History of Science*).

It is this conception of perspectival space that Hobbes adapts in order to build his vision of the body politic. It is this 'imaginary space', homogeneous and empty 'because it might be filled',[69] that he develops to create the leviathan.[70] Note that it is precisely the interrelation between object and subject, world and reason, that forms the basis of his distinction between the infinite and the finite. Space cannot be infinite, because reason, through representation, sets limits to the limitedness of space:

> For in an infinite space, whatsoever we take or design in our mind, the distance of the same from us is a finite space; *for in the very designing of the place thereof, we put an end to that space, of which we ourselves are the beginning*; and whatsoever any man with his mind cuts of both ways from infinite, he determines the same, that is, he makes it finite.[71]

It is the *ratio* that, by entering the world of bodies, dissects space to make sense of it. It is as if the modern subject captured the infinity of the world in her own finitude, with no possibility of escaping the boundaries of her perspective.

Space and Sovereignty

In this way, for Hobbes, infinity is equally trapped by the limits of thinking and by the thinking of limits.

The notion of 'limit' plays both an epistemological and an ontological function in Hobbes's work. In fact, just as *knowledge is not possible without limits, existence is impossible without borders*:

> *Extreme parts* and *limits* are the same thing. And from hence it is manifest, that *beginning* and *end* depend upon the order in which we number them; and that to *terminate* or *limit* space and time, is the same thing with *imagining their beginning and end* ... Of infinite space or time, it cannot be said that it is a *whole* or *one*: not a *whole*, because not compounded of parts; for seeing parts, how many whatsoever they be, are severally finite, they will also, when they are all put together, make a whole finite: nor *one*, because nothing can be said to be one, except there be another to compare it with; but it cannot be conceived that there are two spaces, or two times, infinite.[72]

This conception of space also implies that infinity *cannot be represented*. The whole determines the parts and these, in turn, call for the whole to give birth to a finite totality. This is the great leviathan, the God that, to become alive, needs to be finite, that is mortal: 'Nothing can rightly be called a whole, that is not conceived to be compounded of parts, and that it may be divided into parts; so that if we deny that a thing has parts, we deny the same to be a whole.'[73] Here lies the core of Hobbes's social physics, which is characterized by an individualistic atomism and a neutralized social space. And it is at this level that we also encounter the limitations of his conception of representation.

Once the political space has been bounded, it is in fact necessary to create differences within this artificial totality, to produce authority within this isomorphic construction. This is the purpose of sovereign representation. To transform itself into a political unity, the multitude has to be transmuted into 'one sovereign person' by means of representation.[74] To form a whole (the state), the parts (the subjects) must be represented by 'one man, or one Person ... so that it be done with *the consent of every one of that Multitude in particular* ... And *Unity*, cannot otherwise be understood in Multitude.'[75]

Although this 'personalistic theory' of representation seems to contradict the mathematical–geometrical conception previously examined, it is actually grounded upon the same mechanistic–scopic ontology and conceals similar conceptual aporiae. In fact the sovereign, in Hobbes's system, is neither the embodiment of the state nor merely the symbol of its power, but the apex of a conceptual pyramid. Indeed, the leviathan is a *magnus homo* 'whose Acts a great Multitude, by mutual Covenants one with another, have made themselves every one the author, to the end he may use the strength and means of them all ... for their Peace and Common Defense'.[76] Once again, the parts are inseparable from the whole and, in turn, the whole is conceivable only as totalization of its parts.

But how is it then possible to give life to this 'geometrical machine'? How can movement, in other words time, enter this sealed space, the hermetic body of the leviathan? For Hobbes, this is precisely the task of the sovereign, who has the function of starting and governing the political machine. As Carl Schmitt has sharply observed, 'Hobbes transfers ... the Cartesian conception of man as a mechanism with a soul into the "huge man", the state, made by him into a machine animated by the sovereign-representative person.'[77] In this sense, the sovereign gesture is like the 'spark' that instils soul into *homo artificialis*.

What is lost in the Hobbesian doctrine of representation is the dialectic between the two worlds, the visible and the invisible, which is, according to Schmitt, the only relation capable of transforming the representative into a *symbol* of the represented, and not merely reproducing the representative arithmetically or mechanically. The mythopoeic force of representing is realized only when it transcends the historico-geometric givenness of the constituent parts: 'A being that is greater than itself – this is the basic definition of the symbol. A symbol is something that manifests in itself that which is not itself, that which is greater than itself and is nevertheless essentially manifested through itself.'[78] But when this transcendent, metaphysical signifier vanishes, state sovereignty becomes a mere simulacrum; the Leviathan is transformed into a machine, thus disappearing 'from the world of representations'[79]:

> The intrinsic logic of the manmade, artificial product 'state' does not culminate in a person but in a machine. Not the representation by a person but the factual, current accomplishment of genuine protection is what the state is all about. Representation is nothing if it is not *tutela praesens*. That, however, can only be attained by an effectively functioning mechanism of command.[80]

In a certain sense, it is precisely the 'dimension of invisibility' – which Nicholas of Cusa,[81] too, had seen as the 'cement' of the sociopolitical domain – that disappears in Hobbes's system. And this, once again, is due to the 'perspectival vision' of the English philosopher. In his *Leviathan*, Hobbes stages an illusionistic, theatrical representation in which the viewer-citizen is, so to speak, 'paralysed' as he looks at himself in the reflection of the sovereign, thus giving life to the visual composition of a *civitas*. In this space the sovereign is an exceptional point – indeed, the 'monarchical point' of a visual pyramid from which the perspectival lines of force radiate. In the frontispiece image of leviathan, 'the eyes of each one, regardless of position, is [*sic*] directed toward the giant's head'[82] of the sovereign, and it is not difficult to recognize in this geometric scheme the postulates of linear perspective previously analysed. The sovereign optical centre, just as much as the centre of perspective, is in fact conceived as *absolute, unique*, a point through which the entire universe should be legislated.[83] Moreover, the 'lawgiver is thought of as for ever inseparably *chained* to his throne. If he quits this absolutized place or even stirs slightly upon it, then the whole unity of the perspectival construction is immediately shattered and the whole perspectival system falls apart.'[84]

It follows that Hobbes's system must necessarily be free of history and move in empty circles, as an automaton. In it, the world has to be completely *static* and wholly *immutable*. As Florensky has argued, 'In a world subject to a perspectival depiction there can be neither history, nor growth, nor dimensions, nor movements, nor biography, nor development of dramatic actions, nor the play of emotions – nor should there be. Otherwise the perspectival oneness of the picture disintegrates yet again.'[85] Hobbes's conception of space captures time and cages history. It is precisely due to his spatial conception that he had to resort to a meta-historical origin in order to elaborate his philosophical system. The state of nature is in fact a fictitious, ahistorical time (although the time of the leviathan is even more so). Between these two domains – nature and culture, disorder and order – there is no history, and the transition from one world to the other can only happen by means of a theoretical 'leap': 'A spark of reason flashes, and a consensus emerges about the necessity to submit to the strongest power.'[86] The leviathan's is, in short, a time without history, a space without action, a humanism without humanity.

Here we encounter, once again, the conceptual problematic of perspectival space – a space conceived of as abstract and universal, schematic and subjective, static and timeless. This 'picture' of modernity is, as we have seen, based on a paradox: only that which can be objectively represented is deemed to be subjective; and only that which is conceivable by an impersonal subject is objective. In the critical words of Martin Heidegger:

> The modern age has, as a consequence of the liberation of humanity, introduced subjectivism and individualism. But it remains just as certain that no age before this one has produced a comparable objectivism, and that in no age before this has the non-individual, in the shape of the collective, been accorded prestige. *Of the essence here is the necessary interplay between subjectivism and objectivism.* ... This objectification of beings is accomplished in a setting-before, a *representing*, aimed at bringing each being before it in such a way that the man who calculates can be sure – and that means certain – of the being.[87]

This is the power of linear perspective: the gaze is as if hypnotized at a point, forced to recognize, in life, only *the subjective certainty of the object and the secure objectivity of the subject*. In other words, things, bodies, and the world in general 'materialize' into a perspectival form only when the modes and dimensions of being are reduced to one. What is sovereign in modernity, then, is the gaze that looks at and is mirrored into the objectivity of the world; the gaze that, by subjectifying the world, objectifies the subject.

The culmination of this monocular and monocentric conception of space can be found in the painting *The Ideal City* (1480–90). In it, the 'ideal' is nothing but space in itself, an absolutely perspectival space that *never takes place*. Here what is represented is a world dominated by an eternal recurrence of the same, a city seen as a pure, uninhabited space, an *urbs sine civibus* ('city without citizens'), a space enclosed by its internal measure and proportion. In this masterpiece of humanism there is no longer any trace of humans.[88]

Conclusion: Within the world picture

In the previous pages I have tried to reconstruct an alternative path for exploring the interaction between art, space and political thought, as it developed during modernity. The complex of references and reciprocal influences across these fields opens an ontological, epistemic and dialogical space where the oculocentric paradigm realizes itself. In it, humans and what

Space and Sovereignty

they can see – being and seeing – become an infinite reflection of each other. Just as in Velázquez's painting *Las Meninas*, we become the illusion of sovereignty created by our gaze, by our own perspective. Although partially linked to the so-called process of secularization, this dynamic has very little to do with the anthropologization of God, or the replacement of God's sovereignty with a human sovereign.

It is not (only) this exchange of roles between Man and God that is at stake in the modern sovereign perspective. As Heidegger noticed, 'Not the I-ness of an individual person, the subjectiveness of the egoity, but *the pre-formed formlike presence of a species of men (type)* forms the most extreme subjectivity which comes forth in the fulfillment of modern metaphysics and is presented by its thinking.'[89] As has been previously observed, it is this depersonalization of the individual, this objectification of the subject that makes possible the emergence of this regime of representation.

But what, then, lies behind the appearance of this objective and empty form of human being? What does it mean that 'man' must be 'everywhere and at all times determinable and, that means, *representable*'?[90] If we follow Heidegger, it means that the human must disappear as 'mystery' and 'potentiality'; that what is 'invisible' no longer exists and cannot be *represented*; that certainty takes the place of the search for 'truth' – just as in Hobbes's argument where *logos* is concerned only with bodies, that is with what is *generated* and *present*, and thus excludes the 'eternal, ingenerable ... in whom there is nothing neither to divide nor compound, nor any generation to be conceived'.[91] Once transformed into techniques, representation and sovereignty lose their symbolic value, thus inaugurating what Heidegger has called the 'age of the world picture'. The ontological signature of this age is 'presence': everything is to be *visible*. Thus the Earth, which for centuries was conceived of and experienced as the ground that illuminates our dwelling (Gaia, Terra Mater), is replaced with its outward appearance, an *imago*, a phantasm that captures the worldliness of being without grasping its more profound essence.[92] Indeed, the fact that the human being 'grasps' the world as a picture implies that she perceives it as *her* world. The Earth thus becomes the objectified-object of the sole sovereign subject: the human gaze. That the human being projects herself into the objectivity of the world means in turn that she perceives herself not only as a subject, but also as something objective, given, unproblematic.

The emergence of the global age from the ashes of modernity, then, involves the disappearance of 'man' as 'problem' and self-opening 'mystery'. The fundamental philosophical question – 'Why are there beings at all, and why not rather nothing?' – is not only ignored, but literally *disappears*.[93] And thus, when the question of the human, of his being and representing, is eclipsed, what appears is an age of 'total mobilization'. Quantity, measurement and calculation take the place of God, the cosmos, and being. In this way modern technology, as the super-objectification of the world, becomes the predominant force behind the process of planetary conquest.

Yet, paradoxically, this is but a blind horizon: the human being is trapped in the (alleged) unstoppability of the technical apparatus precisely because her infinite potentiality is transferred into the total occupation of terrestrial space and its resources. For Heidegger, in other words, technological objectification is a reduction, not an enlargement, of human existential and imaginative power. Material occupation based on abstract calculation involves the occlusion of the open, infinite horizon of meaningfulness and the devastation of the finite one (the Earth). From this perspective, then, it is possible to understand why the so-called process of rationalization, unleashed on a global scale, cannot be rationally limited, and why the finite resources of the Earth can be constantly exploited by an infinite will to power.

In this crucial historical moment, then, it is more important than ever to problematize our conceptions of space, its sovereign occupation and the way we represent ourselves in it. Indeed, we may ask: what happens to sovereignty in the age of the spectacle – an age characterized by anonymous masses, visual dictatorship, techno-security and millions of impersonal eyes watching the crowds? Rethinking space and its invisibility is an urgent task for both contemporary artists and political theorists.

Part Two

Political Theologies

3

Encounters at the End of a World: Max Weber, Carl Schmitt and the Tyranny of Values

> Evil is the starry sky of the Good.
> Franz Kafka, *Oktavheft* G, II, 2

Worldviews arise from spatial revolutions, and thinkers are always intimately related to the ethos of their age. Both Max Weber and Carl Schmitt would have probably subscribed to these views, convinced as they were of the non-universality of the human sciences and of the radical historicity of ideas.[1] This conception of intellectual history can also be used to explore the epochal background against which the complex relationship between these two German thinkers has gained intensity and momentum. Rationalization and disenchantment, secularization and neutralization, theology and theodicy, legality and legitimacy, charisma and katechon: all these conceptual pairs are in fact the leitmotifs in Weber's and Schmitt's work, and point to a common origin: the crisis of Western rationalism.[2] Nonetheless, it would be arbitrary to assume that Schmitt 'was a "legitimate pupil"' of Weber', or that his work represents the 'response of a political thinker to an economist'.[3] With the first assumption, one underestimates the overall context: the crisis of modernity and the cultural and political horizon from which both Weber and Schmitt drew their themes. The second argument emphasizes personal choices, thus reducing the boundaries of the *mundus imaginalis* that lies beyond their analyses.

The path undertaken here is different. In an attempt to uncover the 'imaginative background' of Weber's and Schmitt's worldviews, this chapter explores them not only from the angle of the problems they faced, but also from that of the solutions they found for those challenges. In so doing, the chapter aims to throw new light on a decades-long controversy over the intellectual relation between Weber and Schmitt.[4] This debate has been characterized by a sharp disagreement between 'Weberians', who exclude the possibility of any continuity between the theorist of *Wertfreiheit* and the *Kronjurist* of the Third Reich,[5] and the proponents of an intellectual filiation between the two thinkers.[6] Without denying the legitimacy of either interpretation, I argue that the similarities between Weber and Schmitt should be sought and located in the larger context of the crisis of modernity. Both thinkers witnessed the dramatic changes caused by the process of rationalization, namely, the neutralization of politics and the emergence of a new polytheism of values. Yet, while for Weber the age of disenchantment represents the end of any possible ideological unity of the world (and the latter's reversal into a 'secular polytheism'), for Schmitt this crisis reveals the origin of politics – in other words it reveals the political (*das Politische*), which becomes the ultimate, pervasive force in modern life.

Catherine Colliot-Thélène has suggested three analytical facets of the confrontation between the two German scholars: the positivization of law; the theory of values; and the role of rationalization in the genesis of modernity.[7] I think it is particularly relevant to engage with the second facet and compare the two along the line of their respective views on values. First, the influence of Weber's theory of values on Schmitt's *Tyranny of Values* (1960) has not yet been fully explored.[8] Second, 'the theory of values' represents a sort of intellectual testament of these authors; indeed, it contains the ultimate conceptual effort, that through which they tried to rethink the question of disenchantment and the nihilistic drift it brings about. In this sense, their 'discourse on values' can be read as an extreme synthesis of the other two – analytical – facets of confrontation. Finally, Schmitt's 1960 essay is the most explicitly 'Weberian' of his works – the one in which he openly acknowledges 'Weber's intellectual honesty', and in which the similarities and differences between the two emerge most forcefully.[9]

By comparing Weber's and Schmitt's work on this conceptual ground, I intend to show that they stand on different 'vocational' sides. Indeed, if for Weber, 'in a time without god and prophet' – the only possibility left is to take 'responsibility before history' and, accordingly, to measure one's own actions by the yardstick of an appropriate individual ethics,[10] for Schmitt, on the contrary, behind modernity and its crisis lies entropy and violence, the latter being the original source of social life – a source that may change form but cannot be completely removed from 'the normative order of the earth.'[11] Here is the rift that separates the atheist theorist of *The Protestant Ethic* from the Catholic author of *Politische Theologie*. The crisis of modernity – and of political mediation – forms the backdrop against which these two thinkers have shaped their conceptual tools; but, as we shall see, the intellectual weapons they used in addressing this epochal crisis are different. Between the Weberian 'ethics of responsibility' and the Schmittian 'neutralization of values' there is an abyss crossed by an ideology: the political.

Reducing polarity: The Weber–Schmitt controversy

The controversy over the intellectual relation between Weber and Schmitt has deep roots: they can be traced back to late April 1964, when, during the Fifteenth Convention of the German Sociological Association held in Heidelberg to celebrate Weber's centenary, a young Jürgen Habermas notoriously stigmatized Schmitt as a 'legitimate pupil' of Weber.[12] His view was shared by György Lukács, one of Weber's old fellow-scholars and a frequent member of the Heidelberg 'circle' in the pre-First World War period.[13] Both Lukács and Habermas were convinced that the charismatic element in Weber's Caesar-like 'leader(ship) democracy' (*Füheredemokratie*) informed Schmitt's theory of decisionism. In truth, the origin of the controversy discussed here can be pushed even further back, being associated with a specific reading of Weber as a theorist of sheer power politics and as a herald of Nazism.[14] It has been pointed out, however, that this line of thought is characterized by an underlying reductionism – something that Leo Strauss has ironically described as *reductio ad Hitlerum*: a polemical interpretation according to which Weber's thought would have led inescapably to Nazi fascism.[15] It was relatively easy, then, for a Weberian like Guenther Roth to label these critics 'ideological' on the ground that, 'for ideological reasons', they 'cannot recognize any dividing line between political sociology and political ideology.'[16]

The linear conception of a teleological evolution, via Schmitt, from Weber's *Führerdemokratie* to Hitler's *drittes Reich* has been reformulated, historicized and carried forward by Wolfgang Mommsen in his pioneering work *Max Weber and German Politics*.[17] According to Mommsen, 'Schmitt merely drew radical conclusions from the premises that were already outlined in Weber's theory of legitimacy.[18] Moreover, for Mommsen, both Schmitt's critique of partisan pluralism and his theory of plebiscitary authority are nothing but a conceptual 'extension of Weber's own program', even though – as Mommsen himself acknowledges – Schmitt developed his radical conclusions on political leadership through 'the thorough repression of all constitutional safeguards that Weber had included'.[19] Although very well documented, this seminal work rests on a problematic methodology. From the outset, Mommsen states that, in contrast to previous studies that have usually interpreted Weber's political thought through the analysis of his scholarly writings, he wants to trace 'Weber's development as a politician by means of a detailed assessment of his position on the day-to-day political issues'.[20]

This approach to intellectual history overlooks the dialectical relation between theory and practice, which is essential to understanding Weber's ideas.[21] In fact, Weber is one of the few thinkers who have emphasized the relevance of theory to conceptually capturing historical contingency; he has done so by showing how, in modernity, critical reflection on political praxis is also related to a momentous metaphysical crisis. As he put it, 'It is always by the demonstration and solution of problems of *substance* that new sciences have been established and their methods further developed.'[22] The union of theory and practice is especially – and 'dangerously' – present in Schmitt's work. For the legal theorist, 'the distinction between theory and practice is one of the consequences of modern political thinking, which no longer possesses a concept of nature.'[23]

John McCormick has shown how Schmitt's work can be read precisely as an attempt to overcome Weber's epistemological categories and to transcend the modern binaries that had opposed 'subject' to 'object', 'nature' to 'culture', 'theory' to 'practice'. This was a radical attempt that did not, however, succeed in overcoming 'Weber's irrational tendencies'.[24] For McCormick, in other words, the target of Schmitt's criticisms and theorizations was Weber's neo-Kantian ideal of a 'liberal' social science. And to support his thesis, he cites a passage from *Die Tyrannei der Werte*.[25] Nonetheless, the citation is misleading, decontextualized, and, if read in its entirety, it would suggest not a critique but, on the contrary, an endorsement of Weber's position. For, in discussing Raymond Aron's interpretation of Weber's vocational conferences, Schmitt stresses that 'it would be obviously wrong to reduce him [*sc.* Weber] to some insightful passages, thus neglecting his broader sociological insights. Moreover, *no one thinks to tie him down [festzulegen] to his neo-Kantian epistemology.*[26] As we shall see, it is precisely by using Weber's 'post-Kantian awareness' that Schmitt attacks the philosophical pretension to construct an objective system of values.

This brief overview highlights a fundamental problem in the existing analysis of the Weber–Schmitt controversy: the polarization of positions and, above all, the ambiguity with which Schmitt confronted himself with the sociologist of Erfurt,[27] to whom he equivocally referred as 'the great German sociologist'[28] or as an 'unbearable thinker' whose 'seething irrationality tries to cover itself with rational fig leaves'.[29] As a matter of fact, Schmitt's opinion of Weber's work – which is itself fragmented and never systematic[30] – has changed and evolved over time. It underwent substantial modifications over the course of Schmitt's long, almost centennial life. Moreover, it has also been suggested that Schmitt's ambiguity may be the expression of his so-called occasionalism, of the groundless foundation of his thinking. As Karl Löwith has argued:

> Schmitt's profane decisionism is necessarily occasional because he lacks not only the theological and metaphysical presuppositions of earlier centuries but the humanitarian-moral ones as well. ... What Schmitt defends is a politics of sovereign decision, but one in which content is merely a product of an accidental *occasio* of the political situation which happens to prevail at the moment.[31]

Without wishing to provide an exhaustive interpretation of the intellectual relationship between Weber and Schmitt – or to resort to the 'spark' of the *occasio* to explain the oscillating ambiguity that characterizes it – in the following pages I will use the 'theory of values' as a sort of 'Trojan horse', to decipher the elements of continuity and discontinuity in the Weber–Schmitt relation. As we shall see, lurking behind their discussion of 'values' are relevant categories that may provide an interpretation – perhaps not unitary, but at least substantive – of their work. The fruitfulness of this approach lies in the possibility of tracing the deep philosophical core upon which Weber and Schmitt rooted their different conceptions of history and politics. The attempt undertaken here requires, therefore, a genealogical reconstruction of Weber's

76   *Genealogies of Political Modernity*

and Schmitt's intellectual apparatuses that has its apex in the 'theory of values'. Their 'discourse on values', as we shall see, is not merely based on a scientific conception or on personal experience but, above all, on a different 'image of history', of its progress and meaning. In this sense, their philosophical views mirror different ontological positions and their understanding of 'value' springs from a historical crisis. In other words, for Weber as for Schmitt, the question of the foundation of values is not in itself ontological. Rather it is a historical problem, which translates into an ontological one when the process of rationalization-secularization has passed a certain critical threshold: modernity.

A short genealogy of the concept of 'value': Origin, evolution, fragmentation

Value has its own self-fulfilling logic: 'Those who speak of value want to valorize and to impose.' In fact, 'no one can evaluate without devaluing, revaluating, and exploiting. Whoever establishes values has thus already positioned himself against non-values [*Unwerte*].'[32] This is, in a nutshell, Schmitt's position on the question of values. To understand its historico-political significance, it is necessary to situate this view within the broader debate on the problematic of values, which emerged in the nineteenth century, matured at the *fin de siècle* and exploded into full force in the twentieth century.[33] Value is in fact a keyword, a symbol of the Western political development, 'one of the best physiognomic features through which to trace the profile of the current age'.[34]

    In effect, the notion of 'value', with its conceptual trajectory, enshrines and condenses the parabola and crisis of modernity. Importantly, two dynamics intersect and overlap within this 'conceptual placeholder': the secularization of ethics and the commodification of the social world. These are two parallel and contiguous developments that tend to merge over time. Thus for Weber, who emphasizes the economic and political origin of the term, 'value' is the 'unfortunate child of misery of our science' – the mature fruit of the 'spirit of capitalism', which has become 'victorious'.[35] For Schmitt, who comes from the other direction, the term indicates a 'crisis of disenchantment': as he sees it, systems of values seek to fill the chasm opened by nihilism, the *horror vacui* created by the decline of morals. In this way, 'value and what is valuable are turned into a positivistic surrogate [*Ersatz*] of the metaphysical.'[36] For the two thinkers, in sum, the category of 'value' emerges when economic rationalization and disenchantment have cloaked the world in a fog, like ghosts of an extinct ethos.

In effect, from an ethical standpoint, the ancients did not possess the notion of 'value'. Rather their moral reflections, especially after Plato, were inspired by the notion of goodness or what is good (ἀγαθός). Plato, for example, has Socrates say in the *Republic* that the 'thing which gives the things which are known their truth [τὴν ἀλήθειαν] ... is the idea of the good [τοῦ ἀγαθοῦ ἰδέαν].'[37] From a different perspective, Aristotle states, right at the beginning of the *Politics*, that 'every community [πᾶσαν κοινωνίαν] is established with a view to some good [ἀγαθοῦ τινος ἕνεκεν συνεστηκυῖαν]',[38] thus reiterating what he had already affirmed in the *Nicomachean Ethics*: that 'the knowledge of the good' is 'the highest [τῆς κυριωτάτης] master science [ἀρχιτεκτονικῆς]' and 'this is obviously the science of politics [ἡ πολιτική].'[39]

In the scholastic era, Thomas Aquinas could still elaborate on the classical notion and draw this conclusion: *summum igitur bonum, quod est Deus, est causa bonitatis in omnibus bonis* ('therefore the highest good which is God is the cause of the goodness in all good things').[40] We are presented with an ethical notion of the 'good', which appears to be transcendent and objective. Whether conceived of as an archetype, as a principle of reason or as an essence (*ousia*), the good is the North Star by which humanity should strive to be guided. It is also a ground (*fundamentum*), and in this capacity can be represented as transcendence that determines and qualifies immanence – or as 'the Good above all that is good', according to Plotinus's well-known definition.[41]

But the ethical meaning is progressively lost with the waning of the medieval age and the transition to modernity. An early variation can be found in Thomas Hobbes's *Leviathan*, in the section devoted to the 'rights of sovereigns', where the 'values men are naturally apt to set upon themselves' are discussed.[42] Nonetheless, Hobbes here still preserves the Latin root of the word. 'Value' is understood as *virtus* and *honor*.[43] It is only with the birth of classical political economy, and with the works of Adam Smith and David Ricardo in particular, that the term 'value' first moves into this new field, then becomes popular and spreads beyond its boundaries.[44] On the basis of this newly acquired popularity, and by expanding its semantic sphere into other realms of knowledge, the concept thus becomes more susceptible of personal interpretations. 'Value' thus turns into a polysemic term that embraces all modes of being: there are always new values emerging in the cultural, aesthetic, political, economic and artistic fields.

During this conceptual revolution, Kant was one of the few philosophers who, by distinguishing 'dignity' from 'value', attempted to bridge the opening rift between the subject and the object. In *Die Metaphysik des Sitten*, in discussing the doctrine of virtue, he differentiates 'a human being' (*homo phaenomenon*) – who, in the system of nature, is merely 'a being of slight importance and shares with the rest of the animals … an ordinary value [*pretium vulgare*]' – from a human being 'subject of morally practical reason', namely regarded 'as a person' (*homo noumenon*).[45] The latter cannot 'be valuated merely as means to the ends of other or even to his own ends, but as an end in himself', because 'he possess a dignity (an absolute inner worth)'. For Kant, it is moral duty that elevates human individuality to universality, compelling the human being to revere his own person, to feel 'his inner worth [*valor*] – in terms of which he is above any price' [*pretium*] – and to 'instill in him respect for himself [*reverentia*]'.[46] As Schmitt was to remark, this fundamental distinction between the *value* of things and the *dignity* of the person was completely lost, because 'a hundred years of rapid industrialization essentially transformed value into an economic category', so that 'a metamorphosis in values, a general valorization (*allgemeine Ver-Wertung*), is now taking place in all spheres of our social existence.'[47]

But there is more. This process of economization of social life is intimately related to the collapse of the Christian ethos and to the secularization of its ethics. For, if we witness an economization of life through which everything becomes potentially commensurable and disposable, we also observe the specular process of fragmentation of traditional ethics in a myriad of 'ethically devalued' values; and we see how both happen under the pressure of the 'capitalist spirit'. This crucial moment in Western history has been described, with extraordinary force, as marking the advent of the 'uncanniest of all guests' – nihilism.[48] Through his 'transvaluation of all values' (*Umwertung aller Werte*), Nietzsche brings the category of value to the forefront of philosophical and political discourse. As Heidegger has acutely argued, 'in the nineteenth century, talk of values became frequent, and it became customary to think in values. However, it was only as a consequence of the broadcasting of Nietzsche's writings that talk of values has become popular.[49]

'What does nihilism mean?' – asks Nietzsche at the beginning *Der Wille zur Macht*. He famously responds: 'The highest values devaluate themselves. The aim is lacking; "why?" finds no answer.'[50] It is in this chasm opened by nihilism, in this loss of meaning of ancient morality, that the notion of 'value' takes the centre of the philosophical stage. Nihilism erodes the place of Christianity, as Nietzsche points out, because it plunges its roots into the corpse of Christendom.[51] Nonetheless, the abyss uncovered by the 'death of God' cannot be easily replenished. Nihilism not only reveals the fundamental groundlessness of morality, but also leaves all ethical questions open and unanswered. For what happens to ethics after the 'death of God'? What is the relevance of 'values', once they have been stripped of the alleged objectivity of Christianity? What does living and thinking in terms of values entail for the domain of politics?

Nietzsche's philosophy, then, brings to the forefront of philosophical debate the problematic of values, which he articulates through the conceptual divide between 'subject' and 'object', the 'antithesis between an interior which fails to correspond to any exterior and an exterior which fails to correspond to any interior'.[52] On the one hand, this dualism opens the way to the question of how to reestablish an ethical personalism and how 'to bear the entire and ultimate responsibility for your actions yourself and to relieve God, world, ancestors, chance and society of the burden'.[53] On the other hand, it raises the issue of how to reconstitute an 'objectivity', a solid foundation, in a world in which even the notion of 'necessity' has become nothing more than a 'conventional fiction'; in a world – Nietzsche remarks – where there is no 'thing in itself' or rule of 'law'.

It is from these issues that an actual *Wertphilosophie* emerges. Its roots lie in the neo-Kantianism of the Baden School and, more specifically, in the work of Wilhelm Windelband and Heinrich Rickert. The latter, in his book *The Limits of Concept Formation*, tried to establish a philosophy of history basing it precisely on axiological foundations. Rickert believed that, in a world in which 'neither empirical actuality [*Wirklichkeit*] nor a metaphysical reality [*Realität*] is qualified to endow ... science and history with objectivity', it was possible to reintroduce a new 'foundational ground' by means of 'the validity of theoretical values'.[54] This way of thinking led him to conclude that 'historical science must be allowed to assume that the unique development of reality stands *in a necessary relationship to some unconditionally and generally valid values*'.[55] In this manner, the 'objectivity' of history was recovered through a novel category of 'value', endowed with general and universal validity.

It is well known that, in developing his epistemological ideas, Weber was initially influenced by Rickert's notion of *Wertbeziehung* ('value relation').[56] However, what is less widely acknowledged is that Weber succeeded in developing an original 'theory of values' only by breaking away from the neo-Kantian positions of the Baden School.[57] As we shall see, it is from the inadequate perspective of *Wertphilosophie* that Schmitt and Weber seek to rethink the boundaries and meaning of the category of value.

The end of a world: The value of history in the history of value

On 2 April 1913 Weber wrote to his friend Robert Wilbrandt: 'I hold the view that what dominates the sphere of values is the irresolvable *conflict*, and consequently the necessity of constant *compromises*; no one, except a *religion* based on "revelation", can claim to decide in a *binding* form how those compromises should be made.'[58] This position, vigorously questioned already in Weber's time, appears in several of his writings.[59] In the Anglo-Saxon world, it has been described as positing an antithesis between 'facts' and 'values', or 'facts' and 'decision'.[60] For example, by analysing what they call the Weberian doctrine of the irreconcilability between facts and values, Factor and Turner have argued that Weber's value positions are themselves 'ultimately non-rational' and, accordingly, not susceptible to compromise.[61] Moreover, they suggest that Weber would have developed his position without discussing, let alone confuting, other relevant philosophical doctrines (such as Mill's, Durkheim's, Hobhouse's etc.), which maintained that value positions might be subject to rational justification. In short, by excluding the possibility of 'rational dialogue between valuative positions and other positions', Weber would have exposed himself to the risk of irrationality.[62]

Here we encounter a typical misunderstanding of Weber's position. When Weber argues for 'the impossibility of "scientifically" pleading for practical and interested stands', he is not implying that the spheres of value, due to their incommensurability, are not subject to rational discussion.[63] In fact, Weber's point about the apparent 'irrationality' of values is not related to valuative positions, to their potential discursivity or intelligibility, but rather to their *foundation*. What is worthy of being known, lived and loved cannot be ascertained objectively by means of science, but 'can only be interpreted with reference to its ultimate meaning, which we must reject or accept according to our ultimate position towards life'.[64] In other words, for Weber, rationality cannot establish itself as the ultimate sovereign point of ascription; it cannot *objectively* take root in history and cannot scientifically prove its necessity. The attempt to understand the logical and historical limits of 'reason' is therefore far more important than the one of criticizing the limitations of the Weberian conception of rationality. In discussing this problematic, for example, Herbert A. Simon has argued:

> In the domain of reasoning, the difficulty in finding a fulcrum resides in the truism 'no conclusions without premises'. Reasoning processes take symbolic inputs and deliver symbolic outputs. The initial inputs are axioms, themselves not derived by logic but simply induced from empirical observations, or even more simply posited. ... Axioms and inference rules together constitute the fulcrum on which the lever of reasoning rests; but the particular structure of that fulcrum cannot be justified by the methods of reasoning. For an attempt at such a justification would involve us in an infinite regress of logics, each as arbitrary in its foundations as the preceding one. ... The corollary to 'no conclusions without premises' is 'no ought's from is's alone'. Thus, whereas reason may provide powerful help in finding means to reach our ends, it has little to say about the ends themselves.[65]

The problem of valuative positions lies therefore in their *foundation*. At stake here is not merely the rational and universal justification of values. The question is not, in Nietzsche's words, 'how are synthetic a priori judgments possible?', but rather 'why is belief in such judgements necessary?'[66] As we shall see, for both Weber and Schmitt, rationality – once it has entered the world of historical becoming – is not necessary at all and, if anything, cannot avoid the irreconcilability between the various subjective points of view that, being all equally ungrounded, are considered dangerously 'objective'.

Leo Strauss has described the Weberian thesis as 'nihilistic' because, if one embraces it, 'every preference, however evil, base, or insane, has to be judged before the tribunal of reason to be as legitimate as any other preference'.[67] For Strauss, it is intolerable that one considers it 'equally legitimate to will or not to will *truth*, or to reject truth in favor of the beautiful and the sacred. Why, then, should one not prefer pleasing delusions or edifying myths *to the truth*?'[68] Strauss's critique, however, is based on notions of 'truth' (understood as logical adequacy) and 'rationality' that are *geographically* and *historically* limited. And yet these historically situated notions become the fulcrum of a universalist vision of ethics and nature.[69] Nonetheless, 'good' and 'evil', 'truth' and 'justice' are concepts that Strauss inherits from a tradition that entered into crisis after all former illusions – 'the "way to true being", the "way to true art", the "way to true nature", the "way to true God", the "way to true happiness" – have been dispelled'.[70] What is the 'true Truth' that reason must inspire, strive for and preserve in an age in which the intellectual and spiritual centre is lacking? 'What meaning does *our* being have, if it were not that that will to truth has become conscious of itself *as a problem* in us?'[71] As Löwith has correctly argued,

> both opponents and advocates of the separation between knowledge and evaluation misjudge Weber's central argument of this distinction: i.e., the recognition that today we live in a world that is objectified by scientific technology and that, on the other hand, the objective rationality of science has freed us from moral and religious universally binding norms. Accordingly, our old values can no longer rely on traditions or be scientifically justified because good and evil are now a matter of personal choice.[72]

Strauss's critique, then, misses its target because the problem raised by Weber is not the negation or rational justification of a universal fulcrum (e.g. Strauss's understanding of 'natural law') in order to cope with the spread of nihilism and extreme relativism. The thesis of the heterogeneity of values illuminates a substantive historical–ontological problem rather than a formal one: the fragmentation brought about by 'disenchantment' through technology involves both a subjective liberation *and* the destruction of a collective centre. After the collapse of the allegedly objective Christian ethos, it becomes difficult to find a new fulcrum capable of recomposing the fragments of values, because the techno-scientific process of rationalization transforms its infinite progressivism and groundlessness into a new ontology of the real. In effect, for

Weber, disenchantment means the end of 'the faith in some kind of "objective" meaning ... Since all objectives have lost their objective meaning as a result of the rationalization carried through by human beings, they are now available to human subjectivity in a new way: *for the determination of their meaning*.[73]

In sum, rationality is no ethos. It is unable to condense actions and perceptions into concrete *and* universal forms of life. It is unable to transform a syllogism into life conduct. Despite the fact that supreme and ultimate value judgements give meaning and direction to our lives (and, for this reason, they are experienced as something 'objectively' meaningful), their ultimate foundation lies in the sphere of individuality. In the realm of history there are no universally 'just' and necessary values, but only valuative positions that are believed to be such. 'It is the fate of our culture, however, that we are again becoming more clearly aware of this situation, after a millennium during which our (allegedly or supposedly) exclusive orientation toward the sublime fervor of the Christian ethic eyes had blinded us to this situation.'[74]

It is from this perspective that Weber rejects the 'metaphysical anchorage' (*metaphysische Veränkerung*) proposed by Windelband (and, in a different guise, by Rickert). For the neo-Kantian philosopher, 'truth is not our discovery or our illusion, but a value that is rooted in the ultimate depths of reality'; and this means that 'the life of values demands a metaphysical anchorage, and, if we give the name God to this super-empirical vital connection of personalities, we may say that his reality is given in the reality of conscience itself.'[75] But Weber cuts the Gordian knot that binds the metaphysical universal to the historical particular. For, once 'God is dead, there is no grounding by which one perspective could have legitimacy over other perspectives.'[76] In other words, there is no a priori and no axiology to hold reality back, once truth – understood as certainty and necessity – has become a problem for us, a meaningless abyss:

> The fate of an epoch which has eaten of the tree of knowledge is that it must know that we cannot learn the meaning of the world from the results of its analysis, be it ever so perfect; it must rather be in a position to create this meaning itself.[77]

Weber's departure from neo-Kantian philosophy is determined therefore by a historical crisis – disenchantment – that reveals an ontological problematic – the groundlessness of the centre. His position emphasizes the de facto impossibility of an objective evaluation by means of science and, at the same time, the impracticability of finding a universal pivot upon which to establish an 'objective' ethics, a new morality capable of guiding political and moral action. As predicted by Rickert, 'Such a doubt, however, if carried out consistently for all values, would destroy the concept of truth itself.'[78] And in fact the crisis of disenchantment opens up new, abyssal questions: how does one create unity out of the fragmentation of subjective values? Is it actually possible to re-establish an ethical order in the age of secular polytheism? And what is the relationship between the domain of the political and the domain of values? These are the intricate issues that Schmitt had to grapple with after Weber's death.

The value of politics and the politics of values

The problem of groundlessness, just explored, raises two interrelated questions, which have the same ontological root, namely the lack of a metaphysical fulcrum. The first is an epistemological–methodological question: science cannot decide for us, by its own means, what values we should embrace. The second is an ethical–political question: since valuative positions are subjectively perceived as something universal and 'objective', they tend to promote ideological absolutism and moral exclusivism.

As we have seen, this second, ethical–political question springs from a historical crisis: once the sky has lost its transcendental cover, it tends to be repainted, as it were, in the subjective colours of ideology; in an age of immanence, the ancient gods, stripped of their enchantment and taking an impersonal form, dominate people's lives again. As Weber puts it, 'the ultimately possible attitudes toward life are irreconcilable, and hence their struggle can never be brought to a final conclusion.'[79] According to him, the 'temperate objectivity' of Kantian apriorism is unable to resolve this tension between values and actions brought about by the age of disenchantment. In a very dense passage, which is worth quoting in full, Weber expresses his dissent from the Kantian perspective in the following terms:

Formal ethics has to face the fact that its propositions do not enable it to deduce substantive conclusions – even within the ethical domain itself, let alone concerning conflicts between value spheres. An attempt to perform such a deduction would be just as sterile as if one wanted to deduce, say, substantive chemical facts from logical propositions. The Kantian imperatives, too, are valid analyses of certain elementary facts concerning the way in which ethical judgments are made. Irrespective of the function that they may consequently have in connection with substantive decisions in the field of ethics, they in any case do not support any kind of decision concerning the ethically irrational conflict of the value sphere.[80]

There would be a sort of *hiatus irrationalis* between *formal* ethics, which rests on abstract assumptions, and *historical* values, which are embodied in concrete subjectivities. From this perspective, formal ethics is unable to restrain desires, passions and ideologically motivated action. For, once valuative positions are actualized by being translated into action, we enter 'the meaningless infinity of the world process': in other words, we have to accept the fact that the consequences of our actions are not completely rationalizable within the stream of history. Formal logic is therefore unable to guide and restrain what Weber aptly calls *das Konkretissimum des Erlebens* ('the hyper-concreteness of experience').[81]

Carl Schmitt essentially agrees with this position. In his view the logic of values is characterized by an 'immanent aggressiveness', because values, although believed to be high, sacred and just, need to be constantly actualized, and this can be done only by an agent against another agent: 'Whether something has value and how much, whether something is worthy and to what extent can be determined only from an assumed point of view or particular vantage point. The philosophy of values is thus a perspectival-philosophy [*Punkt-Philosophie*]; the ethics of values is a perspectival-ethics [*Punkt-Ethik*].'[82] This 'perspectival pointillism' is intrinsically dangerous, in that 'values as such are brought by actual [*konkreten*] people to bear upon other actual people.' Consequently, 'the genuinely subjective freedom of value-setting leads [...] to an endless struggle of all against all, to an endless *bellum omnium contra omnes*.'[83]

The main target of Schmitt's critique here is Max Scheler's philosophy of values. It is well known that Scheler, in order to 'square the circle of practical philosophy', and to mediate between the concreteness of action and the need for an ethics, had attempted to overcome Kant's 'empty apriorism', which in his view 'bars us from any true insight into the place of moral values in man's life'.[84] To Scheler, overcoming Kant's formalism meant building a system of values based on 'the living center of the individual' without, however, depriving her of a historical–relativist habitus or renouncing to the universal 'idea of an absolute ethics'.[85] Schmitt attacks Scheler's pretension to build a non-formal (*material*) and universal axiology because, in the realm of the political, the values' positions are constantly subject to a fatal reversibility: the 'meaning and function' of valuative positions 'change with the changing planes', that is with the transformation of the axiological horizons.[86] Accordingly, it is not only insufficient but also dangerous to establish scales of values or axiologies – as Scheler tried to do – in order to contain the crisis of nihilism and the perils brought about by modern subjective freedom. As Schmitt argues:

> To claim an objective character for values which we set up means only to create a new occasion for rekindling the aggressiveness in the struggle of valuations, to introduce a new instrument of self-righteousness, without for that matter increasing in the least the objective evidence for those people who think differently. The subjective theory of values has not yet been rendered obsolete, nor have the objective values prevailed: the subject has not been obliterated, nor have the value carriers, whose interests are served by the standpoints, viewpoints, and points of attack of values, been reduced to silence.[87]

The thetically grounded structure (*thetisch-setzerischen Struktur*) of values emerges in all its strength when one considers the Weberian concept of *Angriffspunkt*. According to Schmitt, Weber uses this expression to refer to those 'points of attack' that are intrinsic to valuative positions.[88] To think with values implies – knowingly or unknowingly – to think 'attack strategies'. In the realm of axiology, therefore, there would be no room for a weak relativism: the potential aggressiveness inherent in purely subjective freedom dominates reason by means of valuative judgements.

This latent conflictuality becomes even more explosive in the domain of politics. As is well known, Weber maintained that 'from no ethics in the world can it be concluded when and to what extent the ethically good purpose "justifies" the ethically dangerous means'; and this is because 'the specific means of legitimate violence as such in the hand of human associations … determines the peculiarity of all ethical problems of politics'.[89] The sphere of politics is therefore different from that of morality and ethics because in it lurks the constant possibility of violence, the tragic tension between different worldviews. This understanding, which is typical of 'political realism', can be traced back up to Machiavelli. According to Isaiah Berlin, for example, Machiavelli's cardinal achievement would be 'the recognition that ends equally ultimate, equally sacred, may contradict each other, that entire systems of value may come into collision without possibility of rational arbitration.'[90] Politics (the sphere of conflict) and ethics (the sphere of values) would be two worlds *toto caelo* different, which it is necessary to keep apart – and at a distance no less. This is one of the reasons why, for Weber, it is essential to structure conflict within the political boundaries of the parliamentary system. For, if all politics is essentially struggle, it becomes crucial to select able political leaders through a 'battle' that is circumscribed to parliament. The parliament provides a public arena where 'political struggle' turns into discussion, selection and eventually decision.[91]

It is at this conceptual juncture, then, that we encounter the first difference between Weber and Schmitt. Where the former speaks of 'struggle' and 'political conflict', the latter reads 'violence' and 'annihilation'. While for Weber politics is a 'struggle' (*Kampf*), for Schmitt *das Politische* implies 'the real possibility of physical killing'.[92] For Weber, in short, political tensions and value positions do not automatically translate into violence and into a *bellum omnium contra omnes*, as they do for Schmitt, because the fragmentation of values can and should be caged within the institutional and democratic arenas. Although between spheres of value there is an 'irreconcilable death-struggle … like that between "God" and the "Devil"', Weber maintains that 'there are, of course, as everyone realizes in the course of his life, compromises, both in fact and in appearance, and at every point. In almost every important attitude of *real human beings*, the value-spheres cross and interpenetrate.'[93]

As this passage clearly indicates, Weber did not think that a 'clash' among spheres of value was unavoidable: social fragmentation – the pluralism of values and, correspondingly, of political positions – can be repaired, its shards reassembled in political forums. Perhaps Weber's view was influenced by his liberalism, as his emphasis on the role of the individual seems to suggest – an emphasis that is visible both in his methodological and in his historical reflections on the charismatic and religious leader. In his vast

Religionssoziologie, the individual plays a central role in the exploration of historical tendencies. In Schmitt's work, on the contrary, there is no trace of methodological individualism, presumably owing to Schmitt's intense anti-liberalism.

Nonetheless, Weber's and Schmitt's different methodological positions should not be considered mere reflections of contrasting epistemological ideas. Quite to the contrary, Schmitt's anti-liberalism, although ideological, is rooted in a specific ontological vision: for him, in the void of meaning that characterizes the age of disenchantment, the individual is unable to represent herself, incapable of creating any politically meaningful unity or order. This anti-individualist position can already be found in Schmitt's early works. In *Der Wert des Staates*, for example, he states: 'If anything can be said of individuality, this is because the object of the predicated individuality has already been defined as an attribution point for a normative evaluation.'[94] Behind the legalistic jargon hides the idea that the individual would not exist outside the law that constitutes her as a legal persona. And, since the *idea* of law is not self-grounded but needs to be constantly actualized, the state becomes the *form* to which Schmitt entrusts the establishment of justice: 'The purpose of the state consists exclusively in the task of actualizing law [*Recht*] in the world [*in der Welt*]' and, in this sense, 'the state is not a human construction but, on the contrary, *the human being is a construction of the state*.'[95]

Weber maintains a rigid dualism between public and private morality, emphasizing the former's primacy over the latter via the dictum 'the state's welfare is the highest law' (*salus rei publicae suprema lex*). If, then, Weber can be considered an exponent of the so-called realist tradition, Schmitt's political dualism is of a different origin and nature. As we have seen, Weber posits a political and institutional unity (parliamentary democracy), which is given and unproblematic, as the foundation of the public sphere. The parliament plays a selective and discursive function precisely because it is sealed, as it were, within the boundaries of the democratic state. But in Schmitt's eyes, this mechanism entered into an irreversible crisis 'because the development of modern mass democracy has made argumentative public discussion an empty formality'.[96] Parliamentary democracy is unable to contain the popular energy that flows out of institutions in an age characterized by the 'revolt of the masses'. At this juncture, then, the ethics of the state becomes an ethics of emergency, a 'hunt of the political'. Schmitt puts it like this: 'Political unity is the highest unity – not because it is an omnipotent dictator, or because it levels out all other unities, but because it decides, and has the potential to prevent all other opposing groups from dissociating into a state of extreme enmity – that is, into civil war.'[97] Behind the necessity and ethical superiority of the state lies, once again, the deconstructive power of the political. Here the preservation of state unity is not presented as 'a greater good' merely because, for Schmitt as for Weber, the nation is 'higher' than the individual, the collectivity counts more than the subjective ego and private morality would not exist without public order. Rather Schmitt sees individuals and their valuative positions as carriers of the deconstructive potential of the political, as the bearers of its latent violent intensity.

This view reveals what Karl Löwith has aptly described as *the catastrophic manner of thinking* characteristic of the generation of Germans after the First World War'.[98] But it also conceals an important difference between Schmitt's and Weber's positions. While for Weber, as we have seen, the era of disenchantment is characterized by a fragmentation of values and a deconstruction of the religious order, for Schmitt this process of secularization assumes, paradoxically, a theological form. In the modern age, in other words, the disappearing theological background leaves an irreducible remainder: the compulsion towards order.[99] To Schmitt, the problem of political unity is a sort of white shadow that the theological matrix casts on modernity. And, since this unity is no longer representable through transcendence, it has now to be reconstituted through a void of meaning. The state – unfounded yet constantly forced towards order – must represent itself vis-à-vis nothingness, that is in the face of death (the enemy). It follows that the modern political form cannot but be nihilistic representation, a constant opening before death – a sort of murder suspended in time, eternally possible and (sometimes) postponed.

Schmitt's decisionism, too, should be read in this light. For the sovereign, who is a concrete agent but not a specific person, is the one who is capable of identifying the enemy in order to constitute his own political unity. To preserve such a unity, sovereignly created but always exposed to the risk of disintegration, the totality (the friends) has to remain open in the face of death and to represent itself vis-à-vis its constitutive negation (the enemy). Here we touch upon the extreme limits of Schmitt's 'biopolitical conception': to preserve itself, life, conceived of as biototality, must constantly be exposed to killing. The state 'cannot permit its members to die for their beliefs or to commit suicide, when the political unity of those members demands the sacrifice of life'.[100] The living being is thus sucked into the leviathan's maw.

It is at this point, then, that the second – and crucial – difference between Weber and Schmitt emerges in full force. Weber too, as is well known, advocates a form of decisionism. For him too, the decision is the means by which we 'open' the stream of history. Yet in his conception the ontological significance of decisions lies in the *individual* search for meanings in an age that is devoid of meaning. *Qua* cultural being, the human being is a seeker and a creator of meanings; and decision represents the more appropriate ethical choice of searching for meaning in the age of disenchantment:

> Life as a whole, if it is to be lived in full awareness and is not just to unfold like a natural event – involves a series of fundamental decisions through which the soul, as Plato describes it, chooses its own fate, – the meaning, that is, of its activity and being.[101]

It is therefore over an ontology of decision – and in the middle of the 'void of meaning' that characterizes it – that Weber and Schmitt cross paths for the last time and reveal their differences. Ultimately, the Schmittian 'decision on the form' and the Weberian 'decision on the meaning' rest on different ethical worlds, which are far apart from each other.

Conclusion: Ethics in the immediacy of the world

Weber's and Schmitt's theories of values represent two different – if contiguous – attempts to respond to the crisis of meaning in the age of immanence. As we have seen, while Schmitt promotes a leviathanic vision of ethics and politics, Weber attempts to safeguard the rationality of the individual on the grounds that reason, once it is uprooted from its foundation, becomes all the more important. In this sense, in the modern age, freedom becomes an absolute negative: freedom from any foundation. Knowing how to accept – and measure with responsibility – the risks and potentialities that this freedom involves means being able 'to countenance the stern seriousness of our fateful times'.

Schmitt, on the other hand, cannot accept this view because in the 'mystery of the political' and in the violence it entails he sees the last remaining historical force. This violent 'destiny' becomes all the more dangerous in the age of 'unstructured immanence' and of the crisis of the state, where values, like loose cannons, collide with one another. If, as he puts it, 'the idea needs mediation', then 'value demands much more of that mediation'. If the spiritual centre and its boundaries are vanishing, then the purpose of justice becomes 'to prevent the terror of the immediate and automatic enactment of values'.[102]

Nonetheless, Schmitt's vision seems anachronistic to us. In the so-called global age, at the wane of the *jus publicum Europaeum*, one can no longer hide the individual within the frame of the state and entrust the formation and mediation of values to the pretence of sovereignty. The unlimited potential of man can no longer be chained to a political form (as Schmitt argues in his *Political Theology*). The real problem of sovereign power, then, does not lie in having stripped human life – that is in having transformed security into control and freedom into biopolitics, as in Hobbes's *Leviathan* – but rather in having considered the human potential and human freedom a universal threat. In effect, Schmitt's vision of modernity can be read precisely as the desperate attempt to control what is uncontrollable, namely the infinite human capacity for action, conceived of as contingency. In this way he ended up stripping life of its form of life, transforming it into bare existence. Today, however, the friend–enemy dialectic can no longer generate any form or unity but, if anything, a violent and unlimited confrontation. In the post-Auschwitz world, it is no longer acceptable to entrust humankind and its political fate to the 'power of the elements'. As Jacob Taubes poetically wrote, *pace* Schmitt, 'earth and sea – without human beings, the elements after all remain "matter" (not even "matter") – When humanism has been depleted ... then that only means, does it not, that the question concerning human being is just posed more radically.'[103]

Today, paradoxically, we find ourselves in a situation similar to that acutely described by Schmitt in 1914:

> There are times of mediation and times of immediacy. In the latter, the devotion of the individual to the Idea is something people take for granted. There is no need for a highly organized state to support the recognition

of law [*Recht*]; on the contrary, the state seems to stand, like in Angelus Silesius's saying, like a wall before the light.[104]

In the immediacy of the global world, we can no longer nullify our individuality in the limited totality of the state, in the hope of being protected from our political anxieties by giving up our ethical, individual choices. Today, in a novel and immediate form, history calls us forcefully to choose our 'fate'. In the *mare magnum* agitated by contemporary planetary mobilization, the individual – if she does not want to sink in the chaotic flow of events – is called to a moral decision: to gaze into this formless tide in order to find guidance, meaning and, above all, a sense of her otherness. In substance, Max Weber's problem is still with us. And yet the question of values, of their implementation and constant reversibility, presents itself to us in a more radical and post-state form and therefore requires even greater personal responsibility. In the enigmatic words of a poem by Theodor Däubler, which is central to understanding Schmitt's work:

> The enemy is the embodiment of our own question.
> And he becomes us; we chase him to the same end.
> Yet violence comes from people's prudence.
> The ancestors gather on the promontories
> And remain silent when the tide clashes with the tide.[105]

4

Until the End of the World: René Girard, Carl Schmitt, and the Origins of Violence

*Every real thing has an inclination and desire for something that befits itself.
But everything that has the nature of being desirable has the nature of good.
Therefore, every real thing has a conformity with some good, and evil as
such is not in harmony with good but contrary to it. Therefore, evil is not an
entity. And if evil were a real thing, it would neither desire anything nor be
desired by anything, and so have no activity or movement, since nothing acts
or moves except because of the desire of an end.*

Thomas Aquinas, *De malo*, q. I, a. 1

In the preface to the new German edition of *The Concept of the Political*,
Carl Schmitt – by now retired in Plettenberg, from where he observes the
slow sinking of the *nomos* of the earth – pulls the strands of his pessimistic
argument together:

> The evolution, which began in 1939, of warfare and of the concept of enmity
> has led to new and more intensive forms of war, to quite confusing definitions
> of peace, and to partisan and modern revolutionary warfare. If we remove
> from scientific consciousness the reality that there is hostility [*Feindschaft*]
> among people, how can we theoretically account for these phenomena?[1]

Lurking behind this seemingly clear passage is an 'incommensurable problem',[2]
which has plagued Schmitt throughout his life, and which also represents his
most controversial intellectual achievement: the discovery of the political
(*das Politische*). In fact, besides the apparent simplicity of the friend–enemy
distinction, this concept conceals the 'unsaid' of political theory, its dark side
– a force that 'is not delimitable' and that therefore requires to be theoretically
distinguished from what seems wholly 'inaccessible to distinctions'.[3]

The pages of this chapter have been written as an exploration of this 'dark' and 'incommensurable' side of politics. More specifically, in what follows, I attempt to trace a theoretical genealogy of political violence – a history of its evolution and containment – through an analysis of the work of two radical thinkers: Carl Schmitt and René Girard. The discussion is divided into four parts. In the first section, I examine Schmitt's concept of the political and Girard's mimetic theory against the background of classical theories of violence. This analysis highlights both the radicality of Schmitt's and Girard's theoretical perspectives, and the reductionist readings to which they have been subjected. The argument here is that there is a divergent agreement between the Schmittian concept of the political and the Girardian notion of mimesis. Indeed, mimesis can be interpreted as the hidden mechanism that leads to the intensification of the political, while the political can be seen as the historicization of the mimetic, its concretization in the realm of history. In the second part, in an attempt to reveal the hidden assumptions and the ontological structure that characterize the two thinkers' work, the comparison between them is pushed to its extreme limits. This exploration takes the form of a backward journey into the field of 'Political Theodicy', where I focus mainly on the differences rather than on the similarities between the two thinkers.

In the third and fourth sections I continue the investigation of these parallel and contiguous paths by analysing Schmitt's and Girard's understanding of the birth, sacral meaning and eventual secularization of juridico-political institutions. This final part offers an alternative insight into the genesis of the unsettling and violent chaoticity that characterizes the global age. Finally, in the conclusion I will show that Schmitt's and Girard's theoretical apparatuses rest on different philosophies of history and that this 'distance' between the two thinkers corresponds to distinct ontological and epistemological ways of rethinking politics in the age of technology and depoliticization. In effect, the contemporary age can be described *literally* as 'apocalyptic', provided that one reverts to the ancient meaning of *apokalupsis* as a revealing or an uncovering of all those contradictions that, having matured during modernity, ended up exploding in the age of globality. How is it possible, then, to reconceptualize the chaotic multitude and social undifferentiation triggered by the dynamics of globalization? What political form should communities take in the 'liquid' age? Analysing the work of Schmitt and Girard might help us shed some light on these epochal questions.

The 'mimetic' and the 'political'

It has been authoritatively argued that the causes of war can be traced essentially to three loci or 'images': 'within man, within the structure of the separate states, within the state system'.[4] This now-classic analytical distinction has become paradigmatic in political theory and international studies. Nonetheless, behind the apparent conceptual clarity of the three Waltzian images lies a fundamental problem: its ideal-typical concepts (i.e. human nature, the state and the state system, regarded as sources of conflict) are in themselves problematic and subject to historical change. 'Change' is to be understood in the twofold sense of: (1) transformation of the historical shapes of phenomena; and (2) metamorphosis of the perception, theoretical reception and conceptualization of phenomena. Thus, for example, Augustine's concept of 'human nature' is completely different from that of a neo-Kantian philosopher, just as the evolutionary notion of 'nature' has nothing to do with the meaning Hobbes attributes to this word. 'When Hobbes speaks of *nature* in the sense of *physis*, he thinks in the traditional way, inasmuch as he assumes the fixity of types. He thinks in pre-evolutionary, pre-Darwinian terms.'[5] This means that putting a diverse range of thinkers and concepts within the same analytical framework implies making a strong simplification. It has been affirmed by many scientists and philosophers that 'human nature' is the cause of conflict; yet Thucydides's idea of war is not Lenin's, and a theologian's understanding of human nature is not the same as that of a revolutionary socialist.

Waltz partially acknowledges this problem when he states that 'our estimates of the causes of war are determined by our presuppositions as much as by the events of the world about us.'[6] Nonetheless, the problem that remains to be solved is that of ontological assumptions, *presuppositions*, which suffer change constantly and, in turn, modify our understanding of 'human', 'history', 'nature' and (organized) 'violence'. As Schmitt aptly puts it:

> All concepts such as God, freedom, progress, anthropological conceptions of human nature, the public domain, rationality and rationalization, and finally the concepts of nature and culture itself derive their concrete historical content from the situation of the central domains and can only be grasped therefrom.[7]

It is of course possible to think in terms of historical constants, as Thucydides himself suggested. But one often forgets Thucydides's cosmological conception of time, according to which 'the visible order and beauty of the cosmos, and the cosmic law of growth and decay [were] also the pattern for [his] understanding of history.'[8] Only in a world imbued with a cyclical cosmology can one understand why, in Thucydides's vision of a *time without history*, what happened 'will happen again at some time in the same or a similar pattern.'[9]

The problems highlighted here are essential to understand the originality and radicalism of Carl Schmitt's and René Girard's theoretical apparatuses. Unlike the classic (and Waltzian) approaches to the study of violence, which postulate an *ahistorical* fixity of categories such as human nature, war and political institutions (the state), what prevails in Schmitt's and Girard's thought is the genealogical, dynamic element. Violence for them is not simply a *problem* but, above all, a *morphogenetic* dimension – a sort of secret engine that creates and destroys the symbolic (rites and concepts) and political forms (kingdoms and states) devised to restrain its energy. To understand this position, it is necessary to move beyond a reductionist conception of causality and beyond a 'universal concept of man.'[10] In other words, we must face a *descensus ad inferos*, a *katabasis* into the realm of the political. To do so, we need to start exploring the mechanisms implicit in Waltz's 'first image'.

According to Girard, '[t]he principal source of violence between human beings is mimetic rivalry, the rivalry resulting from imitation of a model who becomes a rival or a rival who becomes a model.'[11] This means first of all that conflict is not innate or part of human 'nature' but is *relational*, dialectically determined. Girard uses the neologism 'inter-individual' to describe this dynamic.[12] For him, the relational structure of conflict – and of the kind of mimesis that leads to rivalry – is triangular: 'Rivalry does not arise because of the fortuitous convergence of two desires on a single object; rather, *the subject desires the object because the rival desires it*. ... The rival, then, serves as a model for the subject ... in regard to desires.'[13]

In this sense, then, violence is neither an original phenomenon nor an 'ineradicable trait of human nature'; rather it is generated by a double transference – mediated by an object – that takes place between the Self and the model.[14] Girard opposes those theories that postulate a 'human absolute' and that describe violence as a surrogate of aggressive instincts and

Until the End of the World 97

impulses.[15] Violence is a by-product of intersubjective mimetic rivalry and in this capacity can take several forms and serve different purposes, as we shall see.

Schmitt's view is close to this anti-absolutist conception of human nature. Some scholars, including Leo Strauss, have interpreted his position, particularly as he developed it in *Political Theology* (1922) and *The Concept of the Political* (1932), as a form of 'negative anthropology'.[16] Here, however, it is argued that this reading is simplistic. For, if Schmitt vigorously criticizes those political conceptions that rest on 'an anthropological optimism', he also argues that the question of the political cannot be solved 'by psychological remarks [*psychologischen Bemerkungen*] on "optimism" and "pessimism"'.[17] Indeed, the friend–enemy distinction cannot be reduced to a mere anthropological concept but should be placed in the concrete situation of violence, physical killing and death. Reinterpreting Hobbes's understanding of the 'state of nature', Schmitt argues that whether a particular state of affairs is 'good or bad', in terms of normality or corruption, depends on the *situation*' and 'the state of nature is an abnormal situation [*abnorme Situation*].'[18] The questions are therefore as follows: why do human beings sink into this situation of absolute degradation? How can existential nihilism be the centre of gravity of politics? And whence does the political derive its intensity?

I will explore these issues in the next section: here it is worth pointing out that Schmitt does not situate the origins of violence in human nature. Like Girard, he regards conflict as relational and dialectical; indeed, as we shall see, violence lies at the core of the friend–enemy relationship. To clarify this point, it is worth quoting *in extenso* a passage from one of Schmitt's more personal works, *Ex captivitate salus*:

> So I wonder: Who can ever be my enemy? So much so that I recognize him as an enemy, I must equally recognize the fact that he recognizes me as an enemy. In this mutual recognition of the recognition lies the prominence of the concept. ... Whom can I recognize as my enemy at all? Obviously, only the one who can question me. While I recognize him as an enemy, I recognize that he can question me. And who can really put me into question? Only I myself. Or my brother. That's it. The other is my brother. The other turns out to be my brother, and the brother turns out to be my enemy. Adam and Eve had two sons, Cain and Abel. Thus begins the history of mankind.

Thus looks the Father of all things. This is the dialectical tension that keeps the history of the world moving, and the history of the world has not yet come to an end.[19]

For Schmitt, therefore, the friend–enemy dialectic represents the secret engine of universal history, the 'energy' that, as we shall see, constructs and deconstructs (through violence) political forms and institutions. But, again, it is important to note that this energy cannot catch fire by itself, so to speak, but ignites only when it comes into contact with the other, dialectically; when the encounter or clash between 'friends' and 'enemies' reaches a certain 'degree of intensity' (*Intensitätsgrad*).[20] Girard, for his part, uses exactly the same words in an early work to describe a situation of 'mimetic crisis', which translates into arbitrary violence precisely when rivalry 'reaches a certain degree of intensity'.[21]

These similarities prompt the question of whether there might be a relation between the mimetic and the political, that is between the violent mimesis envisioned by Girard and the 'mystery of the political' imagined by Schmitt. This is an interesting line of research, which will be explored in the next sections. Meanwhile it must be emphasized that Schmitt's and Girard's conceptualizations of conflict differ significantly from classic theories of violence. According to the latter, it is not that human nature (variously defined) is the locus of conflict; rather it is conflict that generates (or corrupts) human nature. For Girard, it is mimetic desire that shapes and changes humankind. He therefore does not posit, at the origin of rivalry, the existence of a fixed and insatiable *animus dominandi* ('desire for power'), as Morgenthau does, or a timeless 'desire for recognition', as in Kojève's reading of Hegel.[22] For him, these phenomena are the expression of a particular passage or *paysage* of mimesis, the adjustment of social relations to historically determined metaphysical systems.[23] Thus, during modernity, political power represents the acme of mimetic desire, whereas the 'desire for recognition' is mainly a product of the maturation of bourgeois society. In other words, for Girard, mimetic desire is not finalistic, ontologically predetermined or univocally oriented. Like the political, it 'can derive its energy from the most varied human endeavours, from the religious, economic, moral, and other antitheses'.[24] Coming from a similar perspective, Schmitt in fact argues that 'the field of relations of the political [*Das Beziehungsfeld des Politischen*] is constantly changing, depending on the forces and powers that are separated or combined together in order to survive.'[25] These two authors, in short, consider violence as a sort of *energy* (the 'political', 'mimetic desire'), which has no predetermined substance, but that gains momentum and takes form in the interdependence of human relationships.

Nonetheless, it could be argued that if conflict is triggered by interpersonal relations, ultimately this means that the source of evil lies in human sociality and, consequently, violence is intrinsic to the human being as *animal politicum et sociale*. An answer to this objection can only be found in the broader discussion concerning the nature of evil and the constitution and dissolution of political order – that is to say, in the realm of (political) theodicy.

Political theodicies: Order, form, sin

Quid est malum? (What is evil?) *Unde malum faciamus?* (Why do we do evil?) These two questions represent the core of Augustine's theodicy. They guide his speculation along two parallel hermeneutic paths that converge into his broader theological system. The Christian theologian distinguishes three categories of evil: ontological, moral and physical. They reflect, respectively, the what, the why and the how of *malum*, that is the way in which evil inserts itself into the world of phenomena.[26] This threefold division is crucial to our understanding of the positions of Girard and of Schmitt on the origins of violence.

Girard has openly acknowledged his intellectual debt to Augustine, particularly in relation to his own conception of 'original sin'.[27] The position can be summarized as follows: if it be true that the human is a *zōon mimētikon* (mimetic animal), then it must be equally true that the human's propensity to imitation is not good or bad in itself; rather it depends on the model that is imitated. Mimetic desire, as we have seen, is not teleologically finalized (i.e. it does not stretch towards a predetermined end) but is always already mediated by the desire of our model. Moreover, 'desire is not driven by a preexisting model; rather it is desire that brings about the model'.[28] This means that the possibility of human redemption and fall is enclosed in individual's free will, in his or her willingness to imitate the righteous model (i.e. *imitatio Christi*). For Girard as for Augustine, original sin is the result of *perversa imitatio Dei*, 'the corrupt imitation of God'. Conflict arises from a wrongheaded imitation of worldly figures and from an acquisitive desire for mundane goods. 'Faced with the choice between following divine and human role models', the human can either embrace evil (by indulging in self-love, *amor sui*, and thus in the sin of *hubris*) or activate a positive mimesis, which finds in God and in the systems of values promoted by religions an inexhaustible and, accordingly, non-conflictual source of satisfaction.[29]

It is precisely from this ambiguous dualism of morality that Reinhold Niebuhr has drawn the conclusion that 'Caesars and saints are made possible by the same structure of human character'.[30] This view may sound Girardian if, paraphrasing Niebuhr, we say that good and evil both belong in the structure of mimetic desire and are shaped by our models. In this sense, Girard's understanding of original sin does not generate an 'ontology of conflict' that requires a doctrine of natural depravity or endless fall of the human being (as in the Lutheran conception and, more recently, in Morgenthau's view). Rather, sin is conceived of as an 'injury' that 'leaves open the possibility of the natural good'.[31] This point has often been overlooked. Yet, for Augustine (and for Girard), humankind is not originally marked by absolute sinfulness – sin is the result of free desire:

> Because sin or iniquity is not the desire of evil natures but *an abandonment of the better things*, this is found written in Scripture: 'Every creature of God is good.' And for this reason every tree that God planted in paradise was good too. Man, therefore, did not reach towards an evil nature when he touched the forbidden tree. *But, by departing from what was better, he himself committed an act that was evil.*[32]

Thus evil is not interpreted as an *essence* that determines social and political behaviour, but rather as a *voluntary* decline, the product of a free choice.[33] 'I hear this question all the time', Girard remarks, '"is all desire mimetic?" Not in the bad, conflictual sense. Nothing is more mimetic then the desire of a child, and yet it is good. Jesus himself says it is good. Mimetic desire is also the desire for God'.[34] Girard's theodicy can be seen as an 'anthropologization' of Augustine's conception of moral evil. Girard traces the origins of conflict to human relations and their models of representation, and the activation of evil to each individual's moral agency. These assumptions, as we shall see, have a significant influence on the way he views violence and its containment. This position also separates his work from Schmitt's. The German scholar's thought does not rest on anthropological assumptions; even the notion of human being (or 'man') is, for him, a transient historical fact. His analysis concentrates rather on the ontological relationship between law (*Recht*) and political form.

When Schmitt affirms that the political denotes only the degree of intensity of an association or dissociation, he is not trying to justify conflict and violence.[35] For the political is not only the breaking of form by the disorder that never vanishes, but also the disorder in search of a form. 'The enemy' – Schmitt argues – 'stands on my own plane. For this reason, I must contend [*kämpfend*] with him in order to determine my own measure [*Maß*], my own limit, my own form [*Gestalt*].'[36] The political is the tragic tension that runs throughout history, the dramatic coexistence of form and breakthrough, peace and war, order and disorder. This means that Schmitt considers conflict as morphogenetic, dialectical, functional to the search for order: 'The political entity presupposes the real existence of an enemy and, therefore, *coexistence with another political entity*.'[37] Coexistence is difference: the political world rests on this constituent conflict.[38]

What emerges from this brief discussion is an anti-deterministic vision of conflict: violence is not necessary (although always possible), the political (the friend–enemy opposition) is 'morphogenetic nihilism' – the problem of political order is, in other words, the shadow that God cast on the imperfection of the immanent, creatural world. Once again, in order to understand Schmitt's political theodicy, we must return to Augustine's account of evil.[39] For the Christian theologian, the existence of evil appears to be, in the immanence of the world, the result of a *corruptio optimi*, 'corruption of the best':

> If we ask, therefore, whence comes evil, we should first ask what evil is. Evil is nothing but *the corruption of natural measure, form, or order*. In fact, what is called an evil nature is a corrupted nature: for if it were not corrupted, it would be, at any rate, good. But, even when it is corrupted, insofar as it is nature, it is good. It is bad only insofar as it is corrupted.[40]

Schmitt's 'tragic vision' of politics rests on this Augustinian account of evil. He envisages the corruption of political unity as an abandonment of *ordo boni*, 'the order of what is good'. Evil inhabits the effort of organized polities to put the chaotic multitude into form (the state) and to contain the potentially violent horde into a unity in plurality (the antagonistic world of states). Conflict is therefore ontological. It is an 'energy' inherent in the mystery of creation and multiplication of matter – an oscillation of the One towards the manifold and of the manifold towards the One.[41] The political is the 'repressed memory' of this tragic tension, a wound that never heals because the ontological hiatus between transcendence and immanence, God and history, creator and creature remains unbridgeable:

> If corruption takes away from corruptible things all measure, form and order, there will not be any nature at all. And for this reason no nature that gets corrupted can be the supreme good, the way God is. However, any nature which can be corrupted has some good in it; for corruption could not harm it except by taking away or diminishing what is good in it.[42]

Unlike Girard, then, Schmitt conceives of evil as an ontological (and not simply moral) condition, which is inherent in the creatural world. This condition is in fact determined by the creatures who, by the power and freedom they are endowed with, transform 'God's world, which does not need salvation, into a world in need of salvation'.[43] In his view, the phenomenal world appears primarily as contingency abandoned by God – a decadent state in which, however, we sense His presence and seek to imitate his forms (order, sovereignty, the state). Modernity, in other words, is theopolitically structured as a relentless pursuit of necessity (unity, order), which is only possible in absolute immanence (the political). Indeed, for Schmitt, the sovereign (*qua* human being) is unable to create his own world – as God did – *ex nihilo*, but can only do so *de substantia sua*, that is out of the immanent state in which he has been abandoned. Accordingly, political and legal institutions, *qua* human organizations, are incessantly exposed to the power of immanence and violence, that is to the political. Human beings and their relations can never be entirely encapsulated in a political unity but merely order themselves by directing their immanent power against another immanent power. This is the dialectic of the political.

As we shall see, by rethinking the relation between transcendence (law), state and immanence (individual), Schmitt elaborates further this 'ontology of conflict' in the theological–political domain. Here it is important to note that both Girard and Schmitt move along similar theoretical paths, described by the problem of disorder and evil, but use different interpretive categories: Schmitt focuses on ontology, Girard on anthropology. And this is the key to understand the differences between the two of them on the problem of law, politics and, more generally, historical meaning.

The sacrality of politics and the contingency of institutions

In the beginning was the sacrifice. This statement condenses the core of Girard's thought, oriented as it is towards the 'origin'.[44] For him, as we have seen, human beings are *animalia imitantia* – mimetic animals. But this characteristic does not set them apart from other species. As a matter of fact, other primates possess the very same mimetic features.[45] The question is rather this: how can we explain that human beings, and *they alone*, are both symbolic *and* mimetic animals? More specifically, 'how can one explain the ubiquitous existence of rites and prohibitions? ... Why the belief in the sacred?'[46] According to Girard, an answer to these questions can be found by exploring our human origins, that is to say, by turning our attention to the process of hominization.

The starting point of his genealogical analysis is the notion of 'acquisitive mimesis' – the conflictual inclination to possess someone else's object. This feature is subsumed to the triangular logic of desire discussed earlier in this chapter. In the animal kingdom, the violent potential of mimesis is controlled by dominance patterns, through the hierarchization of social roles. Violence is thus contained, *differentiated*, split and channelled in many directions. Nonetheless, in the phylogenetic transition from the animal to the human world – in the process of hominization – there must have been a moment when intra-group rivalry 'became strong enough to break animal dominance networks and unleashed contagious violence'.[47] According to Girard, there must have been a time when, by overstepping this threshold, the infectious power of acquisitive mimesis translated into violent conflict. From that point on, animal societies become impossible. If this is true, then it means that human order must have been generated out of this primeval chaos, from which it was impossible to escape unless violence was redirected against a surrogate victim, a sacrificial substitute or a scapegoat. As Girard puts it,

> Order in human culture certainly does arise from an extreme of disorder, for such disorder is the disappearance of any and all contested objects in the midst of conflict, and it is at such a point that acquisitive mimesis is transformed into conflictual mimesis and tends toward the unification of conflict against an adversary.[48]

At the moment when conflict reaches its maximum intensity, the object – the ostensible reason for conflict – loses its power of fascination and attraction, thus leaving enemies entangled in a web of rivalries and violence. In order to avoid complete annihilation and self-destruction, this tension carried to the extremes – this *bellum omnium contra omnes* – needs to be unified and rechannelled towards a scapegoat. This is the role of the sacrificial victim, who is held responsible for the destructive disorder but at the very same time has the power to restore order. She is the carrier of destruction and salvation, chaos and order, guilt and sacrality at once: a creature ready to be killed and deified, guilty because is sacrificeable, yet venerable because her sacrifice restores the lost order.

This 'mechanism of the sacred' would be at the origin of archaic cultures and religions. Its paradoxical dialectic, which Girard calls *double transference*,[49] would also be the source of that ambiguity of the sacred that many scholars have tried, unsuccessfully, to account for.[50] Indeed, for Girard, archaic rituals and prohibitions would preserve the 'memory' of this founding murder. More specifically, prohibitions (e.g. 'Thou shalt not covet thy neighbour's wife') would possess an anti-mimetic character, while rituals would serve to re-enact, in a non-violent manner, the foundational and original chaos, thus preventing 'the return of the sacrificial crisis'.[51]

It may be appropriate at this point to consider in greater detail some of the key issues that have been discussed so far. As we have seen, for Girard 'humanity results from sacrifice; we are thus children of religion.'[52] This means that archaic religions and their institutions, rites, and myths would be nothing but the result of a huge (metaphysical) effort to maintain order. At the same time, however, the contingent foundations upon which sociopolitical institutions have been established continually compromise this conciliatory effort. Archaic religions are unable to devise ethical systems truly capable of containing mimetic violence, which is always lurking in the shadows: '*The sacred is violence*, but if religious man worships violence it is only insofar as the worship of violence is supposed to bring peace; religion is entirely concerned with peace, but the means it has of bringing it about are never free of sacrificial violence.'[53]

Equally important is Girard's insight that violence, owing to its mimetic origin, is closely connected with two other dimensions: social undifferentiation and psychophysical proximity. Mimetic conflict is all the more acute as there is greater proximity, physical and symbolic, to the model-rival; and violence is widespread when hierarchical, social and political distinctions have faded.

It is through this lens that Girard examines the formation of sovereignty. For him, this concept describes the process of sacralization of political order, which is the attempt of human communities to restrain violence by hierarchizing power by splitting the world into two separate spheres: the 'high' and the 'low', the sacred and the profane. From this perspective, then, the main task of politics would be the creation of 'power distinctions', symbolic separations, anti-mimetic institutions. As Girard writes:

> In all human institutions it is necessary to reproduce a reconciliatory murder by mean of new victims. The original victim is endowed with superhuman, terrifying prestige because it is seen as the source of all disorder and order. Subsequent victims inherit some of this prestige. *One must look to this prestige for the source of all political and religious sovereignty.*[54]

Needless to say, over time, the sacral source of political authority becomes institutionalized, visibly detached from its violent origins. Yet, according to Girard, sovereignty would still be marked by the sacred; it would still preserve the memory and the sacral signs of its violence. Indeed, in ancient times the sovereign was precisely the one who, mediating between two separate worlds (the 'high' and the 'low', transcendence and immanence, necessity and contingency), exposed himself to the risk of being killed. He was literally a mortal god, an ontologically guilty figure, a potential scapegoat, a dead man walking.[55] Perhaps it is this arcane narrative of sovereignty that resonates in Shakespeare's play *Henry IV*: 'The time of life is short ... And if we live, we live to tread on kings.'[56]

Coming from a similar perspective, Schmitt reaches different conclusions. For the German jurist too, violence creates political distinctions, exclusionary inclusions, friend–enemy groupings. As we have seen, he describes the political as the origin of political life and of its exclusionary but ordinative institutions (the state and its separation into an inside and an outside). Nonetheless, there are substantial differences between Girard and Schmitt. First, it should be noted that Girard's work is entirely focused on the problem of origin, on what happened before the 'first coming', while Schmitt concentrates almost exclusively on modernity, which for him represents literally a historical threshold, a new era, a *Neuzeit*.[57] Second, their ways of thinking politics rest on different ontological, epistemological and historical premises. Although both authors deal with the question of origin and end – that is the birth of institutions and the advent of the *parousia*, politics and its crisis in the global age – this convergence of themes does not imply that there is any ideological complementarity between the two scholars. Schmitt, as we shall see, is first and foremost a 'political thinker' (the thinker of the 'political'), while Girard considers the problem of violence through the lens of religion.

Schmitt's thought is in fact entirely based on a powerful intuition: human existence strives to be put into form, to be enclosed in a space dialectically constituted by order (*Ordnung*) and localization (*Ortung*), unity and difference, political form and social substance – that is by the friend–enemy morphogenetic dialectic. Schmitt elaborates on this idea by shaping it in different ways: as a friend–enemy distinction, then as an opposition between land and sea, and as a relation between *Großräume*, and, finally, through the concept of *nomos*, understood as unity [*Einheit*] of *Ordnung* and *Ortung*.[58] Nonetheless, all these categories rest upon the same foundation: violence is all the more dangerous when social and political distinctions have disappeared, for example during civil wars, and politics is all the more effective when a political form manages to enclose itself by remaining open to conflict. The hermeneutic categories through which Schmitt rethinks modern politics – space, decision, form – are all oriented in his mind towards this chiastic reasoning: order is a unity open to conflict.

This is a conceptual level at which we find another fundamental difference between Schmitt and Girard. For the German jurist, in fact, the political form should not be conceived as a 'one-dimensional space' determined by a clear-cut division (which establishes an order by separating the inside from the outside, the 'high' from the 'low'). Rather, a political community is a cosmos that *represents itself* as a unity. A political decision is in fact a 'cut' (*Scheidung, caesum*) that, by isolating a part of land, creates a new unity. The sovereign is the one who, through his decision, concretizes the ideal order in an existential unity, in an *ethos*. In one of his earlier works, Schmitt already presents an ontological conception of his decisionism: 'Between the concrete [*jedem Konkretum*] and the abstract [*jedem Abstraktum*] there is an insurmountable gap, which cannot be filled by any gradual transition. ... In order to serve as a guide for the transformation of reality, the idea of law [*der Rechtsgedanke*] must become positive; that is, its content has to be laid by a sovereign decision [*einen Act souveräner Entscheidung gesetzt*].'[59]

The sovereign is therefore not only the apex of a sacral pyramid (as in Girard's account), but also the embodiment of a *represented* unity. The state is not merely a political form generated out of the power of contingency (violence, the political, pure *Macht*), but a cosmos suspended between the transcendence of the idea and the immanence of history. As Schmitt aptly put it, the state is 'not an *interindividual* but a *superindividual* [*überindividuelle*] entity which does not owe its dignity to any individual creation: it stands before us in its original authority'.[60] For Schmitt, in short, to be truly effective, the state *qua* political form must be equally open to transcendence and to immanence, and at the same time it must be capable of transfiguring a mass of individuals into a totality encapsulated in the legal system. The state is not the realization of the spirit in the world, but the union of history and spirit that realizes the political unity: decision is the moment when this 'sublime short-circuit' occurs.

From this angle, then, Schmitt's thought is at odds with Girard's mimetic theory. As we have seen, Girard considers institutions and rituals nothing more than the fallout of a quasi-natural mechanism: the sacred. According to him, even the law is a by-product of our origins in violence: 'Violence *produced* law, which still is, like sacrifice, a lesser form of violence. This may be the only thing that human society is capable of.'[61] For Schmitt, on the contrary, immanence *qua* immanence is not capable of generating any form or unity. *Nomos* in fact does not refer to positive law, but describes 'the fundamental principle of distribution of terrestrial space' – a space that is intensified and qualified by law.[62] In other words law is not *natural*, if by 'nature' we mean something immanent in history. Rather *nomos* is *natura non naturans*, material constitution, a constant actualization of the idea: for 'every political unity must somehow be integrated because such unity is not by nature present. Instead, it rests on a human decision.'[63]

For Girard, nature and history coincide: the origin of the sacred lies in nature, and it is the sacred that determines human nature. For Schmitt, however, the human is a 'naturally artificial' being. Through representation, humans, *qua animalia politica* ('political animals'), are concerned with making natural something that is devoid of naturalness:

> Representation is not a normative event, a process, and a procedure. It is, rather, something existential. To represent means to make an invisible being visible and present through a publicly present one. The dialectic of the concept is that the invisible is presupposed as absent and nevertheless is simultaneously made present.[64]

In sum, while for Schmitt politics is an 'artificiality' that qualifies and defines humanity (perhaps as its highest symbolic expression), Girard's mimetic theory, on the contrary, is devoid of a dialectic between transcendence and immanence, nature and history, law and politics. Indeed, in Girard's intellectual system, contingency plays the same role as random mutation in evolutionary theory: the world develops and changes *from below*, and the process of social stratification and differentiation is but the result of chance, which collides with the ubiquity of the sacred. Girard's thought is a sort of pendulum that produces different understandings of myths and institutions as it swings, but always returns eventually to its starting point – the sacred. In contrast to Schmitt, then, Girard does not seem to recognize that symbolic power of transcendence without which it would be impossible for us to explain the crisis of modernity and the emergence of a global age.

The global age: History and apocalypse

Girard sees history as a movement marked by two events: the founding murder and the crucifixion of Christ. These events, in turn, gave rise to two key moments in world history: the advent of humankind – that is the transition into a symbolic animal; and the birth of modernity – the age of artifice. And if sacrifice is the violent mechanism through which mankind has tried to contain mimetic conflict, Christianity represents a demystification of the sacred, an unveiling of its violent roots: 'Christ brought to light what had been "hidden since the foundation of the world", in other words, the foundation itself, the unanimous murder that appeared in broad daylight for the first time on the cross.' Thus, 'by revealing the victims' innocence, the Passion makes positive what was still negative in myths: we now know that victims are never guilty.'[65] Because it unveils violence that archaic myths attempted to conceal, Christianity can be literally seen as a process of desacralization and ethical humanization, 'a founding murder in reverse'.[66]

This avowedly Christian 'anthropology of the cross' opens out two paths that, like spirals, radiate from the event of the crucifixion. For the liberation brought about by Christianity releases both a positive and a negative potential: it represents both the exaltation of individual liberty and the creation of individualism; it can be seen both as a humanization or secularization of the sacred and as a deification of the individual. Modern Western history, however, is characterized by the progressive neglect of the ethical message of the cross in favour of a new metaphysics of individuality and secularism that ended up undermining the ancient political institutions and their systems of values. The loss of ethical striving towards 'divine models' (and their external, transcendental and peaceful mediation) thus causes them to be slowly replaced by artificial, immanent and mundane figures.

According to Girard, the disappearance of ethical restraints triggers a dangerous drift. On the one hand, at the institutional level, political organizations (the state), their interactions (*la guerre en dentelle* between sovereign states) and the various universalist ideologies (communism, liberalism, progressivism) would be nothing but surrogates of the sacred, through which communities attempt, without ever succeeding, to hold back an ever-increasing conflict. On the other hand, at the individual level, human beings, in the absence of exemplary models, follow a 'descent into matter', an immanentization of desire, a process of self-reification:

> The Other is more fascinating the less accessible he is; and the more despiritualized he is, the more he tends toward an instinctive automatism, the more inaccessible he is. And the absurd project of self-divinization ends up by going beyond the animal to the automatic and even the mechanical. The individual becomes increasingly bewildered and unbalanced by a desire which nothing can satisfy and finally seeks the divine essence in that which radically denies his own existence: the inanimate.[67]

In modernity, this dynamic of secularization–reification is pushed to the extremes because no symbolic barriers are left to keep in check the power of *homo desiderans* over nature and its resources, and the world's tendency towards violent undifferentiation. Once all the sacred mechanisms – for example the ritual and political sacrifices – that restrained mimetic violence are exhausted, political communities are presented with a radical ethical choice: 'Abstain completely from retaliation, and renounce the escalation to the extremes'; or succumb to the inevitable march of acquisitive mimesis.[68]

At first glance, Girard's apocalyptic theory, which we have here briefly expounded, seems to explain many of the phenomena that characterize the age of globality: states' inability to restrain forms of violence that are growing more and more immediate and asymmetric (e.g. 'terrorism'); the rise of mimetic conflicts and ideologies based on the 'clash of civilizations' motif; and humankind's tendency towards technological perfection and the automated and inanimate hyperproductivity of the world, as illustrated by cyberspace and global finance. Nonetheless, the alleged explanatory power of mimetic theory may be the result of an epistemological lacuna. First, it should be noted that Girard's *scientific theory* of the human – his mimetic anthropology – eventually translates into *religious eschatology* – the so-called anthropology of the cross. The distinction and relationships between these levels of analysis appear extremely problematic. In effect, a 'general theory of religion' is transformed into a Eurocentric philosophy of history, and one based on Christian revelation.[69]

Moreover, in my opinion, mimetic theory suffers from a common methodological flaw: it presents itself as a scientific theory, grounded on a universal mechanism (mimesis, the sacred), but actually it attempts to explain the infinity of the historical process deductively. And therein lies the problem. For the logical ideal of such an approach 'would be a system of formulas that would have absolutely general validity and that would, in abstract form, represent what was common to all historical occurrences'.[70] But this scientific goal is only achievable through 'an increasing remoteness from the empirical reality, which is, everywhere and at all times, only given and *perceivable* as concrete, individual, and qualitatively differentiated'.[71] Paraphrasing Weber, we may say that it is impossible to reduce the endlessness of the historical process to a universal anthropological law, which is always historically situated, unless we strip history of its infinite multiplicity and potentiality. Such a goal, however, would be achievable only if we *conceptually transformed history into an emanation of our own theoretical system*, into a sort of eternal return of the same (e.g. the sacred).

Needless to say, such a theory is not 'scientific'; it looks rather like a form of radical essentialism. Girard in fact confuses his premises with his deductive conclusions, or it might be better to say that he makes the explanandum and the explanans coincide in the mimetic mechanism. As the American philosopher Charles S. Peirce once wrote, 'If we look over the phenomena to find agreements with the theory, it is a mere question of ingenuity and industry how many we shall find.'[72] From this perspective, then, Girard's mimetic theory is 'involuntarily' Eurocentric because it claims to be universal, and it is openly universalist because it is devoid of historical consciousness.

Conversely, Carl Schmitt's genealogical method is *consciously* Eurocentric. His beliefs are instrumental to the analysis of the theopolitical categories of modernity. At least since the publication of *Roman Catholicism and Political Form* in 1923, it became clear to Schmitt that the state is a cosmos made up of concreteness and representation: a political form that is all the more effective as it is *represented* – which is to say, capable of embracing opposites (transcendence and immanence, justice and power, politics and the political). Before the advent of modernity, the Church was considered the fulcrum of this *complexio oppositorum* because, by embracing fundamental antithetic pairs such as reason–spirit, art–industry or nature–machine, it was capable of sublimating these dualisms in different spheres of life, for example in aesthetics, law or politics.[73] The crisis began when this cosmos collapsed under the pressure of the Reformation, thus releasing the dualisms it contained. The theological domain got mixed with the political domain, violence with justice; the defeat of the enemy was now confused with the annihilation of the opponent. These tensions produced the Wars of Religion of the sixteenth century. It is at this historical level, then, that the theological–political questions were asked afresh, and perhaps with greater intensity:

> *Quis judicabit? Quis interpretabitur?* [Who will decide? Who will interpret?]
> Who answer *in concreto*, on behalf of the concrete, autonomously acting human being, the question of what is spiritual, what is wordly and what is the case of the *res mixtae*, which ... constitute ... the entire earthly

existence of this spiritual-wordly, spiritual-temporal, double creature called a *human being*?[74]

The answer to the crisis is the principle *cuius regio, eius religio*, which signals the respatialization of religion within the sovereign territory of the state. Thus, from Westphalia onwards, the state comes to hold a monopoly on the political. But even so, it suffers from a fundamental problem inherent to its new role and status. By secularizing politics, the state has in fact become a 'decapitated leviathan': it has lost the memory of its transcendental and representational function.[75] By being erected in the 'shadow of transcendence', the state loses its representational force and is now at the mercy of the power of contingency – the political. It is for this reason that, according to Schmitt, the state can function as a katechon only if, making itself aware of its own 'imperfection', of its own 'original deformity', it closes its borders by remaining open to conflict, to the possibility of death. This is the essence of Schmitt's tragic vision of modernity.

Once access to transcendence and to its symbolic resources is closed, the modern political form tends to develop within itself all those immanent energies (individualism, liberalism, progressivism, i.e. new abstract universalist ideologies) that, according to Schmitt, will lead the state to self-destruction. Initially, the state overburdens itself with potentially nihilistic energies, say, of nationalism and mercantilism, then releases these forces externally in all their dangerousness, producing something like economic and political globalism. At this stage not even law, spatially oriented and localized as it is, can hold back the emergence of the new universalisms. Indeed, law, too, falls prey to this nihilistic tendency, which moves from the concrete to the abstract, from legitimacy to mere legality, from political form (the state) to economic formlessness (globalization).[76]

In discussing the relationship (and the divide) between law and religion, Harold J. Berman once wrote: 'At the highest level, surely, the just and the holy are one, and our sense of each rests partly on our sense of the other. It is necessary to say this because conventional wisdom has separated them to the point of disaster.'[77] Schmitt would have agreed with this conclusion. As we have seen, for him, the neglect of the vertical, transcendental dimension of politics leads to secularization and loss of symbolic meaning. In absolute immanence, there begins a regression that will ultimately bring the modern age to an end. In the desperate attempt to politically and legally 'cage' the political (which is now ubiquitous and fed by new universalisms), the state starts a 'process of continuous neutralizations of various domains of cultural life', that reaches its conclusion in the technological age.[78]

For Schmitt, globalization is not simply a form of *deterritorialization* and, therefore, a dismantling of the katechonic, restraining function of the state. Above all, the global age represents the occupation and exploitation of the earth in its entirety – an occupation that destroys all the checks and balances, the political distinctions and symbolic resources, created during modernity. Paraphrasing Heidegger, Schmitt in fact writes that in the age of globality 'it is not the world that is in space but rather is the space that is in the world'; that is to say, 'space has become the field of man's energy, activity and creativity.'[79] Technology is at the heart of this global, permanent revolution. It has occupied and at the same time emptied the last *Zentralgebiet* (central domain), thus bringing modern politics to a close, to the unpolitical. It is as if, while looking for a neutral ground as it was on the run from the political, humankind ended up neutralizing itself, thus falling into 'the cultural nothingness.'[80]

At this conceptual level, Schmitt's pessimistic vision takes on even darker tones. In the smooth and undifferentiated space produced by technology there are no handholds to cling on to if you want to arrest the sinking of the *jus publicum Europaeum*. The katechon and all the other mythopoetic resources have by now been exhausted and are no longer able to hold back the technological wave. Space and time seem to have merged into a new 'global mobilization', which fails to produce new political forms and symbolic meanings. As Schmitt poetically writes in his *Glossarium*: 'Space is magic; time is spell; speed is nothing but sorcery. Time flows; space stands still or lies down. Movement erases space in that it transforms space in an empty container of its own progress.'[81] Paradoxically, in the 'age of fire' the power of the elements and the dialectic triggered by them runs out of steam. The rift between idea and action, justice and law, transcendence and immanence is by now unbridgeable.

In his earlier writings, Schmitt had anticipated this political drift: 'To the political belongs the idea, because there is no politics without authority and no authority without an ethos of belief.'[82] Yet the 'global' is an ethos with *mobile foundations*. In this disunity of the world, there is no authority capable of creating an idea of order out of the new metaphysics of infinity and processuality. Thus the future now becomes – as Schmitt put it – 'the creation *of* nothingness as the condition for the possibility of the self-creation of an ever new worldliness'.[83] In sum, in the 'age of world picture', as Heidegger strikingly called it, human beings have lost their own measure, their symbolic power, their capacity for political representation.

As should be clear by now, Schmitt's counter-philosophy of history sketches a genealogical trajectory that differs from the one traced by Girard's mimetic theory. For Girard, as we have seen, history is a sort of motionless, timeless process characterized by an extraordinary event: the revelation. From his anthropological perspective, it is as if immanence (the sacrificial mechanism), by trying in vain to rise up to transcendence, always ends up falling back on itself (in violence). Immanence is a sort of prison that has only one way out: the sacred – which is in fact another prison. For Schmitt, on the contrary, it is the dialectic between transcendence and immanence, necessity and contingency, 'idea' and 'law' that determines political history and its mediatory forms (cities, empires, states). It was the *putting into form of the political* that constituted the secret engine of Western history.

It can therefore be argued that Girard's mimetic theory – in order to explain historical change, and precisely because it is conceived of as a scientific anthropology – needs to be anchored in an extra-rational and meta-historical event (the revelation). In contrast, Schmitt's political theology, precisely because it describes modernity as an age devoid of transcendence, is unable to provide a worldly, immanent solution to the crisis brought about by globalization. In short, Girard's 'immanental individualism' and Schmitt's *complexio oppositorum* are halves from two different wholes. Although these thinkers deal with the same 'crisis' – namely global undifferentiation – their assumptions about the origins, evolution and destiny of Western politics are divergent and at times conflicting. Ultimately, the conceptual trajectories drawn by Girard and Schmitt represent two parallel paths that converge only towards the end.

Conclusion

In this chapter I have presented two alternative theories of the origins and evolution of political violence. Their differences notwithstanding, Schmitt's and Girard's radical insights allow us to investigate some of the complex dynamics that characterize the so-called global age. Their genealogies are, in my view, obligatory points of passage for those who want to explore the 'mystery of the political' and the violence it entails. It goes without saying that recognizing a problem is not the same as solving it. For, if the genealogies sketched by these two authors are useful for framing at least some of the causes of the latent conflictuality that affects the global age, the theoretical solutions they propose are far from being effective. In the age of global mobilization – of goods, services, values – and of mixing cultures and religions, Schmitt's proposal of a juridical–political respatialization sounds anachronistic, as much as Girard's new Sermon-on-the-Mount ethic appears ineffective.

Nevertheless, their radical visions have at least the merit of making us see more clearly the roots of the new global disorder. Through their reversed perspectives, Schmitt and Girard in fact highlight a crucial conundrum: there can be no order without a transcendental dimension, a tension towards the 'idea' (of God, of justice, it does not matter here). In the *mare magnum* produced by technology, in the age of unstructured immanence, the Idea is all the more necessary as the new global process–progress presents itself as uncontrollable. But, in order to reach it again, it is not sufficient to share purposes and ideals or to create a new, globally dispersed political agency, which should be multifunctional and pluralistic, like a sort of 'postmodern Prince'. To represent, Schmitt reminds us, involves the union of Idea and reality, order and *localization*, in a space that becomes public only when it is *elevated*. It seems difficult to achieve this goal in the virtual space of private networks that, by penetrating into the public sphere, disrupts its very foundation. The common good, in fact, cannot be simply embodied from below: our idea of the commons needs to be placed in a physical space in order to be shared and protected.

In our 'liquid' times, then, Schmitt warns us (*contra* Girard) that 'eternity cannot be reached with one's own ladder'; that is to say, we cannot escape from this condition of absolute immanence by pulling ourselves 'by the hair from the swamp of nothingness up into existence'.[84] In this horizontal dimension, we cannot save ourselves by following an individualist ethic or by instrumentally restoring transcendence. What 'global space', then, can give form to our always-evolving idea of justice? What order will be 'representable' in the age of uncontrolled immanence and global undifferentiation? These are the momentous questions that Schmitt and (in part) Girard have bequeathed to us as a disquieting legacy.

5

Religion and Political Form: Schmitt *contra* Habermas

A state is not made up only of so many men, but of different kinds of men; for similars do not constitute a state.

Aristotle, *Politics*, II, 1261a23–5

It has been argued that the birth of modernity resembles an explosion or, it would be better to say, an implosion. The collapse of the ethical–political architecture of the *res publica Christiana* produced a fragmentation that the territorialization of faiths and churches was unable to repair by reassembling the pieces into one whole (and, when so, only for a limited period of time). Moreover, this pluralism in fragments – grown in the shadow of the 'death of God' – was shaken even more by the subsequent wave of globalization, which replaced the old principle of territorialization (*cuius regio, eius religio*, discussed in the previous chapter) with one of total mobilization (*cuius oeconomia, eius regio* – 'the religion will be that of the person whose economy it is'). Today we live in a world that is literally made of slivers of worlds (values, symbols, objects) mixed without guidance (apart from the randomness driven by private interest). Accordingly, the question of pluralism is not merely theoretical, but also practical and political, as shown by the heated debate on 'Euro-Islam', the 'headscarf affair', the complex problem of migrants and asylum seekers, and the overwhelming resurgence of nationalisms and identity politics that we have witnessed in recent years. A critical reflection on pluralism, from both a conceptual and a practical point of view, is, in short, more urgent than ever. But how is it possible to reconceptualize this unstable pluralism in terms of a new unity in plurality that is no longer based on classical and exclusionary models – the so-called particular universals: the nation state, the 'free' market, citizenship?

It is precisely this urgent question that animates the current post-secular debate. According to Jürgen Habermas, who is one of the leading voices in the debate, the description of modern societies as 'postsecular' refers in fact to a 'change in consciousness' that can be attributed to three interrelated phenomena: the perception that religion is regaining worldwide influence, its 'return' within national public spheres (which were supposed to have been 'secularized') and the pluralism of ways of life typical of immigrant societies.[1] Whether or not this description is consistent with reality and whether or not this 'change in consciousness' is an actual historical development is not essential here.[2] In fact, the historical premises of Habermas's analysis are used instrumentally, to support his normative vision. The fundamental issue at stake is not whether Western societies are secularized – for they mainly are – but rather how we can 'ensure that in firmly entrenched nation states, social relations remain civil despite the growth of a plurality of cultures and religion world-wide'.[3]

The postsecular *arcanum* does not seem so mysterious after all. The problem is still how to solve the 'riddle' of pluralism – an issue that had already intensified the debate between Habermas and the Canadian philosopher Charles Taylor on the theme of multiculturalism.[4] The only difference this time seems to be the emphasis placed on the 'religious spirit' of that pluralism and on Habermas's 'conversion' and 'change in consciousness' towards religion, as he puts it in his dialogue with the then Cardinal Joseph Ratzinger.[5] Habermas is now ready to recognize that a 'complementary learning process' between secular and religious sides must be fostered, that 'secular citizens in civil society and the political public sphere must be able to meet their religious fellow citizens as equals'.[6] In order to promote this new 'political openness', however, religious worldviews and utterances must be translated into a publicly accessible language and then introduced into a secular discourse.[7] Of course, according to Habermas, 'the domain of the state, which controls the means of legitimate coercion, should not be opened to the strife between various religious communities, otherwise the government could become the executive arm of a religious majority that imposes its will on the opposition'.[8] Under this aspect, therefore, religion is considered *useful*, 'particularly [with regard] to vulnerable social relations ... [as it] possesses the power to convincingly articulate moral sensitivities and solidaristic intuitions.[9] Religious beliefs, however, given their potential for conflict, should be 'rationalized' and not allowed to have any power over the *res publica*.

Habermas's recovery of religion – his post-secular discourse – implies nothing but the possibility of movement of religious beliefs, which, in the public sphere, should be channelled towards secular and instrumental ends. This means that the potential contained in the 'religious irrational' should be used rationally, to contrast the sociopolitical fragmentation produced by instrumental rationality; and then one should expel this 'irrational' element when it attempts to enter the decision-making process. From this perspective, the 'novelty' promised by the post-secular framework does not seem to justify the use of the prefix 'post-'. The logic used by Habermas is still tied to dichotomous categories of modernity such as inclusion–exclusion, public–private, secular–religious, and so forth.

Nonetheless, lurking behind this post-secular discourse – which can also be seen as a normative response to the phenomenon of the 'return of religion' – is one of the greatest conundrums in the history of Western political thought: the problematic relationship between transcendence and power.[10] In fact, as a result of migration flows and the failures of instrumental rationality, the return of religions (in the plural) to the public domain brings back to the fore, in a new guise, the old problem of political unity and its internal cohesion and legitimacy. What sort of unity is possible in the plurality of cultures and religions? What identities and types of legitimacy are formed through the contingent fragmentation created by the dynamics of globalization? What political form can give shape to community in an age in which state borders are becoming more and more 'porous'? It is not difficult to see that the post-secular discourse both conceals and reveals some of the most profound questions of the Western political tradition and challenges us to wrestle with them again.

In what follows, through an analysis of the post-secular envisaged as both an intellectual and a historical challenge to Western thought, I aim to problematize Habermas's analytical–normative proposal and to highlight its underlying difficulties. This critical analysis is not an end in itself; it attempts to frame, in the context of international politics, the radical issue of the relation between the sacred and the political. This problematic relation has re-emerged in full force as a consequence of what can be described as the second great crisis of the political space – and one triggered by the 'border-crossing' dynamics of globalization. In fact the contemporary age is characterized by a continuous mobilization and hybridization of borders, which makes ineffective the conceptual and political divisions established during modernity (inside-outside, private–public, religious–secular etc.).[11]

As we shall see, faced with this challenge, which encompasses the problem of pluralism, Habermas makes an instrumental use of religion; and he does so, paradoxically, in order to combat the 'iron cage' set up by instrumentally oriented action. Besides, his responses to the challenge of religious and cultural pluralism are covertly Western-centric and fall into what might be called the 'isomorphic fallacy': an attempt to preserve the liberal–democratic identity by transforming the public sphere into an abstract tabula rasa – a space deprived of the *concrete* plurality and social differences that constitute the *respublica*. This once again demonstrates the difficulty of overcoming the mechanism of inclusion–exclusion on which the political architecture of modernity was established. Moreover, Habermas's post-secular project presents an additional risk: the possibility of failure of our political systems, which, if based once again on abstract and universalist categories, could end up polarizing the concrete and irrepressible plurality generated through the global mobilization of cultures and religions.

In an attempt to address these issues in a more systematic fashion, this chapter seeks to go further than Habermas's neoliberal project by placing the post-secular discourse within a broader genealogy of the relation between religion and political space. In so doing, its aim is to show how religion has been an inescapable dimension of Western politics, both in the process of formation of the modern state and in that of transforming its secular foundations into a new form of universalism.[12] If we wish to understand the strength of this twofold bond created by an absence–presence of religion in modern politics, I believe it is worth revisiting Carl Schmitt's genealogy of political modernity. Schmitt's political theology is a far-reaching analysis of the origin of modernity and of its central political form – the state. It offers an intellectual journey that begins with a crisis of space (and of its relationship with 'transcendence') and ends with a new beginning, which is marked by another spatio-political crisis, namely the advent of the global age. The intent is therefore to revalue the negative and critical part of Schmitt's thought and not the positive and constructive part – *pars destruens*, not *pars construens*: to follow his deconstruction of the political categories of modernity, not his 'dangerous' respatialization of *jus publicum Europaeum*. The aim here is to rethink – through Schmitt, but really beyond – the place of the sacred in the political space.

The discussion proceeds in three moves. In the first section I revisit the relation between religion and politics as described in Schmitt's *Political Theology* of 1922, which also presents an alternative theory of secularization. The purpose of this exploration is to outline the theological roots of modernity, that is, the 'remains' of sacredness that Christianity, according to Schmitt, has left in the secular sphere and in the modern notion of sovereignty. This analysis is useful for addressing critically the modern rationalistic separation between public and private, religion and politics, church and state.

The second part examines Schmitt's theological–political ideas from two different but interrelated perspectives: one domestic; the other international. It will be shown that the modern state, once severed from its religious foundations and in order to preserve its unity in the absence of a 'transcendental signifier', is constantly exposed to the risk of destabilization – that is, to the problem of how to reconstitute an idea of a 'common good' on which it could itself be grounded *qua* political community. As we shall see, for Schmitt, the process of secularization–neutralization, which is driven by globalizing forces and ideologies (individualism, global economy, technology), has brought about a disintegration of the unity and functions of the state (decision, legitimacy, order), both at the domestic and at the international level.

The third section illustrates, in light of Schmitt's political theory, the conceptual and practical problems that underlie Habermas's post-secular project; and it emphasizes the latter's homogenizing and hidden universalistic logic. Finally, on the basis of this critique, I seek to go beyond Schmitt's analysis, in an attempt to overcome the dialectic of inclusion–exclusion that shaped the modern state form (by now hopelessly 'deformed' through the dynamics of globalization) and to suggest some alternative lines along which one can reflect on the role and contribution of religious and cultural pluralism in Western democracies.

Genealogy of a crisis: The theological roots of modernity

According to the character Socrates as construed by Plato in the *Republic*, one of the fundamental characteristics of a *politeia* (civil polity, state) is its tension towards 'unity'. For 'can we think of any greater evil for a city than what tears it apart and turns it into many cities instead of one? Or any greater good than what unites it and makes it one?'[13] This ideal unity towards which the Republic (*Kallipolis*) should strive is, however, a dual unity. For politics in general and the classical city (*polis*) in particular can only be a reflection or representation (*mimēsis*) of the original purity of the Form. So the problem of the 'political' envisioned as a mixture of unity and duality goes back as early as Plato. Politics is a spurious unity because of the incommensurability between Form and reality, transcendence and immanence, foundation and movement. This is the reason why, according to Plato, the philosopher, who spends 'his time with what is divine and ordered', has the 'duty' to mediate between the two worlds, between the Form of the Good and social plurality, thus seeking to achieve harmony.[14]

The ancient world was imbued with this kind of dualist metaphysics. The Stoic philosophers, for example, use the term *cosmopolis* precisely to refer to the specular relation between the divinely ordered universe (*kosmos*) and the humanly ordered space of the *polis*.[15] Political harmony is a mirror of the universal harmony. For even the city 'is born representing itself as a "world" that reproduces the sacred order of the universe on a small scale'.[16] Its boundaries enclose an indivisible order, made up of space, sacredness and politics. And it is no coincidence that this *cosmos* is endowed with meaning through omens and auspices, even by means of ritual sacrifices.[17]

With the advent of Christianity, however, something changed forever. 'God become man in historical reality',[18] and what had hitherto been conceived of as a symbiosis of eternal and temporal, this world and the hereafter, was transformed into a friction between transcendence and immanence, sacred and profane, the kingdom of God and the kingdom of Caesar. Herein lies the origin of the concept of 'Political Theology' *stricto sensu* and of the 'fundamental dualism that has dominated the world since the beginning of Christianity'.[19] In contrast to the dual unity that characterized the ancient world, Christianity represents itself as a unitary duality in which this world is significantly devalued vis-à-vis the kingdom of heaven. This metaphysical separation can be traced back to Saint Paul, but it was Augustine who – following Christ's maxim 'my Kingdom is not of this world'[20] – fully elaborated upon the division between two kingdoms, one of God, *civitas Dei*, and the other earthly, *civitas terrena*. Christianity had to present itself as an alien creed in a secular world and, at the very same time, to adapt itself to the 'realm of sin' by rethinking the conceptual and practical relation between God, church and empire.

Carl Schmitt's theological–political reflections are rooted precisely in this problematic tension between sacredness and political order – a tension that traverses two intertwined axes: one vertical, namely openness to transcendence; and one horizontal, namely closure of political unity. Since his early works, Schmitt has meditated on the bond between transcendence and politics and, above all, on the historical rift between these dimensions that had taken place during the modern age. In his view, as we shall see, modernity is born out of a crisis or, it would be better to say, out of a spatial revolution that reverberates to the other fundamental spheres of social life: politics and the sacred.[21] On the one hand, this crisis is cosmological – a consequence of the Copernican Revolution and of the momentous shift that characterizes the transition from the closed world to the infinite universe.[22] On the other hand, this crisis is also a geo-political one triggered by the discovery of the New World and marked by a radical change in the human perception of the Earth.[23]

But the revolution that took place in the sixteenth and seventeenth centuries is, first and foremost, a 'theo-political crisis of the *res publica Christiana* spurred by the Lutheran Reformation'.[24] And this transition represents an epochal and paradoxical change. For, if the Reformation facilitates the fragmentation of the Christian ethos and the unleashing of the productive energies of Protestant individualism, on the other hand, by mixing together *civitas Dei* and *civitas terrena* and by making ineffective the spiritual and political mediation of the Church, this crisis reopens, in an intensified form, some radical theological–political questions: *Quis judicabit? Quis interpretabitur?* Who will decide? Who will interpret? The civil Wars of Religion are, accordingly, the unavoidable corollary of this crisis, out of which modernity and its political form, the state, emerged. The response to this violent reaffirmation of 'political theology' is in fact the neutralizing principle *cuius regio, eius religio*: an attempt to reassemble religious fragmentation through the territorialization of churches and religious orders.

At this conceptual level, then, Schmitt's thinking is, and will always remain, focused on the problem of the creation and preservation of political order. As he writes in one of his latest works, 'substances must first of all have found their *form*; they must have been brought into a *formation* before they can actually encounter each other as contesting subjects in a conflict, that is, as *parties belligérantes*'.[25] In order to create such a unity, the political space must necessarily remain open to the notion of the good. To consolidate political immanence within the artificial borders of the state, such a notion must transcend empirical reality and its parts. Schmitt, however, is well aware that the fragmentation brought about by the civil Wars of Religion can no longer be repaired and the whole recomposed with the help of theological categories. Indeed, by leaving their normal ethos and entering into the energetic realm of the political, religious beliefs beget violence. In the absence of an overarching political and ethical framework, opposing values tend to polarize along the friend–enemy continuum.[26]

The state, therefore, at the moment of its historical–conceptual formation, was created to restore unity in the European fragmentation triggered by the Reformation. Its principal aim was to produce an internal homogeneity and an external balance between political entities that were now considered legally equal. But, in order for this goal to be achieved, 'theology, the former central domain, was abandoned because it was controversial, in favor of another – neutral – domain'.[27] This period can be considered the beginning of a new (and supposedly) detheologized epoch marked by Alberico Gentili's famous dictum – *Silete theologi in munere alieno!*[28] – and by 'the rational and human cultivation of war between states'.[29] The birth of the European state system, the *jus publicum Europaeum*, as Schmitt called it, was first and foremost just that: an attempt to transform the civil wars of the sixteenth and seventeenth centuries into state rivalries (*la guerre en forme*) through the consecration of political limits (inside–outside, police–army, domestic–international) and through the non-discriminatory mutual recognition of that right and territorial limitation.

Nonetheless, the new modern political order, which is established inside and outside the state, in interstate relations, is fragile and unstable. The European state system is not a perfectly balanced network, but rather a field of forces that contains within itself the violence of its origins, the latent disorder from which it was generated. Indeed, if the state served to restore order by removing the 'political' from the theological domain, modern politics lost its foundational substance by establishing itself in the 'shadow of transcendence'. According to Schmitt, the modern state, if compared to the ideal–typical model of the Church, both lacks and seeks to replicate its essential power: the capacity for public representation. In his *Roman Catholicism and Political Form* (1923), Schmitt describes the Church as 'a unity-in-plurality, which clearly has both a metaphysical structure and a concrete significance'.[30] The Church's two bodies, the mystical and the collegiate, would allow this institution to mediate between transcendence and immanence, idea and reality, publicity and individuality, whole and its parts.[31] The Church is a perfect *complexio oppositorum* (combination of opposites), being able to harmonize the disunity between the sphere of the sacred and the sphere of the political by connecting together *veritas, auctoritas* and *potestas*.[32]

But by cutting its ties with the vertical, transcendental sphere, the modern state 'becomes a leviathan' and thus 'disappears from the world of representations'.[33] Political modernity – of which the state is the vital core – is 'acephalous': in order to survive, the state – structured as it is around the absence of a transcendental and foundational substance – is constantly forced to chase the shadow of a disappeared order. In other words, for Schmitt, the process of secularization, understood here in its temporal dimension, 'deforms', but does not transform, the sacred into the secular. These two spheres are analogically related in the form of a constant presence in absence: on the one hand, modern politics is structured 'by the absence of foundational "divine substance", and is therefore contrary to theology. On the other hand, modern politics reproduces, although only in a formal–rational way, theology's monistic ordering function'.[34] In short, the structural correspondence between transcendence and power continues not only in *space* (i.e. within the state) but also in *time* (i.e. in the Western conception of order and unity).[35] And this continuity is characterized by a presence in absence – an aporia that liberal scholars seek to erase theoretically but cannot exclude from the domain of the political.

This relationship of formal continuity and substantial discontinuity between modern politics and theology is clearly reflected in the conceptual structure of law. When Schmitt writes that 'the exception in jurisprudence is analogous to the miracle in theology', he means that 'exception' is the secularized name by which political science, from Hobbes onwards, refers to the lack of a founding political principle.[36] In the beginning, therefore, during the process of state formation, there was neither a rational mediation nor a social contract. The actualization of law (*Rechtsverwirklichung*), which took place through the form of the state, was in fact a 'cut', a 'leap', an original decision that eradicated politics from the realm of the 'political' – the primeval violence from which the modern state emerged.[37] Indeed, 'the legal idea cannot realize itself' but needs a concrete space in which it can be 'translated into reality', and the decision is in fact the gesture by which 'authority proves that to produce law it need not be based on law'.[38]

It should be clear by now why Schmitt regards legal positivism *à la* Kelsen, which equates law with sovereignty, as 'the antechamber of jurisprudence'.[39] For this approach is unable to account for the actual 'origin' of the state form and for the fact that, normatively, political 'decision emanates from nothingness'.[40] For Schmitt, in the foundational emptiness that characterizes modernity, the sovereign decision serves precisely to concretize the idea of Justice within the borders of the state. This does not mean, however, that Schmitt is opposed to the rule of law, or that he is a warmonger who wants to abolish the legal order by means of exceptional decisions. In fact, as he clearly puts it, 'Both elements, *the norm as well as the decision, remain within the framework of the juristic*'.[41] And he believes that, to preserve order, it is necessary to deal with the original disorder of modernity, and that behind the state lurks violence and not the 'nirvana of law' – the political and not the social contract. This is in fact how he interprets Thomas Hobbes's dictum *authoritas, non veritas, facit legem*[42]: 'The truth does not actualizes itself [*vollzieht sich nicht selbst*]; it requires enforceable commands [*vollziehbarer Befehle*]. This is the function of the *potestas directa*, which – in contrast to the *potestas indirecta* – assures the execution of commands, requires obedience, and protects those who obey.'[43]

The sovereign, therefore, should never lose sight of the 'constituent nihilism' that lies at the origin of the state. In order to preserve political order, the state should always remain open to conflict (i.e. to the political). It is as if the transition from the state of nature to civil society were not only impossible but also incautious: for the political is like an energy without place that needs to be handed out in small doses in order to be located and therefore controlled. Or, speaking more directly, the modern state, given its groundlessness, can act as a katechon only if it is able to face its own existential insecurity, the always present possibility of violence and death.[44]

Schmitt's genealogy, although imbued with reactionary and anti-liberal ideas, reveals a fundamental point of crisis in modern political thought, which never succeeds in closing itself. As we have seen, the modern political form is always exposed to the unformed, to an archetypal remnant, to the exception. This point of indifference explodes the rationalistic conception that sees politics and the state as self-grounded and autotelic. Indeed, Schmitt suggests that immanence – the realm of the political – cannot govern itself, but needs to open up to a 'higher' idea. This is one of the reasons why he is critical of liberalism: society and the market are not self-governing entities, just as private subjectivities are unable to create public representations. In the plurality of private interests there is room only for conflict and for the tyranny of values.[45] Modern individualism and its corollaries, capitalism and neo-liberalism, are incapable of giving rise to a stable political unity; on the contrary, they can only accelerate the dissolution of the ancient forms of order, *christianitas* first, and then the state.

Schmitt therefore conceives of the state as a historical *necessity*, which is, however, constantly exposed to *contingency*, in other words, to the dangers of the political. As will appear later on, the state – precisely because of the illusory closure of the immanent order on itself – begins an entropic process through which its political unity is fragmented by the globalizing and neutralizing forces of capitalism and technology. And this dynamic will eventually lead to another spatial revolution, and to the emergence of a new relation between sacredness and political space.

Within and beyond unity: Universes and pluriverses

Schmitt's 'political theology' is a reflection on the origin of the modern political form – the state – and on the absence of transcendent support that characterizes its precarious unity. In consequence, his analysis opens another problematic: that of the (ostensible) closure of the state and of how to preserve the state's political unity. Here again Schmitt does not conceive of transcendence and immanence, religion and politics, ethics and the state as polar dimensions. According to him, as we have seen, modern politics and its institutions have been constituted by duplicating religious concepts and structures, after a process of emptying, but not of exceeding, the theological categories. The illusory ideology that sees the modern state as self-grounded and autotelic – with the corollary that it is capable of fully neutralizing conflict and rationalizing social life – is challenged by the same rationalistic forces (individualism, economy, technology) that the state, *qua* supreme mechanism (*machina machinarum*), has first nurtured and then unleashed. For, if the aim or *telos* of the state, in its European expansion, was political unity, this principle was the result of *historical contingency* (the situation created by the civil Wars of Religion) and of *genealogical necessity* (the legacy of the Greek and Christian conceptions of order). However, once the state cut itself loose (although only outwardly) from the theological domain, 'the ethical question of fidelity and loyalty must get a different answer from the one it gets in the case of a univocal, transcendent and comprehensive unity'.[46]

If we wish to maintain unity within the new, secular borders of the state, then the relationships between legitimacy and legality, between political unity and the plurality of the social body have to be thought anew. In the absence of a transcendental signifier and of a unifying principle, the new ethics of the state should now attempt to produce a homogenization of social differences. As Schmitt has it, 'Political unity is the highest unity – not because it is an omnipotent dictator, or because it levels out all others unities, but because it decides, and has the potential to prevent all other opposing groups from dissociating into a state of extreme enmity'.[47] Pluralism, understood as sheer plurality and multitude, is possible only between states, but not within the state. Domestically, different sources of legitimacy involve a plurality of obligations and loyalties and, accordingly, a risk of implosion of state unity. The only stable form of pluralism is to be found in a world of rival states. As Schmitt writes in *The Concept of the Political*, 'The political world is a pluriverse, not a universe. In this sense every theory of the State is pluralistic even though in a different way from the domestic theory of pluralism'.[48]

By deciding who the enemy is and by containing plurality within its borders, the state becomes the decisive political unity, since it is able to control the political. Internal pluralism is possible because the state guarantees and preserves social diversity. In other words, for Schmitt, the state is a higher moral entity, because it ensures survival and reconciles social differences. The priority assigned to the state is therefore not opposed to pluralism. Schmitt's political monism seeks to contrast the dangers that might result from multiple fidelities:

> 'In the plurality of loyalties', there is no 'hierarchy of duties', no unconditional prescriptive principle of super- and subordination. In particular, the ethical bond to the state, the duty of fidelity and loyalty, appears as only one instance alongside other bonds – alongside loyalty to the church, the economy, or the family; loyalty to the state has no precedence, and the ethic of state is a special ethic among many other special ethics.[49]

'The world of objective spirit', as Schmitt puts it, is always made up of a diversity of peoples, religions, cultures, languages and legal systems. Nonetheless, pluralities need to find a space to express themselves and to coexist – a space that the higher-order violence of the state renders impenetrable to violence. Externally, therefore, the international system is conceived of by Schmitt as a plural universe made up of political monads that, in order to remain self-enclosed, should stay open to the possibility of conflict. This is in fact the meaning of the political: order is possible only if it preserves a certain openness to disorder. Internally, however, Schmitt understands plurality as a universe of associations that, in order to be harmonious, must be homogenized by the unifying and unconditional loyalty to the state.

It is at this conceptual point that Schmitt's 'ethics of the state' becomes truly dangerous. Given the lack of a common ethos and of a transcendental ground, political order and state homogeneity cannot be maintained 'automatically'. Rather they must be politically constituted. A political community is not merely a 'juridical artifice' based on 'natural law', but a unity shadowed by the ever-present threat of an enemy. As Schmitt has it, the state is a unity composed of movement (population) and foundation (the sovereign), exception and decision, friends and enemies.[50]

Thus, much like Weber, Schmitt thinks of the state as a *primus inter pares*, an institution that has monopolized violence and whose legitimacy is rooted in a system of law.[51] But, to become the 'holder of the most astonishing of all monopolies' (*erstaunlichsten aller Monopole*), the state needs to be recognized as a 'higher' entity.[52] The social body has to conceive of itself as a whole and homogeneous unity. And this homogeneous collectivity must mirror itself, so to speak, in the state's legitimate power and in the legality of its enclosed political system.

But it is precisely here that we encounter the *nodus letalis* ('deadly knot'). Since the nineteenth century, the unity and homogeneity of the state and especially the identity between the people and the state begin to collapse. New identities and loyalties, which are considered 'higher' or more important than those related to the state, emerge from the fractures of its broken unity. Universalist ideologies (e.g. Marxism, capitalism, anarchism), together with the productive and uncontrollable forces of technology and of international economy, challenge the system of checks and balances established by states. Historically, states found their *nomos* through the neutralization of their shared political space (Europe), replacing the arbitrary use of power with the rule of law. But this process of rationalization of politics and violence could not be contained within the geographic limits it had helped to establish. The scientific, technological and industrial forces eventually transcended the boundaries of their political ethos, igniting a novel spatial revolution.

From this perspective, then, the age of globalization represents a quantitative, but also a qualitative transformation of politics. All classical distinctions, checks and balances developed during the modern age to guarantee order and security become increasingly ineffective. At this stage, social plurality turns into chaotic contingency. Modern categories – inside and outside, public and private, religious and secular – lose their practical and conceptual value, and new universalist and private subjectivities are now free to move across the international system. In the new preface to *The Concept of the Political*, Schmitt writes: 'The classic nature [of the modern categories] lies in the possibility of clear and unambiguous distinctions: inside and outside, war and peace and – in warfare – civil and military, neutrality and non-neutrality. These concepts were clearly separated and could not be intentionally confused.'[53] But in the age of globality these distinctions have lost their effectiveness. Modern technology and global economy have transformed the world by launching what Schmitt sees as a permanent revolution: 'This transformation is no less profound than that which occurred in the sixteenth and seventeenth centuries. At that time man believed that the world found itself in an empty space. Nowadays ... space has become the field of man's energy, activity and creativity.[54] For Schmitt, this spatial revolution is incapable of generating a new (and stable) political system and of transforming the chaotic plurality brought about by the age of mobilization into an ordered pluriverse.

It is from this crisis that the issue of pluralism and political unity really emerges afresh. The problem is intensified by the global scale of the phenomenon, and cannot be easily solved through a forced closure of state borders or a respatialization of politics (as Schmitt himself seems to suggest). As a matter of fact, the new *nomos* must be able to contain what is uncontainable: the constant mobility of values and powers, which are the very essence of the processes of globalization. The major question that Schmitt bequeathed to us is therefore the question of how to conceive of a new unity in plurality, in a world that is now crossed by the formless and destabilizing dynamics of globalization.

Plurality, universality, identity

Schmitt's genealogy of modern politics, although heavily conditioned by a Christian conception of history,[55] has the undisputed merit of making explicit the aporiae and the underlying weaknesses of Western statehood and liberal democracy. His analysis helps us identify with greater clarity the problems raised by contemporary pluralism (in both its religious and its cultural forms) and the limitations of Habermas's post-secular project. It goes without saying that Schmitt's genealogy is useful only if we neutralize its dangerousness and recognize its anachronism, that is, only if we seek to find a different solution to the problems raised by his reflections. As will be disclosed, however, there is a specular polarity between Schmitt's deconstruction of modern political categories and Habermas's post-secular discourse. Faced with the crisis of political space and with the resurgence of religious and cultural pluralism, Habermas proposes a theoretical framework that is unable to overcome the dichotomous categories of modernity, as it is deeply rooted in their logic of inclusion–exclusion.

To begin with, Habermas's proposal to reorder religious and cultural pluralism within 'firmly entrenched'[56] states is highly problematic. If it is true that this new plurality has emerged as a consequence of the border-crossing dynamics of globalization (a point that Habermas acknowledges), it is unclear how 'nations' can still be considered 'firmly entrenched'. The plurality of which Habermas speaks is not only created by these dynamics but it is a *modality* of globalization (if by this term we denote a border-crossing phenomenon, which shapes itself through a continuous mobilization and hybridization of cultures and borders). Even when Habermas abandons the political framework of the nation state in favour of a 'constitutional patriotism', he takes pains to define, in concrete terms, the organization of contemporary pluralism. Essentially, whether from a state-centred or from a constitutional perspective, his aim is to transform the public sphere, through rationalizations and translations, into a liberal amalgam. He argues:

> Positions that do not wish to subject the political influence of religious voices to formal constrains blur the limits without which a secular state cannot maintain its impartiality. What must be safeguarded is that the decisions of the legislator, the executive branch, and the courts are not only *formulated* in a universally accessible language, but are also *justified* on the basis of universally acceptable reasons. This excludes religious reasons from decisions about all state-sanctioned – that is, legally binding – norms.[57]

Habermas accepts religious pluralism as a sociological fact, but politically he reduces religious diversity, through translations and reifications, to a flat, abstract and rationalized homogeneity. In his view, the threshold that determines access to power and political participation can be determined and modified only by secular reason. 'The contents of religious expressions' – he writes – 'must be translated into a universally accessible language before it can make it onto official agendas and flow into the deliberations of decision-making bodies.'[58] 'The result of such an operation' – Chantal Mouffe has aptly argued – 'is to reify the identity of the people by reducing it to one of its many possible forms of identification.'[59]

True, Habermas proposes to 'absorb' pluralism thorough the rule of law. However, this new constitutional framework serves as a means of obliterating differences or assimilating diversity. The argument is fallacious for at least two reasons. In the first place, it establishes, in a rather unsubtle fashion, the dominance of Western rationality over other cultures and belief systems (these are 'naturally forced' to follow a universalist, Western-centric model; a model which Habermas describes as an 'end of history', the ultimate and unchanging achievement of mankind). In this sense, Habermas's post-secular logic transforms Western rationality into an authoritarian and exclusivist variety of rationalism, that is, into a sort of abstract universalism.

This is an old problem of his political theory. Discussing Habermas's notion of rationality, Gerard Delanty has rightly argued that 'by conceiving of universal morality in terms of an evolutionary theory culminating in the discourse of Occidental rationalism, Habermas has failed to see how universal morality may be embodied in different forms in other cultures, both historically speaking as well as in contemporary society'.[60] Even when Habermas attempts to circumvent this problem by proposing a plural, intercultural and shared 'space of reasons', his argument cannot but fall, once again, into the same isomorphic fallacy.[61]

And this brings us back to Schmitt's analysis. As we have seen, for Schmitt, concrete plurality is only possible within homogeneous political forms. International politics is a pluriverse made up of a plurality of states. Universality is, therefore, an internally differentiated unity. But, in Schmitt's view, liberal universalism attempts to frame universality in name of a 'higher' concept of humanity. And therein lies the trouble. For the notion of humanity is paradoxical: it is a universal, abstract idea that can only be concretized by particular groups in specific historical contexts. In other words, enforcing universal principles results in discrimination in the name of humanity: we end up thinking otherness – religious, cultural, political – as something inferior, unjust, less universal and less rational. Schmitt clarifies his understanding of 'humanism' and 'humanity' in a dense passage, which is worth quoting in full:

> There is no human and no political life without the idea of humanity, but this idea constitutes nothing, certainly no distinguishable community. All peoples, all classes, all adherent to religions, Christians and Saracens, capitalist and proletarians, good and evil, just and unjust, delinquent and judge, are people, and with the help of such a universal concept every distinction may be negated and every community ruptured … it is a dangerous deception when one single group pursues its special interests in the name of the whole,

and unjustifiably identify itself with the state ... when, for the first time, a supreme and universal concept like humanity is used politically so as to identify a single people or a particular single organization with it, then the potential arises for a most awful expansion and a murderous imperialism. In this regard, the name of humanity is no less abused than the name of God, and it could be that a feeling spreads very widely among many peoples whose authentic expression is to be found in the variation of Proudhon's elegant dictum: 'Who speaks of humanity desires to deceive.'[62]

It goes without saying that Habermas's post-secular project has no intentionally imperialistic or discriminatory purposes. However, by theorizing a strong separation between the state and the public sphere (in which religious beliefs, once rationalized, could be free to move), Habermas, *nolens volens*, follows a liberal universalist and forced assimilationist logic. In order to preserve the formal possibility of communicative action, he ends up removing the substantive identity and the concrete plurality of the religions and cultures by which contemporary democracies are inevitably composed.[63] As we shall see, this argument is not only conceptually weak but also practically dangerous.

If it is true that Western states should now be considered systems 'pierced' by the dynamics of global mobilization, their forced closure might generate dynamics of conflict and rupture, of *exit* from political life instead of *voice* and communicative action.[64] If we tend to exclude formally religious and cultural differences from the public sphere (unless they have been 'rationalized'), and if we categorically deny to religious values the possibility of democratic access to decision-making, the institutional channels of voice could be abandoned in favour of supra-legal actions and obligations. In other words, if the *formal* equality established by the rule of law is perceived as a *substantive* discrimination towards one's own identity or faith, we could witness the failure of interreligious and intercultural dialogue and the emergence of non-democratic or even anti-democratic groups. In short, we could witness the breaking up of liberal democracies into multiple enclaves and subsystems dominated by higher forms of authorities and loyalties. This was one of Schmitt's greatest concerns: the possible return of the political in an exacerbated form.

The problem of a foundational lack that affects the liberal state has been reformulated by Ernst-Wolfgang Böckenförde in his 'theorem of incompleteness': 'to what extent' – he asks – 'can peoples united in a state live solely on the guarantee of individual freedom, without a "common bond" which precedes that very freedom?'[65] To respond to this challenge, Habermas argues that liberal democracies are based, essentially, on procedures and dialogic exchange; that this form of government should be seen as 'a method whereby legitimacy is generated by legality' and therefore 'there is no "deficit of validity" that would need to be filled by the ethical dimension'.[66] This means that for Habermas democratic systems are self-grounded and autotelic, and that unity is constituted and strengthened by a system of laws. Liberal democracies are in no need of ethical or pre-political bonds; on the contrary, it is the system of laws as such that allows citizens to participate in the constitution of the liberal public sphere.

Nonetheless, as we have seen, the type of political participation envisaged by Habermas still follows the logic of inclusion–exclusion and the opposition between 'us' (Western rationalism) and 'them' (religious and other cultural utterances). Furthermore, Habermas's conceptualization runs the risk of reducing the system of legality to mere rules of the democratic games, of transforming the search for a shared public reason into 'a pluralistic dissolution of the unity of the political whole'.[67] In this regard, Schmitt has polemically argued:

> [The 'ethics of fair play'] can found no ethic of state, since the individual social groups, in their role as contracting subjects, are then as such the prescriptive forces, who use the contract to cater to themselves, and are bound only by a contractual association. They stand in relation to each other as independent forces, and what unity there is only the result of terminable agreements (as all agreements and contracts are terminable) …
> In the foreground stands the obvious inadequacy of the proposition *pacta sunt servanda*, which, in concrete terms, can mean nothing more than the legitimation of the contingent status quo, just as in private life it is capable of taking the role of a splendid ethic of usury.[68]

What Schmitt fears is the implosion of political unity under the pressure of a plurality of private interests, which are unable (and unwilling) to establish 'public bonds'. The transcendence and unity of the state vis-à-vis the social body cannot be guaranteed by law (as claimed by Habermas), or by a *Grundnorm* (as claimed by Kelsen), but rather by the self-representation generated by the conflict between concrete pluralities, which can coexist side by side precisely because they wrap themselves within the representation of the state, the 'sovereign mirror' in which they see themselves reflected as a totality *in fieri*, in the process of becoming actual. In this sense, institutional access should not be closed in principle (as Habermas seems to suggest) to some parts of the social body. This would be tantamount to establishing an artificial and dangerous closure of history, a domination of one (secular) part over all others. 'For what remains of the state as a political unity when all other contents – the religious, the economic, the cultural, and so forth – are removed? Were the political merely the result of such a subtraction, it would in fact amount to absolutely nothing.'[69]

Once again, Habermas ends up thinking of political unity as something based on an abstract and universalistic pivot, which is historically determined: Western rationality and its abstract corollaries – that is, the 'liberal subject'. Democracy is thus transformed into a cultural notion. Its public sphere is no longer conceived of as a contingent but ordering process – a real openness to plurality – but rather as a Western identitarian framework. This understanding of democracy is, to quote Schmitt, 'quintessential universalism and monism, and completely different from a pluralistic theory'.[70]

In short, even when he seems to distance himself from the ideals of the rigid Enlightenment, as he describes it, Habermas ends up reproducing their logic of exclusion–inclusion and of marginalization of religious minorities. The final outcome of this reasoning is a *fictio juris* based, once again, on the abstract and aporetic concept of multicultural humanity. This way of thinking not only is linked to, but also covertly replicates, the dark side of modernity. Indeed, if Schmitt entrusted the formation of political communities to a logic of inclusive exclusion, namely to the friend–enemy dialectic, Habermas, in a similar vein though going the opposite way, reproduces that very gesture by conceiving of democratic systems as formally open but substantively emptied of concrete differences.

But there is more. As we have seen, the relation between modern politics and theology is chiastic: it is structured as a presence in absence, as an endless search for a new, transcendent signifier. Indeed, in the attempt to replace the sacred, the ideals of the Enlightenment, which Habermas in part follows, have slavishly imitated the exclusivity and universality that characterized the theological–political domain. The result of this reoccupation is a theoretical reversal that does not exceed the mechanism of inclusion–exclusion but, on the contrary, conceals and incorporates it as founding ground. Only in this way is it possible to understand how Western rationalism has been transformed into a new secular religion and how religious monotheism translated into the monotheism of reason. Karl Jaspers offers a succinct but powerful summary of the contradictory relation between modernity and theology:

> In the great process of secularization – that is, the movement to retain Biblical values while casting off their religious form – even the fanaticism of unbelief shows the influence of its Biblical origin. The secularized philosophical positions within the Western civilizations have frequently revealed this trait of absolutism, this persecution of other beliefs, this aggressive profession of faith, this inquisitorial attitude towards other faiths, always in consequence of absolute claims to a truth which each one believes he possesses. In view of all this, philosophical faith must reluctantly recognize that where discussion is broken off and reason countenanced only under certain conditions, the best intentions of maintaining open communication are doomed to failure.[71]

Towards a new unity in plurality

Drawing on the previous discussion, in this final section I briefly examine four challenges mounted by pluralism: (1) the problem of how to think the state no longer as a closed, entrenched system but rather as a space inevitably crossed by transnational actors and activities; (2) the problem of how to rethink the public sphere as an arena open to dialogue and communication between concrete pluralities (and not as a space 'policed' by mono-cultural universalism); (3) the problem of how to rethink the common good in relation to political legitimacy and loyalty; (4) finally, the problem of how to identify the plural subject entitled to decide the political destiny of a political community. This task implies nothing less than 'to consider democracy as something essential but not universal, a polity to which no one should be forced, but of which everyone must be respectful as long as they share its space'.[72] It goes without saying that it would be impossible to treat these matters satisfactorily in the limited space of this work. My aim is therefore to present some lines of reflection on the political challenges raised by religious and cultural pluralism.

It is obvious that, as regards the first two points, the state can no longer be conceived of as an all-encompassing leviathan. Technological forces and the mobile complexity of globalization constantly cross its borders. Democratic public spheres can no longer accommodate pluralities (of values, beliefs, cultures) as abstractions. The public sphere should now be rethought as a form of enlarged communication, which can become truly reflexive only if it is open to concrete entities. Communication, in other words, can no longer be understood merely as a rational translation and reification of our Western identity. Instead, it should be conceived as an expression of multiple forms of life and historical traditions that jointly contribute to real democratic education and deliberation. Today the mutual learning process of which Habermas speaks cannot be founded on rational and abstract premises. It should rather be open to and based on the concrete plurality of experiences and historical paths that combine together within the democratic space. This conception of democratic development was dear to Karl Jaspers, according to whom mankind's journey is always determined by encounters between historical and opposing realities:

> Everything real in man is historical. But historicity means also multiple historicities. Hence the postulates of true communication are: 1) to become concerned with the historically different without becoming untrue to one's own historicity; 2) to reveal the relativity of scientific truth, while fully recognizing its just claims; 3) to abandon the claim of faith to exclusivity because of the breach of communication it implies, yet without losing the absoluteness of one's own fundament; 4) to take up the inevitable struggle with the historically different, but to sublimate the battle in the loving battle, in communication *through the truth that develops when men act in common, not as abstract individuals*: 5) to orient ourselves toward the depths that are disclosed only in the division into manifold historicities, to one of which I belong, but which all concern me and which all together guide me to that source.[73]

True, embracing this form of open communication would inevitably lead to conflict between social groups. It is necessary, however, to see conflict as a creative moment of democracy, and not merely as a crisis of its communicative space. One should transform the democratic public sphere into a space 'of contestation forever open, instead of trying to fill it through the establishment of a supposedly "rational" consensus'.[74] For conflict does not necessarily translate into violence. On the contrary, conflict represents a vital dynamic of any political systems, as it highlights the limitations and moments of constructive crisis of the democratic process.[75]

In order for participation in the democratic game to be possible, then, the only prohibition imposed from above, the lowest common denominator, so to speak, would be renunciation of the use of violence. By following this path, the democratic process would no longer be based on a single and stable identity or on a culturally embedded idea of humanity. Rather it would be nurtured by an ever-changing and open-ended plurality – a movement within which the various projects of life can flourish 'through multiple and competing forms of *identifications*'.[76]

If such a plurality is to work as a unitary multitude, it should strive towards an ideal of the commons. But this ideal, contrary to what Schmitt suggested, cannot and should not be historically predetermined. As Aristotle argues in the *Politics*, 'Every state is a community of some kind, and every community is established with a view to some good; for everyone always acts in order to obtain that which they think good'.[77] In this sense, then, not only is it that the idea of the common good is necessary but, in order to be truly inclusive, 'the elements out of which a unity is to be formed' must 'differ in kind'.[78] Even the ideal of the commons, then, is the result of the plural and creative encounter between different – even opposing – social tensions. Aristotle also reminds us that communication involves a plurality of languages. Along with the language of logic (which he classifies as 'demonstrative' or 'apophantic'), there are the languages of the passions, of poetry and of rhetoric, of philosophy and of religion. For 'a prayer is a sentence', even if it 'is neither true nor false'.[79] It expresses one of the infinite possibilities of being in the world. Aristotle suggests, in short, that the common good cannot be created out of nothing – out of immanence *qua* immanence – or achieved by adding up arithmetically different opinions; it is instead constantly formed through the multifaceted participation and critique of its ideal and meaning. As Chantal Mouffe has argued from a similar perspective, 'Without a plurality of competing forces which attempt to define a common good, and aim at fixing the identity of the community, the political articulation of the demos could not take place'.[80]

In this vision of a democracy that is ontologically plural, a movement in search of a novel and broader foundation and not a foundation that obstructs

140   *Genealogies of Political Modernity*

the movement, religions and cultures have a fundamental role to play. They should not be seen as mere bearers of exclusivist and potentially violent values. Taken in their plurality of forms, these ethical systems of belief represent what has been called a *philosophia perennis*: a perennial philosophy at the heart of which lies an 'ethic that places man's final end in the knowledge of the immanent and transcendent Ground of all being'.[81] Religious beliefs and utterances are fundamental to fostering a new and plural notion of the commons, thereby overcoming the logic of inclusion–exclusion and balancing the mechanisms of subjectivation generated by Western rationalism. Revitalizing the dialectical tension between the sacred and the secular is crucial if we want to give breath to democratic life and rule of law.[82] Against the sacralization of the law and the advent of the one-dimensional-right, which is self-founded and unable to create a stable political unity, it is necessary to recover the dualistic tensions between law and conscience, norms and ethics, pluralistic ethos and democratic *nomos*. Accordingly, the space between the sacred and the political remains open – and rightly so in an age where the universal human need to come to terms with the meaningless infinity of the world has not yet been filled by instrumental rationality.

Conclusion

Under a new name, the post-secular discourse conceals an old problematic: the game of mirrors between the sacred and the political. Following the border-crossing dynamics triggered by globalization, the relation between these two spheres has taken the form of a difficult coexistence between religious and cultural pluralism and Western secular universalism. In a certain sense, Habermas's post-secular project can be seen as an unconvincing response to the question of 'how much' and 'what' religious pluralism (given the re-emergence of religious forces in Western public spheres) should be allowed in our democratic systems. Faced with this challenge, which is historically new because generated by novel historical forces and dynamics, it is essential to attempt to identify new political categories instead of relying on the exclusivist logic of those forged in the modern age. From this perspective, we need to abandon the idea of a homogenizing universalism in favour of a political vision that could open our public spheres to concrete diversity and to the various historicities that inhabit them.

Schmitt remarked that 'in a spiritual world ruled by the law of pluralism, a piece of concrete order is more valuable than many empty generalizations of a false totality. For it is an actual order, not a constructed and imaginary abstraction, a total situation of normal life, in which concrete people and social groups can have a concrete existence'.[83] This insight is still relevant today. Nonetheless, it is no longer possible to follow the identitarian and nationalistic logic advocated by Schmitt. It is dangerous to try to solve twenty-first-century problems using the conceptual tools and categories developed in the nineteenth. To pursue a new vision of unity in plurality – one not based on an empty and formal equality that conceals too many substantive differences – we need to rethink the democratic space, already smashed by the dynamics of globalization, and our forms of communication and dialogue vis-à-vis the challenge of otherness. This implies rethinking the very concept of openness. Democratic communication, in fact, can no longer be seen as the pursuit of a rational consensus, or as the reification of diversity through the language and limits imposed by Western rationalism. Open communication implies a continuous reflection on otherness and on identity, a constant dialogue that shows the way to the commons through the infinity of its dialectical movement. To find an alternative between 'tribalism' and 'universalism', the most sensitive if tortuous way seems to be a novel democratic openness. All things considered, it is worth remembering that 'boundless openness to communication is not the consequence of any knowledge, it is the decision to follow a human road'.[84]

Part Three

History and Archaeology

6

The Myth of Origin: Archaeology and History in the Work of Giorgio Agamben and René Girard

Nothing at first can appear more difficult to believe than that the more complex organs and instincts should have been perfected, not by means superior to, though analogous with, human reason, but by the accumulation of innumerable slight variations, each good for the individual possessor.

Charles Darwin, *On the Origins of Species*

The theory of the ambivalence of the sacred has been famously formulated by Émile Durkheim. In *The Elementary Forms of Religious Life* (1912), he writes: 'All known religious beliefs display a common feature: they presuppose a classification of the real or ideal things that men conceive of into two classes – two opposite genera – that are widely designated by two distinct terms, which the words *profane* and *sacred* translate fairly well. The division of the world into two domains, one containing all that is sacred and the other all that is profane – such is the distinctive trait of religious thought.'[1] In Durkheim's view, these domains are 'two forms of life that are mutually exclusive' and yet endowed with the mysterious property of transmuting into one another, because 'sacredness is highly contagious, and it spreads from the totemic being to everything that directly or remotely has to do with it.'[2] The ambiguity that characterizes the sacred, therefore, would be the result of its all-pervasive tendency to penetrate into the profane world, 'invading all that passes within [its] reach.'[3]

For the French sociologist, the solution to the riddle of the ambivalence of the sacred lies in the religious mentality of primitive humans. Since there are no *ontologically* sacred things, sacredness has to be attached, superadded to objects. The sacred world would then be constituted by the primitive imagination, which, by enchanting the profane sphere, gains the impression 'of reassurance and dependence that are created in consciousness through the workings of society'.[4] Thus, if objects 'take on religious significance that is not intrinsic to them but is conferred on them from outside', this is because 'contagion is not a kind of secondary process by which sacredness propagates, once acquired, but is instead the very process by which sacredness is acquired'.[5] In other words Durkheim regards the human tendency to sacralize the world as a specific property of religious forces, which are nothing but 'transfigured collective forces, that is, moral forces ... made of ideas and feelings that the spectacle of society awakens in us'.[6] Under this aspect, the religious imagination would tend to enchant the profane sphere in order to strengthen the social cosmos. Sacred contagion is the means by which social life makes the secular world meaningful, transforming it into a network of sacred correspondences.

As is well known, this particular view of religion has been criticized, among others, by Claude Lévi-Strauss. According to the French anthropologist, the aporia lies in Durkheim's paradoxical belief in the 'primacy of the social over the intellect'. As he puts it, 'It is when Durkheim claims to derive categories and abstract ideas from the social order that, in trying to explain this order, he finds at his disposal no more than sentiments, effective values, or vague ideas such as contagion or contamination'.[7] For, if it is true that the 'social' has shaped humans' intellectual capacity, how and where did society first emerge? On what conceptual schemata and categories was it established? In effect, for Lévi-Strauss, modes of thought and intellectual categories are precisely what is used 'by the social order in its formation'.[8] In consequence, Lévi-Strauss traces the sacred–profane dichotomy back to those binary oppositions (night and day, right and left, nature and culture etc.) that characterize the human cognitive apparatus.[9] The dialectic of the sacred and the profane would be just a by-product of differential thought, which finds its ontological anchoring in the rift between two sides of the same reality, the continuous and the discontinuous: 'The passage from nature to culture [is based] on the emergence of a logic operating by means of binary oppositions and coinciding with the first manifestations of symbolism'.[10]

In 1949, a few years before the publication of Lévi-Strauss's *Totemism*, Mircea Eliade had addressed the same riddle of the sacred in his *Traité d'histoire des religions.* But, instead of inscribing its ambiguity in the social sphere, like Durkheim, or in the human mind, as Lévi-Strauss would do, he preferred to explore the morphology and structure of the religious experience through the analysis of what he called 'the modalities of the sacred'. Since 'every manifestation of the sacred takes place in some historical situation', Eliade argues, sacredness should be considered a liminal event open on two worlds: 'Because it is a hierophany, it reveals some modality of the sacred; because it is an historical incident, it reveals some attitude man has had toward the sacred'.[11] For Eliade, therefore, the origin of the divide between the sacred and the profane would lie in the contradictory tension produced by hierophanic manifestations, in their capability of revealing the infinite in the finite, sacredness in history: 'The dialectic of hierophany implies a more-or-less clear choice, a singling out. A thing becomes sacred insofar as it embodies (that is, reveals) something other than itself'.[12]

According to Eliade, this dialectic possesses a paradoxical character: it reveals the universal by historicizing it; it actualizes the sacred by profaning it: 'The thing that becomes sacred is still separated in regard to itself, for it only becomes a hierophany at the moment of stopping to be a mere profane something, at the moment of acquiring a new "dimension" of sacredness … The fact that a hierophany is always an historical event … does not lessen its universal quality'.[13] The ambivalence of the sacred would lie, then, in this tension between, or at the intersection of, human and world, religion and history, immanence and transcendence: sacredness is the short-circuit in which this dual experience takes shape.

The three images of the sacred just examined – Durkheim's, Lévi-Strauss's and Eliade's – constitute as many distinct scientific paradigms, which lead, in turn, to different methodological, epistemological and ontological visions. Durkheim's pan-sociologism rests on an ontology that essentially treats the human being as *homo sociologicus*, whereas Lévi-Strauss and Eliade anchor their discourses respectively on *homo gnoseologicus* and *homo religiosus*. For Durkheim, it is the social that lays the groundwork for a 'science of man'. For Lévi-Strauss, on the contrary, the cognitive apparatus establishes the foundation; whereas for Eliade, this is the work of religious consciousness (with its internal structure), which provides us with an Archimedean point.

Once ontologically anchored, these discourses can flow only into particular epistemological and methodological positions. It is not by chance that linear and chronological time forms the background of Durkheim's search for a (social) 'beginning'. In effect, his ontological vision pushed him to trace the origin of religious phenomena back to the simplest of the original social forms (which he thought he had discovered in the Aboriginal Australians of Aranda). For Lévi-Strauss, by contrast, it is the human cognitive apparatus that plays an ontological function: if dichotomous thinking is an original phenomenon, this would explain its constant re-elaboration, from *la pensée sauvage* to Aristotle, from Hegel to Bergson. Accordingly, Lévi-Strauss's structural anthropology is the epistemological precipitate of such an ontological conception.[14] Finally, in Eliade's view, the sacred is a manifestation of universal history and of the transhistorical consciousness of humankind, and this implies that a hierophany, as universal and constant, transcends time and roots itself in 'spaces' (which in this way become 'places'). It is for this reason that Eliade's comparative history offers a synchronic survey of the various modalities of the sacred.

However, despite the differences just noted, Durkheim, Lévi-Strauss and Eliade share the same cognitive gesture: they all seek a myth of origin to moor their investigations to. In order to develop their analysis, these scholars need to posit a foundation's foundation, something that grounds the ground, so to speak – be it the 'social', the 'cognitive' or the 'religious'. But to search for an origin in time or space also means to postulate an *essence* of things, to tie them to an ontological plane that is always historically determined. As Michael Foucault has argued:

> This search assumes the existence of immobile forms that precede the external world of accident and succession. This search is directed to 'that which was already there', the 'very same' of an image of a primordial truth fully adequate to its nature, and it necessitates the removal of every mask to ultimately disclose an original identity.[15]

It is precisely against the tendency to essentialize history that René Girard and Giorgio Agamben have developed their methods. As we shall see, their 'archaeologies of the sacred' attempt to evade the problem of ontological anchoring through a demystification of origins. In what follows, I aim to show that Girard and Agamben offer two similar and alternative ways of

The Myth of Origin 149

doing philosophy: they seek to explain human symbolic nature without predetermining its essence. Although different in style and philosophical breadth, the two thinkers are in tacit agreement on the nature of the sacred and on how to analyse the traces that it has left on the Western political order. Like two parallels that can never meet, Girard's and Agamben's narratives are the positive and the negative of a philosophical film that seeks to capture the infinity of the historical process in its foundational, paradigmatic moments.

The quest for origin, or towards an archaeology of the sacred

Drawing on Foucault's epistemology, Agamben defines the purpose and practice of philosophical archaeology as follows, in his book *Signatura rerum* (2008):

> We may call 'archaeology' that practice which in any historical investigation has to do not with origins but with the moment of a phenomenon's arising and must therefore engage anew the sources and tradition. It cannot confront tradition without deconstructing the paradigms, techniques, and practices through which tradition regulates the forms of transmission, conditions access to sources, and in the final analysis determines the very status of the knowing subject. The moment of arising is objective and subjective at the same time and is indeed situated on a threshold of undecidability between object and subject. It is never the emergence of the fact without at the same time being the emergence of the knowing subject itself: the operation on the origin is at the same time an operation on the subject.[16]

According to Agamben, therefore, philosophical archaeology also looks for an origin, an *archē*. But this original moment is not conceived of as an absolute event, but rather as a threshold – a geological *plan de clivage*, or an *Entstehung* (origination). From this perspective, history should not be frozen into a beginning because 'origin', as we shall see, is not merely a point in a chronology or an event that happened *illo tempore* but, above all, 'a field of bipolar historical currents stretched between anthropogenesis and history, between the moment of arising and becoming, between an archi-past and the present'.[17] The archaeological gaze does not seek the essence or origin of historical phenomena, hypostatizing them into a subject (an *ego cogitans*) or into an object (the historical 'fact'). Rather it tries, through analytical regression, 'to go back to the point where the dichotomy between conscious and unconscious, historiography and history (and, more generally, between all the binary oppositions defining the logic of our culture), was produced'.[18]

In this way it might be possible to avoid the question of origin *qua* Origin, which is in fact historically unknowable. For, in historical research, it is not unusual to project on the 'primordial chaos' or 'beginning' the historical attributes of the singularities produced by a conceptual scission. For example, following this logic, it is usually argued that there was an 'age without law', which is then defined precisely through the absence of the historical features that characterize positive and secular law. In a similar vein, it is argued that our pre-human ancestors were not *homines sapientes* and had not yet developed their potential intelligence and brain volume. This methodological gesture casts the shadow of the present upon the past, thus anchoring the origin to an immutable ontology of the human and of the knowing subject. In this regard, Girard has argued, of evolutionary theorists, that 'as soon as they start discussing human culture, they seem to assume that the modern individual is the prototype of the primitive human being that produces and transmits culture'.[19] In this manner, chance and contingency are removed from the historical stage.

In political theory, the methodological lacuna involved here was already highlighted by Carl Schmitt, who lamented the (ab)use and arbitrary repositioning of concepts outside of their 'central domains' (*Zentralgebiete*):

> All essential concepts are not normative but existential. If the center of intellectual life has shifted in the last four centuries, so have all concepts and words. It is thus necessary to bear in mind the ambiguity of every concept and word. The greatest and most egregious misunderstandings (from which, of course, many impostors make their living) can be explained by the erroneous transfer of a concept at home in one domain (e.g., only in the metaphysical, the moral, or the economic) to other domains of intellectual life.[20]

The attempt to trace the origin of historical phenomena leads to the following fallacy: the 'after' becomes the conceptual archetype of the 'before', the distinctive sign of a 'beginning'. The typical gesture that results from this logic is to superimpose one's own epistemological–conceptual

The Myth of Origin

plane upon the past, so that the origin cannot but coincide with the end, with what it has already *become*.

Wittgenstein's critique of Newtonian mechanics in the *Tractatus* can be read in this way, too. In order to analyse phenomena, classical physicists superimpose a conceptual framework or network upon an image of the 'world' – which is, in turn, theoretically construed. The result of such an operation, Wittgenstein argues, cannot but be arbitrary, 'because I could have applied with equal success a net' made of different meshes. In effect, 'to the different networks correspond different systems of describing the world. Mechanics determine a form of description by saying: All propositions in the description of the world must be obtained in a given way from a number of given propositions – the mechanical axioms'.[21] In this way, we do not learn much about the 'world' (and its origin), but we learn a lot about the logical structures we use to describe it.

Girard's Mimetic Theory, too, is driven by the search for an 'original' phenomenon. But this *archē*, just as in Agamben's archaeological conception, is not construed as a single, historically determined event. Rather, as Girard puts it, 'in the process of the emergence of cultural elements, one ... needs to stress that there is no absolute beginning. The process is extremely complex and progressive'.[22] In his view, the 'beginning' is a sort of contingent threshold that divides the human from the animal world and at the same time preserves the continuity between these domains: 'it should be possible ... to think through the process of hominization in a truly radical way, that is, by beginning with animal nature itself and by making no use of anything that has been falsely claimed to be specifically human'.[23] In the Girardian conception, the passage from nature to culture – from animal 'natural' violence to human 'symbolic' violence – is gradual and proceeds through accumulation of 'sense'. Indeed, it was the power of mimesis that eventually broke the chains of the animal kingdom, thus superimposing the book of history on the tabula rasa of nature:

> The intensification of mimetic rivalry, which is already very much in evidence at the level of primates, destroyed the dominance patterns and gave rise to progressively more elaborate and humanized forms of culture through the intermediary of the surrogate victim. At the point when mimetic conflict becomes sufficiently intense to prohibit the direct solutions that give rise to the forms of animal sociality, the first 'crisis' or series of crises would then occur as the mechanism that produces the differentiated, symbolic,

152 *Genealogies of Political Modernity*

and human forms of culture ... it must have been the increasing power of imitation that initiated the process of hominization. ... *Beyond a certain threshold of mimetic power, animal societies become impossible. This threshold corresponds to the appearance of the victimage mechanism and would thus be the threshold of hominization.*[24]

Origin is a *point of no return* that coincides with the founding sacrifice, with the act of killing understood as an ordering ritual. In Girard's view, (violent) death is man's first Goddess and inspiring Muse. Indeed, it is by sacrifice and thanks to sacrifice that the animal–human is transformed into a victim, that is, into a transcendental *signifier*. The killing of a human *qua* Human exposes the problem of guilt, it instils a surplus of self-consciousness in the human being: How can the death of our 'double' create peace and order? This means that the murder of the 'other' – which was fortuitous but wanted, unnecessary but wished for – generated the dialectic between identity (us) and difference (the scapegoat), totality (the mob) and particularity (the victim), inclusion and exclusion:

The only thing 'lacking' in animal rites is the sacrificial immolation, and the only thing an animal needs to become human is the surrogate victim. ... Because of the victim, in so far as it seems to emerge from it, for the first time there can be something like an inside and an outside, a before and an after, a community and the sacred ... the victim appears to be simultaneously good and evil, peaceable and violent, a life that brings death and a death that guarantees life. Every possible significant element seems to have its outline in the sacred and at the same time to be transcended by it. In this sense the victim does seem to constitute a *universal signifier*.[25]

Expiatory sacrifice is a *porta inferi* that allows the transition from nature to history, from *animalitas* to *humanitas*. Murder represents the passage, in Heideggerian terms, from captivation to the opening up of the world. Sacrifice is therefore a founding and revealing act, which breaks the 'existential dizziness' of the animal–human. The bloody corpse is a sort of ur-symbol, the 'means of creating a new degree of attention, the first non-instinctual attention'.[26] No wonder, then, that the idea of the ambiguity of the sacred finds in Girard's work a radically new theoretical status and solution. The ambiguity that characterizes this domain is in fact traced back to the twofold nature of the

The Myth of Origin 153

sacred, to its being both a *pharmakon*-poison and a *pharmakon*-remedy, the cause (problem) and the effect (resolution) of an original crisis:

> The word 'sacrifice' – sacri-fice – means making sacred, producing the sacred. What sacrifices the victims is the blow delivered by the sacrificer, the violence that kills the victim, *annihilating it and placing it above everything else* by making it in some sense immortal. Sacrifice takes place when sacred violence takes charge of the victim; *it is the death that produces life, just as life produces death*, in the uninterrupted circle of eternal recurrence common to all great theological views that are grafted on sacrificial practices.[27]

In Girard's view, then, 'the beginning' is an event or, better, a series of events that emerge from historical contingency – sheer violence – and that ends up shaping the *bios* of humans. Random natural events (understood as mimetic crises) create symbolic forms of culture by which humans root themselves in Meaning, that is, in history. In other words, killing is seen by Girard as the power of absolute immanence to generate the transcendent cosmos of the new symbolic species *Homo sapiens*. Chance gave rise to historical necessity because, once set in motion, human's sacrificial power cannot be stopped but only diverted, channelled into surreptitious forms: 'humanity results from sacrifice ... original sin is vengeance, never-ending vengeance.'[28] In sum, according to Girard's scientific theodicy, it is the randomness of violent mimesis that – imponderable like an axe stroke from the unknown – opened the world to humans, consigning them to their intimate, sacrificial destiny.

The structure of Agamben's genealogy of the sacred is in many ways very similar to that of Girard. In his research on the mysterious ambiguity of the category of *sacertas* – research that began with his first major work on the subject, *Homo Sacer* (1995) – Agamben had in fact questioned the specificity of this archaic figure and of ritual sacrifices: 'If *homo sacer* was truly the victim of a death sentence or an archaic sacrifice, why is it not *fas* [licit] to put him to death in the prescribed forms of execution? What, then, is the life of *homo sacer*, if it is situated at the intersection of a capacity to be killed and yet not sacrificed, outside both human and divine law?'[29] In other words, why does this figure literally embody a zone of indistinction – a sort of movable threshold – between life and death, between inclusive exclusion and exclusionary inclusion? Unlike Girard – who sees the ambiguity of *sacertas* as a kind of universal mechanism that remains fluid, open, and, in a sense, beyond good and evil (as it generates both the human and the divine) – Agamben believes that behind this figure of the exception hides a fundamental yet overlooked paradigm of Western politics. This arcanum would be located at the heart of Western philosophical reflection and, if deconstructed, it 'may allow us to uncover an originary political structure that is located in a zone prior to the distinction between sacred and profane, religious and juridical'.[30] Indeed, for Agamben, Western politics and its ontological constructions are based on the logic of the exception and on its mechanisms of exclusionary inclusion:

> It may be that only if we are able to decipher the political meaning of pure Being will we be able to master the bare life that expresses our subjection to political power, just as it may be, inversely, that only if we understand the theoretical implications of bare life will we be able to solve the enigma of ontology.[31]

To decipher this ontological enigma, Agamben has explored in his theoretical genealogies and archaeologies how the various dimensions and modes of being can all be traced back to a hypostatic logic. In his archaeology of the oath, for example, he has shown that, if we analyse carefully this 'most ancient thing', we discover that we 'have to do with a sphere of language that stands before law and religion and that the oath represents precisely the threshold by means of which language enters into law and *religio*'.[32] In other words, there is a pre-religious and pre-categorical 'limit', against which we collide every time we seek to trace the origin of the oath and which leads us from the political to the juridical and from the juridical to the religious, down to a sort of 'indistinct primordial chaos'. According to Agamben, behind this 'veil of indistinction' lies the secret of Western ontology.

The conclusions drawn by the Italian philosopher regarding the relation between language and the function of the oath are somehow different from those of Girard's Mimetic Theory. As we have seen, for Girard, language presupposes sacrifice as its original matrix. Murder is the *archi-trace* that opens the human to the possibility of language. The 'sacrificial scream' is the ur-word that, once uttered, gives life (i.e. meaning) to voice through repetition and reinforcement: 'In order to have symbolical power you must have an origin of it, and to me that is the scapegoat mechanism. ... It is the first moment in which something *stands* for *something else*. It is the ur-symbol.[33] In other words, the 'origin' of human language would not lie in its communicative function but rather in an act of desperation.

For Agamben, too, language presupposes an anthropogenetic moment. Yet this event would not be determined by the sacred – understood as an original sacrifice – but by human exposure to an *ethical challenge*. As Agamben sees it, the essence of language does not lie in the relation between meaning and referent, symbol and thought. Although important, this cognitive aspect of language rests on a more original opening – one through which humans are called into question, exposed to their own being, and forced to *invent themselves ethically*:

> The specificity of human language with respect to animal language cannot reside solely in the peculiarity of the instrument, which later analyses could find – and, in fact, continually do find – in this or that animal language. It consists, rather, no less decisively in the fact that, uniquely among living things, man is not limited to acquiring language as one capacity among others that he is given but has made of it his specific potentiality; *he has, that is to say put his very nature at stake in language*. ... the oath express the demand, decisive in every sense for the speaking animal, to put its nature at stake in language and to bind together in an ethical and political connection words, things, and actions. Only by this means was it possible for something like a history, distinct from nature and, nevertheless, inseparably intertwined with it, to be produced.[34]

The structure of the oath reveals an original, ontological 'gesture'. Language does not merely bind together individual and society, private and public, in a communicative horizon; rather it establishes a *subjectum* on which to place the order of things and by which the living beings are constantly called to language. Human language is the mark of an ethical call: to become speaking beings, humans must make room for the *logos*. They must open themselves *on* themselves, so to speak, thus continually binding things and words together, to avoid their dissolution. Language, for Agamben, is the original short-circuit that allowed the creation of a *generative* and *reflexive* relationship between humans and their world:

> The decisive element that confers on human language its peculiar virtue is not in the tool itself but in the place it leaves to the speaker, in the fact

that it prepares within itself a hollowed-out form that the speaker must always assume in order to speak – that is to say, in the ethical relation that is established between the speaker and his language. *The human being is that living being that, in order to speak, must say 'I', must 'take the word', assume it and make it his own.*[35]

This means that human language should not be considered a mere communicative instrument. Rather it represents a sort of anthropogenetic dispositive. Language is a natural artifice that permits the advent of the 'discourse on man'; it allows us to order, fragment and reconstruct this epical narration with the power of *logos*; it shows that the dominion of *homo faber* over nature and its resources presupposes a *homo loquens* and her capacity for naming. Indeed, only human language is capable of establishing inclusive divisions, exceptions and rules, thus overwriting the book of history on the blank canvas of nature. As Agamben puts it:

It is possible … that the mechanism of the exception is constitutionally connected to the event of language that coincides with anthropogenesis … in happening, language excludes and separates from itself the non-linguistic, and in the same gesture, it includes and captures it as that with which it is always already in relation. That is to say, the *ex-ceptio*, the inclusive exclusion of the real from the *logos* and in the *logos* is the originary structure of the event of language.[36]

Agamben's genealogical work, although developed following trajectories, categories and figures similar to Girard's, reaches quite different conclusions. Yet despite the apparent differences there is a strong complementarity between the works of these authors. In fact, both Girard's and Agamben's narratives rest on, and seek to trace out, a generative event – a sort of anthropogenetic Big Bang that gave life to the cultural–historical process (for Girard, this zero point coincided with the founding murder, while for Agamben it occurred with the event of language). Both thinkers assume that this primordial 'cognitive explosion' has left its marks on human culture, its language and above all its political symbolism. But what distinguishes these theoretical archaeologies from previous studies on the origins of human knowledge and cognition is their 'semiotic method': without presupposing it, Girard and Agamben believe they have traced the original, anthropogenetic event by encountering its signs

The Myth of Origin

in the remains and deposits that it left in history: from expiatory rituals to human sacrifices, from enthronement ceremonies to sovereign power, from political acclamation to the logic of the exception. In other words, according to Girard and Agamben, the event of anthropogenesis is a biohistorical threshold that must be reconstructed backwards, starting from the signs–referents that it imprinted on the political, linguistic and cognitive functions of the human being, and that represent the traces of a lost unity. As Agamben points out:

> The anthropogenetic event coincides with the fracture between life and language, between the living being and the speaking being; but, precisely for this reason, the becoming human of the human being entails the unceasing experience of this division and, at the same time, of the just as unceasingly new historical rearticulation of what has been thus divided. The mystery of the human being is not the metaphysical one of the conjunction between the living being and language (or reason, or the soul) but the practical and political one of their separation.[37]

This analysis leaves some thorny questions unanswered. For example, is it possible to refer to something (say, to origin) without presupposing its existence? And, if so, how is it then possible to encounter – I mean, to find without seeking – the signs of the originary event? Moreover, if, as we have seen, the 'real' origin of phenomena is somehow inaccessible, what is the logical status of the archaeology of the sacred? How should one methodologically approach the genealogy of origins and that of exceptions? To answer these crucial questions, it is necessary to explore Girard's and Agamben's ontological assumptions: one needs to discuss the logical structure of their archaeological methods and the epistemological problems and different historical visions that emanate from their work.

Marks of the sacred: History and politics

As we have seen, Girard's and Agamben's work offers a genetic–genealogical analysis of the domain of the sacred and of the ambiguity that characterizes it. Unlike other scholars, for these thinkers the notion of 'origin' cannot and should not be thought of as that of a fixed point, fundamental ontology, *Satz vom Grund*, or *principium rationis*. Rather, for them, 'origin' refers to the generative event of ontology. The ambivalence and duality that characterize Western civilization would in fact arise from an originary scission. This primordial event, however, just like a cultural Big Bang, is not frozen in time; on the contrary, it continues to produce its effects on the present:

> The 'oldest history' ... that archaeology seeks to reach cannot be localized within chronology, in a remote past, nor can it be localized beyond this within a meta-historical atemporal structure ... it represents a present and operative tendency within historical languages, which conditions and makes intelligible their development in time. It is an *archē,* but, as for Foucault and Nietzsche, it is an *archē* that is not pushed diachronically into the past, but assures the synchronic comprehensibility and coherence of the system.[38]

It is precisely because the origin is, paradoxically, still present that one can investigate its mutations, historical influences and distortions. Although he has never explicitly defined his epistemological apparatus, Girard, too, like Agamben, believes that the originary event is still 'operative' because, having generated human symbolism, it is partially preserved in cultural memory and social constructions. Indeed, for Girard, mythical narratives and archaic rituals would hide and reproduce the same structure of the mimetic mechanism. In effect, he considers these 'marks of the sacred' to be real 'symbolic fossils'. Importantly, in his view political and religious institutions would also retain and preserve the memory of their sacrificial foundation:

> How do we conceive the ritual origin of political power? The origin of such a power was by means of 'sacred monarchy', which we should also view as a modification, minute in the beginning, of ritual sacrifice. ... How can one define ... the paradox of organizations or institutions that are very real but rooted in a transcendence that is unreal and yet effective? ... The ... emperors draw their authority from the sacrificial power that emanates from the deity whose name they bear, the first Caesar, who was assassinated by numerous murders. So like every sacred monarchy, the empire is based upon a collective victim who is divinized. There is something about this so striking, so impressive, that it is impossible to see it as a pure and simple coincidence.[39]

The origin of political power is like a wound under the skin that never heals completely and that, by constantly resurfacing, leaves new signs. Political institutions are marked by the sacred even when, over time, they secularize its substance. This is the logic of the originary dispositive: despite changes in political forms and religious substance, the sacred preserves its expiatory and sacrificial function. Indeed, for Girard, the variegated and multiform appearances that characterize historical becoming are a by-product of the sacrificial mechanism. And likewise, in his genealogy of economy and government, Agamben has argued that the same ancient theological dispositive can evolve morphologically, without substantially changing its operative tendency and power:

> As a matter of fact, the modern state inherits both aspects of the theological machine of the government of the world, and it presents itself as both providence-state and destiny-state. Through the distinction between legislative or sovereign power and executive or governmental power, the modern State acquires the double structure of the governmental machine. … The providential-economical paradigm is, in this sense, the paradigm of democratic power, just as the theological-political is the paradigm of absolutism. … *The economic-governmental vocation of contemporary democracies is not something that has happened accidentally, but is a constitutive part of the theological legacy of which they are the depositaries.*[40]

For both Girard and Agamben, archaeology is a 'science of signs', an inquiry into the traces left by the originary event on the living body of history and power. No wonder, then, that, to justify their methods, both refer to the work of Carlo Ginzburg.[41] For, in an important book, this historian has powerfully reconstructed the logical structure of the evidential method and revealed its epistemological relevance as a paradigm of juridical, criminal and historical inquiry. In Ginzburg's view, the method of the historian and that of the detective are not different: both are semiotic methods, that is, they aim to evaluate the (historical and symbolic) significance of imperceptible signs. The heuristic power of these traces, however, is not immediately apparent. On the contrary, 'secret clues' are often accidentally left by their author. For this reason, any analysis that seeks to trace the original relationship between an act and its author in the form of an attribution, be it of a painting or of a crime, must start with a careful examination of the details, even the most minute and seemingly irrelevant ones. In effect, according to Ginzburg, the art connoisseur 'resembles the detective who' – just like Conan Doyle's Sherlock

Holmes – 'discovers the perpetrator of a crime (or the artist behind a painting) on the basis of evidence that is imperceptible to most people'.[42] The same method and the same logic can be applied by the historian in her search for the meaning of deep historical connections.

Girard has openly embraced Ginzburg's method. In referring to the 'evidential paradigm' analysed by the latter, he writes: 'In a crime one is dealing with the same type of evidence that I am dealing with in my work'.[43] Agamben is even more explicit about the 'evidential' and 'semiotic' nature of his 'paradigmological' inquiry. As he puts it, 'the clue represents the exemplary case of a signature that puts an insignificant or nondescript object in effective relation to an event ([...] a crime ... a traumatic event) or to subjects (the victim, the murderer, the author of a painting)'.[44] In sum, it is the interplay of references between present (the permanence of traces) and past (the power of the origin), external (context) and stylistic data (gestures and characters), act and author that Girard's and Agamben's archaeological methods seek to reconstruct and that represents the central aspect of their science of signatures.

At this juncture, then, it might be prudent to address some of the methodological perils and epistemological lacunae that emerge from the previous discussion. In fact, both Agamben's paradigmology and Girard's Mimetic Theory present some underlying methodological limitations: although informed by the 'evidential paradigm', these authors are unable to clarify the logical and epistemological nexus that binds together *act, action* and *intentionality*. As we have seen, in Ginzburg's work the relation between clues and historical gaze, between traces and their material source may be reconstructed because the agent of an act – be it a painter, an ancient writer or a criminal – is a being endowed with intentionality. For an intentional agent can leave, purposely or accidentally, traces that can then be ascribed to their author precisely because he or she had an intention or an aim (*telos*).[45] The tension inherent in our actions determines the meaningfulness of the signs (i.e. signifiers) that we leave behind and that, precisely for this reason, can be traced back to a signified. But in Agamben's and Girard's work, intentionality – by an audacious epistemological leap – is ascribed to social groups, transhistorical periods and general mechanisms or dispositives (*dispositifs*). The problem here lies in using the language and methods of teleology[46] to describe dynamics that, from an immanent perspective, are nothing but a 'finite segment of the meaningless infinity of the world process, a segment on which *human beings confer meaning and significance*.[47] In other words, from a logical standpoint, ontological dispositives and collective rituals (such as Girard's mimetic cycle) should not be construed as *historical beings* who pursue goals and have intentions, but rather as general heuristic mechanisms that are meant to explain specific self-regulating functions (more on this later).

But, even so, some fundamental questions remain. For example, what is the relationship between ontology and concrete historical agents, collective mechanisms and individual actions? What trans-epochal functions do sacrificial practices and the political capture of life perform? Surely ontological constructions, political paradigms and mimetic mechanisms do not exist in a vacuum. If anything, they are 'performed' and 'enacted' by political elites, artists, slaves, philosophers and so on – individuals who mark and are marked by history and who bear the signs of its origin. At this conceptual level, then, Girard's and Agamben's methods collide with a classical epistemological problem: methodological individualism. Although Girard has tried, with difficulty, to defend himself against this type of challenge, his conception of the problem is not entirely correct.[48] Methodological individualism in fact does not postulate, as Girard believes, a trans-historical and never-changing idea of subjectivity; on the contrary. Rejecting the use of human aggregates and collective concepts (e.g. the state, society, ontology) in historical research, this epistemological position holds that individuals are the only historical agents endowed with *intentio*. Individuals are not seen as unwitting puppets of sacrificial forces and mechanisms, but rather as agents capable of determining, participating in, and being overwhelmed by the *unexpected consequences* of their collective action and meanings.

What I am suggesting here is that Girard and Agamben confound the subtle but crucial difference between the *real* foundation and the *heuristic* foundation of knowledge.[49] The paradigms with which Agamben operates, as well as the mechanisms of the sacred described by Girard, cannot replace or constitute, either intensively or extensively, historical realities or concrete individuals. They are conceptual constructions that may help us to interpret historical processes and phenomena. Indeed, a paradigmatic case (e.g. the sacrificial victim, *homo sacer*, the oath), once it is suspended as historical singularity, becomes something other than, and beyond, itself precisely because it is transformed into a heuristic instrument. A paradigm does not *produce* history; but it may help us to *make sense* of it. For example, Jeremy Bentham's Panopticon is a historical vision of control that can help us understand how a certain conception of power and security operated in late-eighteenth-century England. But when this peculiar idea is abstracted from the course of the events, it becomes something other than itself: it becomes 'panopticism', the heuristic twin concept by means of which we seek to investigate similar types and forms of surveillance and disciplinary power.

It is not a coincidence that, by prefiguring the inapplicability of the Morellian or evidential method to historical aggregates and social groups, Ginzburg eventually acknowledged the limitations of the morphological approach. 'Suddenly I realized' – he writes – 'that in my long research ... I had been pursuing a method that was much more morphological than historical. ... I was using morphology as an instrument to probe depths beyond the reach of the usual historical methods'.[50] At the same time, however, Ginzburg felt the need to distinguish the real basis of historical knowledge from the heuristic instruments employed to describe it; to use, in other words, the formal and stylistic analogies he had discovered in the course of his investigations as a *tool* for exploring deeper historical connections: 'In my plan, the work of classification should constitute *a preliminary stage*, meant to reconstruct a series of phenomena which I would like to analyse historically'.[51]

In their work, however, Girard and Agamben collapse the difference between the real and the heuristic foundation of knowledge, between resemblances in form and in historical reality. The resulting epistemological lacuna misguides them, prompting them to empty their genealogies of historical content. As a matter of fact, the historical substance of sacrificial forms and rituals cannot but change constantly, because the historical conditions of possibility (agents, technological means, worldviews etc.) are never completely identical; if they were, there would be no historical evolution at all. It is not by chance that, for Girard, the course of history is determined by a universal matrix or mechanism that presents itself, continuously and unconsciously (at least until to the Revelation), in new forms.[52] Historical epochs and worldviews – the Greek world, *romanitas, christianitas* – would all be different expressions of the same sacrificial mechanism; their uniqueness, evolution and peculiarities are not even taken into account. In Agamben's work, on the contrary, it is precisely the historical uniqueness of Western onto-politics that becomes the focus of his genealogies. Nonetheless, the different genealogical layers of the historical trajectory are left blank or empty, as if they were constantly *reoccupied* by the same ontological problem – the dialectic of exclusion–inclusion – or as if there were a sort of ontological malfunction behind the movement and evolution of Western politics and history:

> The Aristotelian onto-logical apparatus, which has for almost two millennia guaranteed the life and politics of the West, can no longer function as a historical a priori, to the extent to which anthropogenesis, which it sought to fix in terms of an articulation between language and being, is no longer reflected in it. Having arrived at the outermost point of its secularization, the projection of ontology (or theology) onto history seems to have become impossible.[53]

In short, the work of Girard and that of Agamben seem to invoke, unwittingly, a functional explanation. Used in biology and in anthropology to make sense of collective processes and dynamics, this epistemological position advocates the possibility of analysing collective actions without reference to an intentional agent. As Carl G. Hempel and Paul Oppenheim have it, 'It consists in explaining characteristics of an organism by reference to certain ends or purposes which the characteristics are said to serve … the ends are not assumed here to be consciously or subconsciously pursued by the organism in question. Thus, for the phenomenon of mimicry, the explanation is sometimes offered that it serves the purpose of protecting the animals endowed with it from detection by its pursuers and thus tends to preserve the species.'[54]

In their genealogies, both Agamben and Girard follow closely a functionalist logic. In fact they both think that the mechanisms of the sacred and the logic of the exception are functions of the *ontological problem of order*: for Agamben, the mechanisms of capture (of language, life and labour) are in fact performative structures through which the process of anthropogenesis evolves; similarly, for Girard, the impersonal mechanisms of the sacred are instruments that guarantee social order and the survival of the human species. This is to say that the sacrificial and impersonal forces represent fundamental ordering functions through which the political order regulates and reconstitutes itself. Historical agents would therefore be unknowingly included in – and excluded

164   *Genealogies of Political Modernity*

from – this 'drama of order', which has its origin and purpose in order itself. As Girard puts it, religion is a 'structure without a subject, because the subject is the mimetic principle'.[55]

And this brings me back once more to the point where I started: the problem of origin. In what sense is the origin of humans constantly reflected in their sacrificial ontology?

Repetition and difference: Of ontology

As we have seen, for both Girard and Agamben human history is marked by an ontogenetic moment: the original sacrifice (Girard) or the exception (Agamben). Once revealed or 'exploded', as it were, this original signifier is erected on human phylogeny, as an ontological foundation. The crucial question is, then: How can we explore, historically and conceptually, the relationship between this beginning and concrete agents, between historical a priori and its evolution? Unfortunately fundamental questions of this sort remain unanswered in the work of Agamben and Girard. Indeed, both authors seem to suggest that the original ontological signifier literally *creates the entire constellation of possibilities* for history to happen (see Figure 7).[56]

In the last volume of the *Homo Sacer* project, Agamben addresses this complex problematic by tracing what he calls an 'archaeology of ontology'. He elucidates the issue in a long and dense passage, which is worth quoting at length:

> First philosophy is not … an ensemble of conceptual formulations that, however complex and refined, do not escape from the limits of a doctrine: *it opens and defines each time the space of human acting and knowing, of what the human being can do and of what it can know and say.* Ontology is laden with the historical destiny of the West not because an inexplicable and metahistorical magical power belongs to being but just the contrary, because ontology is the originary place of the historical articulation between language and world, which *preserves in itself the memory of anthropogenesis, of the moment when that articulation was produced.* To every change in ontology there corresponds, therefore, not a change in the 'destiny' but

in the complex of possibilities that the articulation between language and world has disclosed as 'history' to the living beings of the species *Homo sapiens*. Anthropogenesis, the becoming human of the human being, is not in fact an event that was completed once and for all in the past: rather, it is the event that never stops happening, a process still under way in which the human being is always in the act of becoming human and of remaining (or becoming) inhuman. First philosophy is the memory and repetition of this event: in this sense, it watches over the historical a priori of *Homo sapiens*, and it is to this historical a priori that archeological research always seeks to reach back.[57]

From this passage it can be inferred that, for Agamben, a 'universal' process, namely anthropogenesis, created the conditions for our species, *Homo sapiens*, to flourish when our ancestors put their nature at risk in language, thus binding 'together in an ethical and political connection words, things, and actions'.[58] This anthropogenetic event cannot be traced back to a specific point in time, yet it is crystallized into an ontological dispositive: Aristotle's metaphysics. In fact the hypostatic logic of the originary paradigm of Western philosophy exemplifies the ontological (and primeval) articulation between 'language' and 'world' (see Figure 7).

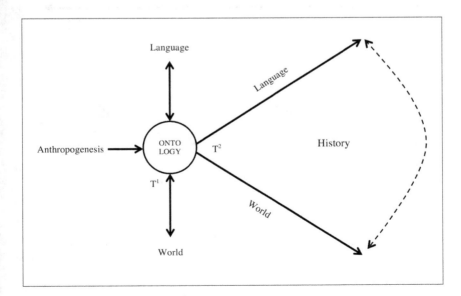

Figure 7 Anthropogenesis: A Figurative Interpretation.

In other words, ontology represents for Agamben the original moment when meaning is disclosed and history opens the doors to human perception and intentionality. The ontological signifier established the boundaries of sense that, since this original event, influenced and directed the course of Western political institutions and culture. Although still operative, however, the echoes or traces of this primeval 'anthropogenetic Big Bang' – which lie embedded in Western ontology – become, over time, more feeble and evanescent (see Figure 8). This means that the 'ontological dispositive' (Agamben conceives of it as a sort of *archi-trace*), that separated being into binary categories (essence and existence, bare life and natural life, *zoē* and *bios*, sacred and profane etc.), is still operating, although in a disfunctional way, but its disclosure becomes increasingly more difficult. This is the reason why philosophical archaeology must engage the sources and traditions and deconstruct 'the paradigms, techniques, and practices through which tradition regulates the forms of transmission, conditions access to sources, and in the final analysis determines the very status of the knowing subject'.[59] In other words, archaeology is a method of philosophical inquiry that, by tracing and disclosing the historical a

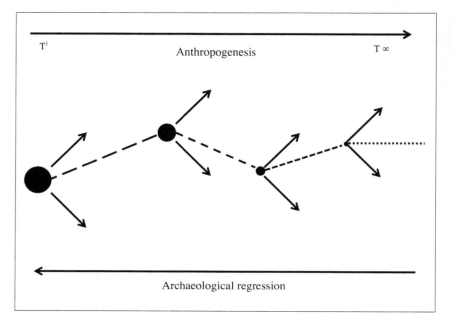

Figure 8 Archaeological Regression: A Figurative Interpretation.

priori 'concealed' in critical (i.e. 'paradigmatic') historical junctures, uncovers the original ontological dispositive and, by so doing, frees up a new (cognitive and political) space for the reinvention of subjectivity.

The careful reader will have noticed that, although following a seemingly different path from that of Girard's, Agamben ends up duplicating the methodological lacunae of Girard's anthropology of the sacred. I will try to illustrate some of the conceptual tensions inherent in their work by restating them in the form of questions. For instance, what is the epistemological and practical nexus between the ontological domain and the historical individuals who live and act within its framework? Is this a merely path-dependent relationship that leads from ontology to history? Or is there a historical possibility to escape from history and get back to the ontological dispositive, from history to ontology? And, if there is, how would such an interaction function? These questions are not fully addressed by Girard and Agamben. In effect, the reader of *Homo Sacer* is left wondering why ontology is subject to historical change – and how. Why has Western ontology taken the current, 'secularizing' trajectory (what Heidegger would call a *Seinsverlassenheit* or abandonment of being)? What accounts for this – and not some other – historical–ontological configuration? In short, what can explain the course, the movement and the specificity of Western onto-politics?

Evidently, it would be reductive to attribute Western exceptionalism to Aristotle's thought and categories, as Agamben seems to do, or to see in the development of Western history a mere oscillation or casual variation of the same mechanism of the sacred, as Girard argues. I mean to say that what operates in Agamben's and Girard's works is a sort of quasi-deterministic, conceptual and transcendent mechanism according to which retroactive access to ontology is denied precisely to the form of life to which ontology was first gifted: *Homo sapiens loquens*. If the entire trajectory of Western history seems to Agamben to be a sort of emanation of its own ontological and philosophical apparatus, for Girard, symbolic systems are, fundamentally, enactments of the sacrificial mechanism, that is, emanations of the immanent history of human violence. But it is difficult, if not impossible, to ascertain when and how human beings' cognitive power initially housed and then determined the (flexible) limits of language and world. Likewise, from a methodological standpoint, it is problematic to assess the ways in which sacrificial mechanisms account for

168   *Genealogies of Political Modernity*

the variety of historical forms, ontologies and centres of power and resistance, and for all those repressed, suffocated and silenced human potentialities that have shaped the course of history.[60]

In this sense, then, it could be argued that Agamben's archaeology of ontology lacks an effective understanding of the history of ontology, just as Girard's history of the sacred is unable to trace theoretically an adequate ontology of history. In the end, both these genealogical analyses appear to deprive historical becoming of its full, contingent and open potentialities: Agamben transforms history into conceptual images (what he calls 'paradigms', which are ideal–typical abstractions and not, as he believes, manifestations of a historical a priori), thus overlooking the dialectical relationship between *mundus imaginalis* and the imaginary, between collective constructions and individual actions.[61] Girard, on the other hand, ignores the intimate nexus between humans and their capacity for self-interpretation, ontology and history, imagination and representation, thus neglecting the fact that the human being is, above all, an *ens repraesentans*. In a sense, then, the work of these authors depicts a sort of chiaroscuro of the magnificent Western philosophical fresco. And yet the intellectual colours they used to trace the contours of this majestic vision are not iridescent enough to give birth to the whole picture.

In following Girard's and Agamben's genealogies, we are thus guided on vertiginous paths that lead us closer to the mysterious relation between agent and action, collective and individual structures of meaning, history and its representation. Despite clear limitations and idiosyncratic epistemologies, the works of these authors give us a powerful insight into the quest for human origins. Nonetheless, the search for the sense of what Max Weber called 'the meaningless infinity of the world' requires the abandonment of any form of philosophical emanationism, from 'above' (Agamben's ontological dispositive) as well as from 'below' (Girard's sacred violence). Today as never before, history seems to have become a sea of meaning that expands at the waning of the old ontological sun.

7

Imago Mortis, Imago Dei:
An Archaeology of Political Sacrifice

The enemy is the embodiment of our own question.

Theodor Däubler, *Hymne an Italien*

In late June 2013, the Icelandic fishing boat *Eyborg*, while sailing the waters of Libya, rescued twenty-three people who were hanging on to fishing cages. After retrieving the dead body of one of the 'migrants' lost at sea, the captain of the boat headed towards Malta; but was ordered to reverse course and to transport the 'migrants' to the Libyan port of Misrata. It was a sovereign order. The captain was in fact threatened with arrest on charges of human trafficking and illegal immigration. Nonetheless, following the conventions of maritime law[1] and his own conscience, he chose to land the surviving 'migrants' in the safest port – and not in the nearest, as ordered by the Maltese authorities. It is well known, at least among those who are sufficiently acquainted with migration issues, that the port of Misrata houses refugee camps from which hundreds of Eritreans, Ethiopians, Nigerians and Somalis are periodically returned to their country of origin, in violation of international conventions. It was only under political pressure from several European countries and through the promise of a subsequent redistribution of refugees among some states of the Union that the resistance of the Maltese authorities was broken and the arrest of the captain prevented.[2]

This story exemplifies the issue that I want to explore in this chapter: the problematic relationship between (bio)politics and sacrifice in the age of forced mobility. Indeed, in the time between the rescue made by the fishing boat and the order to repatriate the migrants to Libya, those twenty-three lives had become embodiments of what Giorgio Agamben calls *homines sacri*:

naked lives that are 'kept safe and protected only to the degree to which' they submit themselves 'to the sovereign's (or the law's) right of life and death'.[3] 'Migrants' who, for example, try to reach the shore of Sicily enter into a zone of indistinction, in which their life is stripped of any rights of citizenship. They are both excluded from law and at the mercy of the sovereign power of states, exposed to a state of exception that, literally, suspends their lives in order to include them in the logic of sovereignty.[4] Their lives hang in the balance, as it were, between the possibility of naturalization and that of deportation, between life and death, between nature and law.

Hannah Arendt was among the first to acknowledge the political relevance of the figures of the migrant and of the refugee. In her *Origins of Totalitarianism* (1951), she writes:

> Every attempt by international conferences to establish some legal status for stateless people failed because no agreement could possibly replace the territory to which an alien, within the framework of existing law, must be deportable. All discussions about the refugee problems revolved around this one question: *How can the refugee be made deportable again?* The Second World War and the displaced persons camps were not necessary to show that the only practical substitute for a nonexistent homeland was an internment camp.[5]

In Arendt's view, the figure of the refugee thus exposes the *dark side* of sovereignty – the long shadow and the intrinsic limits of its power.[6] In effect, as we shall see, the 'migrant' can be seen as a figure of the exception, a paradigm of sacrificiability that discloses the aporiae inherent in the modern political order.

The power of inclusive exclusion that captures the 'migrants' does not, however, release its hold once they have disembarked. On the contrary, it is precisely in the refugee camps (such as those in Lampedusa, southern Chad and Lebanon) that their condition appears more dismal. Indeed, the modern camp is a zone of indistinction in which the 'naked life' of humans, which is trapped by sovereign power, takes place in the absence of law (i.e. in a space and a time of exception).[7] 'If this is true', Agamben has argued, 'if the essence of the camp consists in the materialization of the state of exception and in the subsequent creation of a space in which bare life and the juridical rule enter into a threshold of indistinction, then we must admit that we find ourselves virtually in the presence of a camp every time such a structure is created, independent of the kinds of crime that are committed there and *whatever its denomination and specific topography*.[8]

It is not by chance, then, that 'the camp' has become the political paradigm of modernity.[9] The extraordinary renditions carried out by the United States, the violations of human rights committed in the prison camps at Guantanamo and Abu Ghraib, bear witness to this suspension of law by extraconstitutional means. Indeed, these artificial zones function as spaces of exception in which the 'bare lives' of detainees do not possess any rights but are captured by the exceptionality of power. The Special Interrogation Plans (SIPs) can be read precisely as a symptom of this political evolution: in a memorandum drafted by John Yoo, the then deputy assistant attorney of the US Department of Justice, it is clearly stated that 'federal laws against torture, assault and maiming would not apply to the overseas interrogation of terror suspects'.[10] This means that the United States disapplies domestic law in order to exercise sheer power over the bare life of a suspected terrorist, thus designing a novel 'juridical' area, which oscillates between rights and the absence of rights, violence and law.[11]

This biopower, however, is not just a prerogative of sovereign states but also of international organizations and non-state actors – and sometimes unknowingly so. We read, for example, in one of the most important and paradigmatic documents produced in recent years by the United Nations, that 'human security is *people-centred*. It is concerned with how people *live* and *breathe* in a society'.[12] The language used here cannot and should not be considered accidental. For, with a typical Hobbesian gesture, the bare life of human beings is thus placed at the centre of UN security policies. What is unclear in the document, however, is who should intervene in those cases in which human lives are threatened by sovereign states.[13] As Agamben has rightly argued, 'In the system of the nation-state, so-called sacred and inalienable human rights are revealed to be without any protection precisely when it is no longer possible to conceive of them as rights of the citizens of a state'.[14] When life is stripped of rights – as in the cases of tortured prisoners or migrants over whom states exercise violence by depriving them of citizenship – these rights are suspended because 'there is no autonomous space in the political order of the nation-state for something like the pure human in itself ... Human rights, in fact, represent first of all the originary figure for the inscription of natural

172   *Genealogies of Political Modernity*

naked life in the political–juridical order of the nation-state'.[15] In other words, it is not possible to ensure the effectiveness of law without state protection, just as it is not possible to guarantee human rights without accepting the principle of sovereignty that can always be used to suspend them. This is the (bio) political paradox of modernity.

The present chapter seeks to deconstruct this biopolitical paradigm and to explore what lies behind the contemporary, exacerbated state of exception. Paraphrasing Agamben, I want to understand why we have ended up putting our security and freedom into play into the very place – bare life – that marks our subjection.[16] If it is true, as Agamben argued, that '*the camp is the space that opens up when the state of exception starts to become the rule*',[17] it is, then, crucial to examine what makes this dispositive the 'hidden matrix' of political modernity. Why has 'the camp' become the *locus intimus* of the encounter between norm and exception, life and politics?

In exploring the genealogical origins of this phenomenon, Agamben openly dissociates himself from Carl Schmitt and the theory of *nomos*. Although acknowledging the influence of the German jurist's work,[18] he suggests that the rise of 'thanatopolitics' has been determined by the breaking of the nexus between 'birth' and 'nation', one of the three pillars – along with 'territory' and 'order' – upon which political modernity was established. As he puts it:

> The rupture of the old *nomos* does not take place in the two aspects that, according to Carl Schmitt, used to constitute it (that is, localization, *Ortung*, and order, *Ordnung*), but rather at the site in which naked life is inscribed in them (that is, there where inscription turns *birth* into *nation*). There is something that no longer functions in the traditional mechanisms that used to regulate this inscription, and the camp is the new hidden regulator of the inscription of life in the order – or, rather, it is the sign of the system's inability to function without transforming itself into a lethal machine.[19]

In the following pages I will explore an alternative path to that opened by Agamben. Indeed, I believe that, if we want to understand the roots of the current biopolitical crisis, we need to return to Schmitt. If it is true that the relation between norm and exception mirrors the problematic nexus between sacredness and politics, life and law, it is necessary, in other words, to explore the genealogical origins of this *nodus letalis*.[20] In so doing, I shall discuss another figure of sacrifice that has become paradigmatic in contemporary international politics: the martyr.

Martyrdom: Event and history

In the Palatine Gallery housed in Palazzo Pitti in Florence, there is a painting by the Italian artist Lodovico Cardi, also known as 'il Cigoli'. With its expressive colours and baroque force, the painting depicts a biblical episode that has been fundamental to the self-representation of Christianity: the stoning of St Stephen (Figure 9). The general outline of his story is well known. Stephen, 'a man full of faith and of the Holy Spirit', was doing 'miracles and great signs among the people'; but one day he was falsely accused of blasphemy and brought before the Sanhedrin. By declaring himself innocent, he challenged his persecutors with his faith: 'Can you name a single prophet your ancestors never persecuted? They killed those who foretold the coming of the Upright One, and now you have become his betrayers, his murderers.' On hearing these words, the crowd 'rush at him' and 'thrust him out of the city'. As people were throwing stones at him, Stephen turned his eyes to the sky and saw the 'heaven thrown open and the Son of man standing at the right hand of God'. Bravely facing his ordeal, he uttered the following words: 'Lord Jesus, receive my spirit.'[21]

The painting represents, in images and colours, the story of the man considered to have been the protomartyr, the 'first witness',[22] the one who – in Jacobus da Varagine's words – *fuit etiam norma, id est, exemplum et regula aliis patiendi pro Christo, sive vere agendi et vivendi, vel pro inimicis orandi* (was a norm, that is, an example or rule, for others, of how to suffer for Christ, as well as of how to act and live according to the truth, or of how to pray for one's enemy).[23] Ludovico Cardi depicts here, with intensity, some fundamental theological concepts that form the basis of Christian martyrology and of its notion of sacrifice, which I shall now try to analyse.[24]

In the very moment when the martyr *lets the executioners sacrifice him*, he opens, as it were, the profane world and becomes the intermediary, the mediator, between two dimensions: transcendence and immanence, spirit

Figure 9 Lodovico Cardi (called 'il Cigoli'), The Stoning of St Stephen, 1597.
(*Galleria Palatina, Palazzo Pitti, Florence.* © *Bridgeman Images*)

and flesh, (eternal) life and (earthly) death. In the painting, this vision is emphasized by the angels, who are portrayed in the act of bringing the divine message and laying the crown of immortality on the head of the dying martyr.[25] In the upper part of the canvas, where we can distinguish the dove of the Holy Spirit, the intensity of the divine light is counteracted by the greyness of the city from which the martyr was expelled before being stoned by the mob. Actually the city could not and should not be desecrated by death and murder, in accordance with an ancient tradition that burials had to take place *extra muros*.[26]

The painting fixes in a space, and with intense beauty, the encounter – the 'short-circuit' – between heaven and earth, eternity and secular time, which has become one of the central leitmotifs of the cult of the Christian martyrs and, subsequently, of the saints.[27] Martyrdom and martyrologies performed, in fact, a foundational function in early Christianity. As Peter Brown has argued:

> What appears to be almost totally absent from pagan belief about the role of the heroes is the insistence of all Christians writers that the martyrs, precisely because they had died as human beings, enjoyed close intimacy with God. Their intimacy with God was the *sine qua non* of their ability to intercede for and, so, to protect their fellow mortals. The martyr was the 'friend of God'. He was an intercessor in a way which the hero could never have been. Thus in Christian belief, the grave, the memory of the dead, and the religious ceremonial that might surround this memory were placed within a totally different structure of relations between God, the dead, and the living.[28]

Martyrdom and its narration thus become the metaphysical lens through which once can mediate and redesign the relation between transcendence and immanence, life and death, community and body politic. This epochal change can be considered the *historical* and *theological matrix* that gave rise to a novel understating of sacred time and political geography. In fact the dead, together with what they symbolized through their absence–presence (i.e. through the remains), were now endowed with a new power, thus becoming the fulcrum around which the new religious communities consolidated themselves:

> In the course of the late fourth and fifth centuries, the growth of the cult of the martyrs caused a visible shift in the balance of importance accorded to the areas of the living and the areas of the dead in most late-antique towns.

Great architectures mushroomed in the cemeteries. ... What is even more remarkable is the outcome of this shift. The bishops of western Europe came to orchestrate the cult of the saints in such a way as to base their power within the old Roman cities on these new 'towns outside the town'. The bishop's residence and his main basilica still lay within the city walls. Yet, it was through a studiously articulated relationship with great shrines that lay at some distance from the city – Saint Peter's, on the Vatican Hill outside Rome, Saint Martin's, a little beyond the wall of Tours – that the bishops of the former cities of the Roman Empire rose to prominence in early medieval Europe. ... Furthermore, an ancient barrier between the former generations of Christians as by any other late-antique men, came to be eroded. The tomb of the saint was declared public property as the tomb of any Christian was: it was made accessible to all, and became the focus of forms of ritual common to the whole community.[29]

This new geography of the sacred is gradually accompanied by an enchantment or 'sanctification' of time. For, along with the eschatological and cyclical understandings of time (which are, initially, metaphysical reoccupations of Jewish and pagan cosmological visions), there slowly emerges a peculiarly Christian *tempus sanctorum*. In a sense, if the eschatological promise intensifies the Christian experience of time and liturgy gives rhythm to the annual cycle, it is precisely the 'time of the saints' that endows Christian life with chronological development. In his analysis of the *Legenda aurea*, Jacques Le Goff has masterfully demonstrated how the early martyrs and saints acted, symbolically and practically, as *marqueurs de temps* – markers of a novel experience of time, which is open to the future yet cyclical, ritualistic and linear in equal measure: *les premiers saints sont les premiers ouvriers du temps chrétien ... le passage du paganisme au christianisme a été un moment essentiel dans l'avènement d'un temps chrétien qui, comme l'a fait le Christ par son incarnation, a régénéré le temps dans son essence* ('the earliest saints were the first workers of Christian time ... the passage from paganism to Christianity was an essential moment in the advent of a Christian time that, just as Christ had done by his incarnation, regenerated time in its essence').[30]

This 'incarnation' of the sacred in the time and space of history, the invention of a novel dialectic of absence–presence – grave and altar – should be considered one of the crucial foundational narratives of Christianity. With their bodies, the martyrs signal an impossible presence: God's transcendence, and the invisible eternity in which he dwells, demands representation; and the remains of the martyrs communicate the presence of this absence, in a space where individual death is turned into collective mourning, ritual and life. Thanks to the martyrs, the human urge to represent the world finds a new metaphysical status: transcendence is transformed into a vanishing point through which one can reimagine the immanent condition and the coexistence of time and eternity, heaven and earth (Figure 10).

It is all too easy to notice the profound differences between this archaic vision of martyrdom and contemporary martyrologies. Indeed, today the word 'martyrdom' has extended its meaning to denote other sacrificial figures: those who use their life as an instrument of death, namely suicide bombers. Leaving aside the bitter theological debate about the legitimacy of suicide martyrdom in Islam,[31] it is worth exploring some often overlooked aspects of ancient and contemporary understandings of martyrdom. It has been stressed, for example, that, while Christian martyrs sacrificed their lives by offering

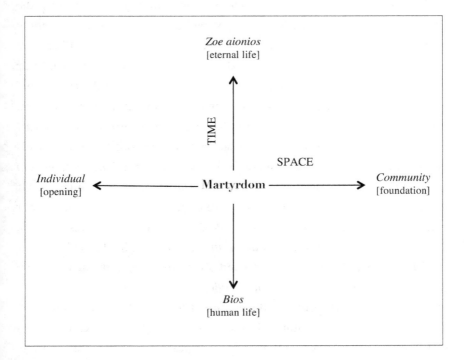

Figure 10 Martyrdom: A Theologico–Political Interpretation.

themselves as witnesses, without killing or committing suicide, suicide bombers give up their lives in order to kill other lives.[32] In this latter case, the human body is used as a weapon to take other lives. Yet, as usually happens in the social sciences, the phenomenon that needs to be explained becomes the explanation, the explanandum turns into the explanans. For this distinction, however true and legitimate, is not explanatory. Indeed, to understand the historical change undertaken by martyrdom, we need to analyse the conditions of possibility that permeate this change and that make the transformation of this phenomenon intelligible (for both actors and spectators).

It is important to highlight, for example, that early Christian martyrs, through their sacrifice, escaped power or Roman *potestas*. Indeed, they claimed the truth (*veritas*) of their faith against the sovereignty (*imperium*) of the Romans. As it clearly emerges from the *Acta proconsularia martyrum scillitanorum* (AD 202), for example, when addressed by the Roman proconsul Saturninus with the injunction '*Nolite furoris hujus insipientia partecipes fieri, sed timete potius reges nostrum, obedenties praeceptis ejus*' ('Have no part in this folly, but rather fear our Emperor, who commands obedience'), the Christian martyr-to-be Cittinus steadily replies: '*Nos non habemus alium quem timeamus, nisi Dominum Deum nostrum, qui est in caelis*' ('We have none other to fear save only our Lord God, who is in heaven').[33] And this statement should not be read as a sign of disregard for secular rules and earthly powers, but rather as a profound profession of faith. In fact the next day, when Saturninus advices the women on trial *honorate regem nostrum, et sacrificate diis* ('honor our Emperor, and make sacrifices to the gods'), the martyr-to-be Donata replies without hesitation: '*honorem quidem Caesari tamquam Caesari; Deo autem nostro honorem et orationem offerimus*' ('we offer Caesar the honour he deserves as Caesar, but [we offer] our Lord God our honour and prayers'). And when Saturninus asked one of the Christians on trial, Speratus, to swear *per genium domini nostri imperatoris* ('by the genius of our Lord the Emperor'), the Christian candidly replied: *Ego imperatoris mundi genium nescio; sed caelesti Deo meo servio, quem nullus hominum vidit, nec videre potest* ('I don't recognize the empire of this world. Rather, I serve my heavenly God, whom no human has seen, or can see').[34] For Speratus, God's invisible and eternal power is definitely more present than the visible powers of this world.

For this reason, then, the sacrifice of the martyrs would not render them 'bare life'. On the contrary, the life of a martyr was *qualified* by martyrdom: offering one's body in sacrifice meant 'reaching the spiritual sensitivity to perceive God's will, his goodness and perfection'.[35] When Tertullian writes *Christus in martyre est*, his words are meant to convey the idea that martyrs reproduce, by their example, the truth of the body of Christ on the cross.[36]

What I want to emphasize through this brief genealogical digression is the fundamental difference between ancient and modern martyrologies. Originally, martyrdom was not simply the expression of a theological order; above all, it signified the creation of a symbolic universe where religious and political powers must confront each other and reconstitute themselves vis-à-vis the imponderableness of an absolute gesture. Martyrdom is based not only on the efficacy of the deed, but also on its imponderable radicalism; indeed, this act is intimately related to death and to the mystery of its inexpressible meaningfulness. A martyr's power is, therefore, that of an absolute renunciation. His ethical–metaphysical example represents the limit that redesigns our vision of the individual and collective body.

From this perspective, there is a close, *structural*, relationship between martyrdom and political power, that is, between the act of self-sacrifice and the dominant political and metaphysical systems in which this act is inscribed. To understand the radical changes undertaken by the narratives and practices of martyrdom (e.g. from the 'sacrifice of one's life' to the 'sacrifice for one's own country'), it is crucial to explore this dialectical relationship between political power and the kinds of exceptions that power allows, protects, or generates and that constitute the 'hidden matrix' of these epochal shifts of perspective. Analysed in this way, martyrdom does not reveal, of course, the personal motivations behind an act, but rather the diverse constellations against which the acts of self-sacrifice have taken their shape and meaning. In other words, only an analysis of the metaphysical conceptions of power and order – and of the dialectical relationship between power relations and the exceptions contained therein – can bring out the differences between ancient and modern understandings of martyrdom. To highlight this point, however, it is necessary to make a short detour through medieval political theology.

***

180 *Genealogies of Political Modernity*

In chapter 5 of *The King's Two Bodies* (1957), Ernst H. Kantorowicz analyses the rise of an ideology that proved to be fundamental to modern European politics: sacrifice for the homeland.[37] Nowadays, it is customary to think that this ideology is as old as the political history of the West and that its roots lie in the Roman notion of *pro patria mori*. But the analogy between these two is misleading. As Kantorowicz points out, when the Romans used the word *patria*, they did not refer to the territory of their republic – or, later on, empire – or to some abstract idea of nation. Rather they had in mind *urbs aeterna*, Rome. For Romans, military and political sacrifices made sense only if they were performed to safeguard the eternal city. Etymology helps us here: *patria* was the land of the *patres*, fathers and forefathers, the soil in which their ancestors were buried (this meaning still lingers in the German word *Vaterland*). It is this very concrete and limited land – a land to which they are genealogically related – that the Romans defended by sacrificing their lives and that is poetically sung by Horace (*Odes*, 3, 2): *Dulce et decorum est pro patria mori* ('It is sweet and proper to die for one's fatherland').

However, to speak of sacrifice for the 'homeland' in the modern sense – an entity that is both abstract and concrete, both emotional and territorial – we have to wait at least until the thirteenth century. For it is around this time that, through the rediscovery of Roman law and theological re-elaboration, an abstract and quasi-religious conception of homeland began to be formed. As Kantorowicz argues, through a slow process of reoccupation of the metaphysical framework of Christianity, 'the "state" in the abstract or the state as a corporation appeared as a *corpus mysticum* and … death for this new mystical body appeared equal in value to the death of a crusader for the cause of God'.[38] To understand this momentous change, Kantorowicz thus places sacrificial practices in relation to the metaphysical worldviews that inform the concepts of political order and authority. Only through the reversal – the immanentization – of the dualistic metaphysics of Christianity is it possible to understand the emotional power and political effectiveness bestowed upon the new concept of homeland and upon the sacrifice that is performed for it:

> Once the *corpus mysticum* has been identified with the *corpus morale et politicum* of the people and has become synonymous with nation and 'fatherland', death *pro patria*, that is, for a mystical body corporate, regains its former nobility. Death for the fatherland now is viewed in a truly religious

perspective; it appears as a sacrifice for the *corpus mysticum* of the state which is no less a reality than the *corpus mysticum* of the church. It all implies a recovery of certain ethical values and moral emotions which with regard to the secular state had been practically absent during the earlier Middle Ages, and yet so dominant in Greek and Roman antiquity. This, however, does not mean simply a paganization of the idea *pro patria mori*. Humanism had its effects, but the quasi-religious aspects of death for the fatherland clearly derived from the Christian faith, the forces of which were now activated for the service of the secular *corpus mysticum* of the state.[39]

It was the merging of two opposing ideas that created the conditions for modern sacrificial practices to emerge. In this process, the ideal of martyrdom for the heavenly, invisible city translated into self-sacrifice for an earthly, visible entity: the modern territorial state. In other words, self-sacrifice for the homeland became a meaningful reality only when the state absorbed into its body politic all the transcendental features of the City of God. Yet behind this transition lies a significant difference: in reality early Christian martyr died neither *pro patria* nor *pro Domino*, but *pro fide*. Their understanding of sacrifice was not *deliberately* or *consciously* political. Their body is described, as we have previously seen, as a tool for transcending the immanent order. By contrast, modern and contemporary forms of self-sacrifice take place in a regime that is entirely political: the search for sovereignty. By being encapsulated in sovereignty and then excluded from it, these martyrs become weapons in a war (whether real or imagined is of no concern here) that immolates the bare life of humans, in a zone of indistinction between the search for and the fight against sovereign power. The essential point here is that, while in the past the martyr gave up her life in order to *escape* the political order, today martyrdom can happen only within it (as the Palestinian–Israeli conflict dramatically shows).[40] As the Tibetan anthropologist Emily T. Yeh has argued, 'Self-immolation is a reclamation of sovereignty over one's own self within a state of siege. Biological life is taken in an assertion of a political life. It is this possibility that is terrifying to the state in its quest to stabilize territorial sovereignty.'[41]

In this difference between ancient and modern martyrdom – and in the disconnection between *veritas, auctoritas* and *potestas* that it signals – it is possible to identify the 'ontological fracture' that has led us into the current biopolitical paradigm. If it is true that, as Kantorowicz has argued, the kingdom of heaven – *regnum coelorum* – has served as a model for the secular and territorial concept of nation, we must then ask: What happens when this political ontology is overturned?

The immanentization of political order

It is well known that ancient cosmology was articulated through the dialectic of two worlds, one transcendent and the other immanent, the latter being considered a mirror or projection of the first (Figure 11). As Eliade, among many others, has argued:

> The world which surrounds us, civilized by the hand of man, is accorded no validity beyond that which is due to the extraterrestrial prototype that served as its model. Man constructs according to an archetype. Not only have his city or his temple have celestial models. The same is true of the entire region that he inhabits … The map of Babylon shows the city at the center of a vast circular territory bordered by a river, precisely as the Sumerians envisioned Paradise. This participation by urban cultures in an archetypal model is what gives them their reality and their validity.[42]

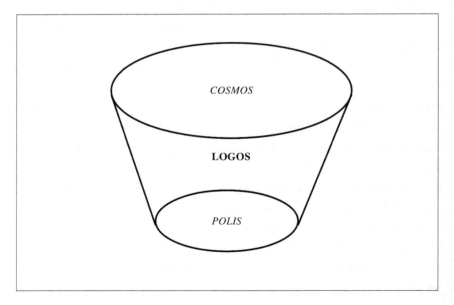

Figure 11 The 'Dual Unity' of the Ancient World: A Figurative Interpretation.

A decisive change takes place with the advent of Christianity. In Augustine's work, for example, the Platonic doctrine of the two worlds is rearticulated through the principle of the fundamental extraneousness of the Christian to the *civitas terrena* (Figure 12).[43] From this perspective, as Carl Schmitt has observed, the Church (*basilica*) is to be considered as *peregrina in saeculo* ('alien in the secular world').[44] 'The Christian government of the world consequently assumes the paradoxical figure of the immanent government of a world that is, and needs to remain, extraneous.'[45] This dualistic metaphysics of order implies that the ancient governmental machine is bipolar, as it were, in that it works by means of a functional correlation between transcendence and immanence, eternity and temporality, providence and contingency. 'The very distinction and correlation between the two levels' – Agamben has argued – 'guarantees that the government is not a despotic power that does violence to the freedom of creatures. On the contrary, it presupposes the freedom of those who are governed'.[46]

It is in this light that we should read the theological and metaphysical revolution brought about by Christian martyrdom. The figure of the martyr should be considered the original matrix that permitted a new type of *mediation* between the transcendent and the immanent level. As we have seen,

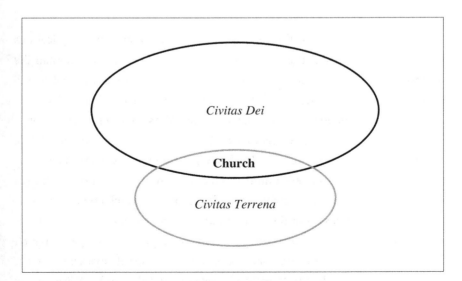

Figure 12 The 'Unitary Dualism' of Christianity: A Figurative Interpretation.

it was possible for martyrs to escape earthly powers, forces or territories in the name of *veritas* precisely because God was considered by them '*regem regum, et omnium gentium Dominum* [the king of kings and lord of all nations]'.[47] From this worldview, there remains a 'space' in immanence that is free from sovereign power precisely because it is tied to transcendence.

The ancient dualism, however, was broken in modernity. We can find one of the most iconic examples of this metaphysical rupture in Thomas Hobbes's *Leviathan* (1651). In this masterpiece of modern political theory, humans' life is regarded as a 'problem' – as the *cause* of existential insecurity (civil war), and at the same time as the *source* of state security. The fundamental performance of Hobbes's system consists in the capture of immanence, namely in the neutralization of human desires and passions. Life is here thought of as absolute contingency. It is for this very reason that Hobbes can write, from the perspective of negative anthropology:

> The attaining of this Soveraigne Power, is by two wayes. One, by Naturall force; as when a man maketh his children, to submit themselves, and their children to his government, as being able to destroy them if they refuse; or by Warre subdueth his enemies to his will, giving them their lives on that condition. The other, is when men agree amongst themselves, to submit to some Man, or Assembly of men, voluntary, on confidence to be protected by him against all others.[48]

Hobbes is perhaps the first thinker to cut all conceptual and metaphysical ties with transcendence, thus transforming contingency and violence – human life stripped of all other transcendent resources – into the real problem of politics (see Figure 13). The modern territorial state is therefore conceived of as a device (the leviathan state) through which human life becomes the source of its own captivity.

What I am suggesting here is that political modernity presents itself as a biopolitical machine because, in this historical moment, two specular views of the world merge by codetermining each other: on the one hand, we witness the emergence of a novel doctrine of sovereign power, which construes life as the reason for politics.[49] On the other hand, as Kantorowicz has convincingly argued, we witness the creation of a new metaphysics of space, which transforms the immanent territory of the state into a giant sovereign body, a mystic–political conglomerate (*corpus mysticum et politicum*).[50] Without the

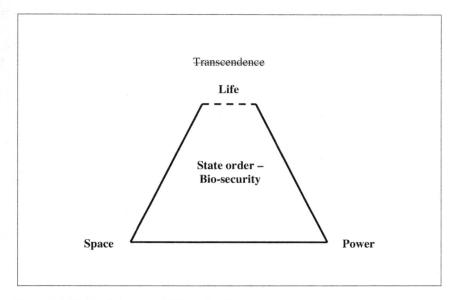

Figure 13 Hobbes's System: A Figurative Interpretation.

reversal that is implicit here, without the fusion between the transcendent and the immanent domain and the transition of the heavenly city into an earthly totality, the modern devotion to the body politic and to worldly sacrifice would be inconceivable. The mechanism that drives this dynamics, which Max Weber called 'disenchantment of the world', is precisely the political attempt to control 'human contingency'. So-called irrational forces (the religious, the non-scientific, the non-measurable) must be somehow 'caged' inside the immanent totality of the state.

It is at this conceptual level, then, that the immanentization of the political order and biopolitics come into contact and blend. Probably no one has sensed the importance of this tendency to understand Western modernity more than Heidegger did:

> The meta-physical of metaphysics, transcendence, changes, when … the *Gestalt* of the essence of man appears as the source of the giving-of-meaning. Transcendence, understood in the manifold sense, turns back into the corresponding re-scendence [*Reszendenz*] and disappears in it. A retreat of this kind through *Gestalt* takes place in such a way that its state of being present is represented and is present again in the imprint of its stamping.[51]

186   *Genealogies of Political Modernity*

In this sense, the protection of 'life' is the form – the *Gestalt* – that modern politics has given itself in order to exist. To paraphrase Heidegger, one could say that the state of being of the *Gestalt* of modern politics is 'life'. The representation and protection of life is the form of dominance of a new and special kind of sovereign power. In modernity, in other words, there is a specular relationship between the immanentization of the body politic and the capture of the biological body. The fulcrum on which this historical–metaphysical intersection rests is the sacrificial paradigm: security is guaranteed by the state through the potential sacrifice of its subjects (or, as Foucault has it, by the right to take life and let live).

However, since the inception of what Foucault has called 'the classical age', the mechanisms of power have undergone a slow but progressive transformation. Through new practices of control and technologies of domination, sovereign power seems to have lost its intimate sacrificial nature, transforming itself into a 'government of the living'. As Foucault puts it:

> The disciplines of the body and the regulations of the population constituted the two poles around which the organization of power over life was deployed. The setting up, in the course of the classical age, of this great bipolar technology – anatomic and biological, individualizing and specifying, directed towards the performances of the body, with attention to the processes of life – characterized a power whose highest function was perhaps no longer to kill, but to invest life through and through. The old power of death that symbolized sovereign power was now carefully supplanted by the administration of bodies and the calculated management of life.[52]

Over the last three centuries, the Western world has experienced an epoch-making political shift: through an invasive politicization of life and privatization of death, the managerial paradigm has progressively replaced the original sacrificial paradigm. The citizen's body thus becomes the centre of new forms of control, care and discipline. Yet this dynamic of privatization of death, which has marked and is still marking the fate of the West, is only the luminous zone around the shadow that biopolitics has cast outside its borders. For how are we to explain the contemporary thanatopolitical drift taken by Western states? Did the current biopolitical paradigm originate in the disconnection of the nexus that tied together 'nation' and 'citizenship', as

Agamben has suggested? If so, how can we make sense of the transition from the idea of *pro patria mori* to the new condition of *sine patria mori* (dying without a homeland)? If one looks at the political world through the gaps of power – for instance from the perspective of the migrant – one will see how the current politicization of the body reveals its intimate connection to the crisis of the body politic, whence the original biopolitical mechanisms had emerged. To understand, then, this genealogical complication of biopolitics, it is necessary, as anticipated at the beginning of this chapter, to pick up the thread of Schmitt's political discourse.

***

In *The Nomos of the Earth* (1950), Schmitt rethinks the original relationship between space and law through two fundamental categories: *Ordnung* (order) and *Ortung* (localization). Every act of land appropriation implies a twofold positioning of the land-appropriating group: a positioning towards the inside (redistribution of resources) and one towards the outside (delimitation of the community from potential enemies). As Schmitt points out, 'Land appropriation is thus the archetype of a constitutive legal process externally (vis-à-vis other peoples) and internally (for the ordering of land and property within a country)'.[53] The dialectical relationship between these two primeval positionings cannot, however, be considered neutral. On the contrary, according to Schmitt, a political–juridical order can be established only by externalizing disorder – by taking it away from the community and into an area of exclusion (the New World, the developing world etc.).

As disturbing as they are, these remarks go straight to the heart of Western geopolitics. In fact the most characteristic signature of the Western political trajectory, in its project of globalization, is the constant shift of the enmity line across its political systems: the discovery and appropriation of the New World, the colonization of Asia, the partition of Africa are all operations through which European nations first, and then the whole Western world, have stabilized their internal political orders through the exportation of disorder, violence and exploitation.[54] From this perspective, the constant exclusion of a part of the world from access to a politically and economically qualified space would represent the condition of possibility for the development of liberal democracies and for the promotion of civil rights in the West.

The dialectic of order and location, however, has now been worn out by the deterritorializing forces of globalization (e.g. financial capital, universalist ideologies, multinational corporations) that, freed from territorial constrains, launched themselves onto the world markets with the aim of conquering them, in line with the new guiding principle discussed in Chapter 5: *cuius oeconomia, eius regio*. At this historical juncture, then, it is crucial to ask what happens when the forces of global capitalism reoccupy and hold the reins of an international state system now atrophied by its territorial limits. What happens when these seemingly uncontrollable universalizing forces superimpose their *global Landnahme* (global land appropriation) on a state's territory? Schmitt formulates the problem thus: 'Has humanity today actually "appropriated" the earth as a unity, so that there is nothing more to be appropriated? Has appropriation really ceased? Is there now only division and distribution? Or does only production remain? If so, we must ask further: Who is the great appropriator, the great divider and distributor of our planet, the manager and planner of unified world production?'[55]

What I am arguing here, upon re-reading Schmitt, is that the political domestication of 'life' in the West, the forced mobilization of 'migrants', and the sacrificial mechanism that shuts them up in 'refugee camps' or immolates them on some border or other are all expressions of the rift that is opening today between sovereign power and economic globalization. The contemporary biopolitical paradigm is situated at the disconnection between sovereign power and territoriality. The transition from the territorial state to what Foucault calls the 'government of the living' is characterized by the fact that globalization, exploding all limits and mediations created during modernity, has reorganized the relation between power and life on a continuum where authority, truth and sovereignty enter into a zone of indistinction (Figure 14). Economic forces, freed from territorial limits and bonds of loyalty, now extend their power over the biopolitical mass ad infinituum, while the 'bare lives' of migrants and economically marginal individuals are, paradoxically, increasingly sucked into the decaying body of the leviathan state. On the one hand, global economy literally mobilizes human lives; on the other hand, sovereign power, by acting as a biopolitical and sacrificial threshold, gives parts of the population access to resources and excludes others from it. In short, *the life of individuals has become the zone of*

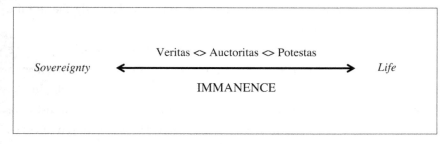

Figure 14 The Biopolitical Threshold: A Figurative Interpretation.

indistinction in which economic and political powers exercise their domination in the name of an undefined idea of progress.

The individual body – the naked life of the individual – is captured by a body politic, which is in turn manoeuvred by politically disembodied economic forces. Thus, to the immanentization of the political space and the never-ending economic appropriation of the earth, there corresponds a transformation of human life into *pure carnality*. Today, in sum, the seemingly unstoppable deterritorialization of power goes hand in hand with the objectification of life and its forms. From this perspective one can appreciate why, in the age of globalization, borders and boundaries have increasingly assumed the function of biopolitical and sacrificial filters.

Conclusion: Towards an 'evenemential' ethics

Political modernity, as we have seen, is characterized by a peculiar metaphysics of presence: corporeity. To be sure, this is the result of the development of the complex relationship between space and sacrifice around which Western politics was organized. Indeed, the control of life, understood as a contingent and dangerous energy, seems to furnish the paradigm of government in modernity. The original signature of sovereign power should not, then, be sought in the process of depriving life of its multiple forms – or, as in Hobbes, in the transformation of security into control and of freedom into biopolitics – but rather in the conceptualization of human freedom and potentiality as *universal threats*. In this sense, political modernity can be read as a desperate attempt to control what is by definition uncontrollable, namely the infinite human capacity for self-transcendence.

Inside this metaphysical apparatus, the paradigm of sacrificiability (of the citizen, of the soldier, of the migrant) proved to be the mechanism through which the modern political order tried to close itself upon itself. In the Western experience, order really means, first and foremost, the expulsion of contingency by means of sacrifice. Yet, having reached the outermost point of its genealogical journey, the sacrificial mechanism seems unable now to guarantee the unity of political systems (which are pierced by financial, economic and universalist forces). By losing its symbolic and sacrificial strength, sovereignty has thus turned into a thanatopolitical device for controlling the foreigner, the migrant and the poor. Today globalization seems to have become precisely what Hobbes feared most: unstructured and uncontrollable immanence.

It is difficult to imagine how we can escape this condition through the power of thought, or through the 'destituent' (i.e. destructuring) potential of what Agamben has designated as 'inoperativity'.[56] Similarly, it is problematic to think that this drift can be countered by mere appeals to the protection of human rights that, as Agamben reminds us, inevitably fall prey to the state's sovereign power. Without pretending to give an exhaustive answer to these momentous problems, I would like to conclude by returning to the story with which I began this chapter. And I would like to do this by discussing the extraordinary reflections that Ivan Illich has left us in his intellectual testament.[57]

Once universal principles (i.e. the true being, the true art, the true God etc.) and categorical imperatives (e.g. 'act according to the universal law') have been disposed with, what is left of ethics and morality? Illich addresses this momentous question with the help of the parable of the Good Samaritan. He sees in the relationship between the Samaritan and the wounded traveller a revolutionary potential: Who is that injured stranger who asks for our help? Who is our neighbour? To these questions Illich replies: the 'other' – our neighbour – is the embodiment of our destiny; he is the one who, by putting us into question, give us an identity. It is important to note that, just like the captain who rescued the migrants near the cost of Libya, Illich thinks that our neighbour is the one whom we *choose* to help, not the one whom we were forced, by power or duty, to rescue. In effect, the careful reader will remember that in the parable two religious figures, the priest and the Levite, avoid the wounded man because they consider liturgy and their duties more urgent than helping a half-dead Jew who lies on the ground. Only the Samaritan saves the wounded traveller – and this in spite of the enmity between Jews and his own tribe.

The message that Illich sends us is clear: human contingency – a wounded man on the road, as well as those migrants lost at sea – represents the moment in which truth manifests itself. Our neighbour is, in other words, an embodiment of the possibility of human morality. But this possibility does not respond to any abstract moral code, duty or Decalogue. The ethical question that a stranger raises through her bodily presence is, essentially, the condition that allows the *immediate* and *contingent* event of brotherhood. *The 'other' is therefore our immediate mediation of meaning.* This is why ethics, according to Illich, cannot be encoded in a norm, in a system of laws, or in a Decalogue: if it could, the moment of truth inherent in the other's bodily call would be atrophied, standardized and decided about by power relations.

Today our reflection on moral duty should therefore start afresh; and it should start from the exception decision of the captain of the boat – a decision that, like the Samaritan, saves the migrants from the power of authority, at the exact moment when the exception suspends sovereign power in order to reaffirm the ethical need of human life.

Notes

Introduction

1 Fernando Pessoa, *Livro do desassossego* (São Paulo: Montecristo Editora, 2012), 103.

2 Martin Heidegger, *Contributions to Philosophy (of the Event)* [1989], trans. Richard Rojcewicz and Daniela Vallega-Neu (Bloomington and Indianapolis: Indiana University Press, 2012), 774, 776.

3 Friedrich Nietzsche, *On the Genealogy of Morality* [1887], trans. Carol Diethe (Cambridge: Cambridge University Press, 2006), xvii.

4 Ibid., 8.

5 Ibid., 51.

6 Ibid.

7 Ibid.

8 Ibid.

9 Ibid., 51–2.

10 Martin Heidegger, *Being and Time* [1929], trans. John Macquarrie and Edward Robinson (Oxford: Blackwell, 1962), 432.

11 Ernst Cassirer, *An Essay on Man: An Introduction to a Philosophy of Human Culture* (New Heaven and London: Yale University Press, 1944), 177.

12 Benedetto Croce, *La storia come pensiero e come azione* [1938] (Naples: Bibliopolis, 2002), 150.

13 Arthur C. Danto, 'Letter to Posterity', *The American Scholar*, 4 September 2012, available at: https://theamericanscholar.org/letter-to-posterity/#.XF2yxmT7SfS (accessed 10 January 2019).

14 See Carl Schmitt, 'The Age of Neutralizations and Depoliticizations' [1929], trans. Matthias Konzett and John P. McCormick, in *The Concept of the Political*, ed. George Schwab (Chicago: The University of Chicago Press, 2007), 81–9.

15 Hannah Arendt, *Between Past and Future: Six Exercises in Political Thought* (New York: Viking Press, 1961), 62.

16 For a discussion, see Mircea Eliade, *Patterns in Comparative Religion* [1949], trans. Rosemary Sheed (Lincoln and London: University of Nebraska Press, 1996), 265–80.

Notes   193

17 Linda Schele and David Freidel, *A Forest of Kings: The Untold History of Ancient Maya* (New York: Morrow, 1990), 66–7.

18 Ernst Pulgram, 'Proto-Indo-European Reality and Reconstruction', *Language* 35, no. 3 (1959): 425.

Chapter 1

1 'In earliest times, before the scribe Gnaius Flavius made knowledge of the calendar available to all, against the senate's wishes, it was a lesser pontiff's duty to watch for the first appearance of the new moon and to report the sighting to the king in charge of sacrifices.'

2 Walter Benjamin, *The Origin of the German Tragic Drama*, trans. John Osborne (London and New York: Verso, 1998), 45. In his Introduction to the English translation of the *Trauerspiel*, George Steiner defines Benjamin's *Erkenntniskritische Vorrede* as 'one of the more impenetrable pieces of prose in German or, for that matter, in any modern language' (George Steiner, Introduction to *The Origin of the German Tragic Drama*, by Walter Benjamin. London and New York: Verso, 1998, 13).

3 Benjamin, *Origin of the German Tragic Drama*, 46, emphasis added.

4 Samuel Weber, *Benjamin's -abilities* (Cambridge, MA and London: Harvard University Press, 2008), 135.

5 Benjamin, *Origin of the German Tragic Drama*, 46.

6 Giorgio Agamben, *Homo Sacer: Sovereign Power and Bare Life*, trans. Daniel Heller-Roazen (Stanford, CA: Stanford University Press, 1998), 6.

7 Giorgio Agamben, *The Use of Bodies*, trans. Adam Kotsko (Stanford, CA: Stanford University Press, 2016), 264; translation slightly modified.

8 Agamben's attempt to trace *theoretically* a super-*archē* is in contradiction both with Benjamin's notion of 'origin' and with Agamben's own methodology (clearly inspired by Benjamin), which he developed post hoc in *The Signature of All Things: On Method*, trans. Luca D'Isanto and Kevin Atell (New York: Zone Books, 2009). By thinking of the process of anthropogenesis as an echo of an archetypal event, Agamben reintroduces metaphysics (the 'primordial indistinction', which he criticizes) into the realm of ontology and human praxis. Benjamin's notion of 'repetition' is not conceived of as a mere reoccupation but implies reinvention, that is a new singularity. It is no coincidence that human practices, understood as sources of meaning, are completely absent from Agamben's project. Genealogical

194 *Notes*

analysis, however, implies a dialectical relationship between ontology and history, theory and practice, as historians like Kantorowicz knew all too well: 'Practice, as usual, precede[s] theory, but existing practice ma[kes] the minds all the more receivable for a new theory' (Ernst H. Kantorowicz, *The King's Two Bodies: A Study in Medieval Political Theology* [1957], Princeton, NJ: Princeton University Press, 1997, 273).

9 For a discussion, see the Introduction to this volume.

10 'The political can derive its energy from the most varied human endeavors, from the religious, economic, moral, and other antitheses. *It does not describe its own substance* but only *the intensity of an association or dissociation* of human beings' (Carl Schmitt, *The Concept of the Political* [1932], trans. George Schwab (Chicago and London: University of Chicago Press, 2007), 38, emphasis added). For a critical discussion, see Michael Marder, *Groundless Existence: The Political Ontology of Carl Schmitt* (New York: Continuum, 2010).

11 Carl Schmitt, *Constitutional Theory* [1928], trans. Jeffrey Seitzer (Durham and London: Duke University Press, 2008), 241, translation slightly modified. In this work Schmitt distinguishes between *Repräsentation* (representation understood in a symbolic sense, as a 'genetic–foundational' event) and *Vertretung* (representation understood in a liberal sense, as a mandate). I have maintained this crucial conceptual distinction here.

12 Ibid.

13 Ibid., 245.

14 Ibid.

15 Thomas Hobbes, *Leviathan, sive de materia, forma, et postestate civitatis ecclesiasticæ et civilis* [1668] (Aalen: Scientia, 1961), 81. The original English version sounds a little different: 'A Multitude of men, are made *One* Person, when they are by one man, or one Person, Represented; so that it be done with the consent of every one of that Multitude in particular. For it is the *Unity* of the Representer, not the unity of the Represented, that maketh the Person *One*. And it is the Representer that beareth the Person, and but one Person: And *Unity*, cannot otherwise be understood in Multitude' (*Leviathan*, ed. G.A.J. Rogers and K. Schuhmann, London: Continuum, 2005, vol. 2, 131). It is important to emphasize that Hobbes uses the term *persona* in its Latin sense. As he puts it: 'The word Person is latine: instead whereof the Greeks have πρόσωπον, which signifies the *Face*, as *Persona* in latine signifies the *disguise*, or outward appearance of a man, counterfeited on the Stage; and sometimes more particularly that part of it, which disguiseth the face, as a Mask or Visard: And

Notes

from the Stage, hath been translated to any Representer of speech and action, as well in Tribunals, as Theaters. So that a Person, is the same that an Actor is, both on the Stage and in common Conversation; and to *Personate*, is to *Act*, or *Represent* himselfe, or another; and he that acteth another, is said to bear his Person, or act in his name' (ibid., 128). This is a central aspect of Hobbes's doctrine of representation, according to which the sovereign is in fact an 'actor' who personifies the unity of the Commonwealth.

16 For a critical assessment, see Hanna Fenichel Pitkin, *The Concept of Representation* (Berkeley and Los Angeles: University of California Press, 1972), 14–37.

17 Hobbes, *Leviathan*, 130.

18 Ibid., 138.

19 Hobbes's doctrine of representation should be contextualized within the historical period that produced it, that is the civil Wars of Religion of the sixteenth century. The problem of political unity – and of its secular representation – is in fact that of the relationship between political *auctoritas* and ecclesiastical *veritas*. As is well known, for Hobbes, *stasis* (civil war) is created by the misguided attempt to place religious faith and beliefs above the political obligation that holds a *civitas* together. To explain the 'injustice' and 'folly' of the English Civil War, for example, he writes in *Behemoth*: 'how came the people be so corrupted? And what kind of men were they that could so seduce them? The seducers were of divers sorts. One sort were ministers; ministers, as they called themselves, of Christ; and sometimes, in their sermons to the people, God's ambassadors; pretending to have a right from God to govern every one his parish and their assembly the whole nation. (Thomas Hobbes, *Behemoth* [1681], ed. Paul Seaward (Oxford: Clarendon Press, 2010), 108–9).

20 *En principe, c'est de l'individu que dérive la réalité collective. Mais alors comment peut-elle le surpasser à ce point? Voilà d'où vient la solution de continuité que présentent la trame de ces raisonnements et le double aspect de sa doctrine: libérale et autoritaire, monarchique démocratique, artificialiste et naturaliste* (Émile Durkheim, *Hobbes à l'agrégation. Un cours d'Émile Durkheim suivi par Marcel Mauss* (Paris: Éditions de l'École des hautes etudes en sciences sociales, 2011), 59; my translation). Starting from these reflections, Durkheim will end up reversing Hobbes's assumptions: society, for the French sociologist, precedes the individual as a meaningful totality.

21 'That an emblem can be useful as a rallying point for any sort of group requires no argument. By expressing the social unit tangibly, it makes the unit itself more

tangible to all. And for that reason, the use of emblematic symbols must have spread quickly, as soon as the idea was born. Furthermore, this idea must have arisen spontaneously from the conditions of life in common, for the emblem is not only a convenient method of clarifying the awareness the society has of itself: *It serves to create – and is a constitutive element of – that awareness*' (Émile Durkheim, *The Elementary Forms of Religious Life* [1912], trans. Karen E. Fields (New York: Free Press, 1995), 231; emphasis added).

22 Here is the full passage: 'le grand problème en Politique, que je compare à celui de la quadrature du cercle en Géométrie, & à celui des longitudes en Astronomie. Trouver une forme de Gouvernement qui mette la loi au-dessus de l'homme" ('the great problem of Politics, which I compare to that of squaring the circle in Geometry, and of longitudes in Astronomy: To find a form of Government that might place the law above man'; Jean-Jacques Rousseau, 'Lettre a Monsieur le Marquis de Mirabeau', in *Collection complète des oeuvres de J.J. Rousseau* (Genève, 1782), vol. 24, 437).

23 This problem is particularly evident in the work of Jean-Pierre Dupuy, who has dedicated numerous essays to the formal and logical justification of the nexus between self-transcendence and order. See, for example, Jean-Pierre Dupuy, *Introduction aux sciences sociales: Logiques des phénomènes collectifs* (Paris: Ellipses, 1992).

24 'The main object of religion is not to give man a representation of the natural universe, for if that had been its essential task, how it could have held on would be incomprehensible ... But religion is first and foremost a system of ideas by means of which individuals imagine the society of which they are members and the obscure yet intimate relations they have with it. Such is its paramount role. And although this representation is symbolic and metaphorical, it is not unfaithful. It fully translates the essence of the relations to be accounted for. It is true with a truth that is eternal that there exists outside us something greater than we and with which we commune' (Durkheim, *The Elementary Forms*, 227).

25 As Kelsen puts it: 'If a man in need asks another man for help, the *subjective* meaning of this request is that the other ought to help him. But in an objective sense he ought to help (that is to say, he is morally obliged to help) only if a general norm – established, for instance, by the founder of a religion – is valid that commands, "Love your neighbor." And this latter norm is objectively valid only if it is presupposed that one ought to behave as the religious founder has commanded. Such a presupposition, establishing the objective validity of the norms of a moral or legal order, will here be called a basic norm [*Grundnorm*]'

(Hans Kelsen, *Pure Theory of Law*, trans. Max Knight (Clark, NJ: The Lawbook Exchange, 2005), 8). The passage clearly shows Kelsen's unconvincing 'epistemic leap' from a historical ethic (established through charisma and by an event) to a logical morality (conceptually and gnoseologically founded).

26 Claude Lévi-Strauss, *Totemism*, trans. Rodney Needham (Harmondsworth: Penguin Books, 1969), 130, emphasis added. As is well known, Lévi-Strauss will trace the dialectic of representation back to 'certain modes of thought', that is to dichotomic thought. He puts it like this: 'The alleged totemism pertains to the understanding, and the demands to which it responds and the way in which it tries to meet them are primarily of intellectual kind. Its image is projected, not received; it does not derive its substance from without. If illusion contains a particle of truth, this is not outside us but within us' (ibid., 177). In so doing, however, he overlooks the sociopolitical problem of order and the question of political unity that it invokes.

27 Schmitt, *Constitutional Theory*, 248. Schmitt also discusses the first relevant political use of the notion of representation as found in Nicolas of Cusa's work. In *De concordantia catholica* Cusa had spoken of *uno compendio representativo* through which *totum imperium collectum est*. But, although the passage emphasizes the totalizing and integrative aspect of sovereignty, it does not clarify the origin of the principle of representation. See Nicholas of Cusa, *De concordantia catholica* [1433], iii, 471: *Primi ordinis sunt reges et electores imperii, patricii. Secundi sunt duces, praesides, praefecti et huiusmodi. Tertii marchiones et lantgravii et similes. Omnes illi, qui ceteris eminent et imperio plus approximantur, corpus imperiale, cuius caput est ipse caesar, constituunt. Et dum simul conveniunt in uno compendio representativo, totum imperium collectum est.*

28 Schmitt, *Constitutional Theory*, 244, translation modified.

29 Ibid., 243, emphasis added. See also Gerhard Leibholz, *Das Wesen der Repräsentation unter besonderer Berücksichtigung des Repräsentativsystems* [1928] (Berlin: de Gruyter, 1973), 30–3.

30 Carlo Ginzburg, *Wooden Eyes: Nine Reflections on Distance*, trans. Martin Ryle and Kate Soper (New York: Columbia University Press, 2001), 65.

31 According to William H. St John Hope, the first use of a funerary effigy dates back to 1272, the year of Henry III's death; see Hope, 'On the Funeral Effigies of the Kings and Queens of England, with Special Reference to Those in the Abbey Church of Westminster', *Archeologia* 60 (1907): 526–8. This hypothesis is now rejected by most scholars. For a discussion, see Ralph E. Giesey, *The Royal Funeral Ceremony in Renaissance France* (Geneve: Droz, 1960), 81; Julian

Litten, 'The Funeral Effigy: Its Function and Purpose', in *The Funeral Effigies of Westminster Abbey*, ed. Anthony Harvery and Richard Mortimer (Woodbridge: The Boydell Press, 2003), 4.

32 Kantorowicz, *The King's Two Bodies*, 421.

33 Ibid., 429.

34 This doctrine is so powerful that, though greatly modified by the flow of time, it can also be encountered in modern political thought. Emer de Vattel, for example, in his treatise *Le Droit de gens* (1758, 291 and 286) speaks of those kings who '*prétendirent avec raison, qu'il n'y avoit rien sur la terre de plus éminent, de plus auguste que leur Dignité*' ['asserted with reason, that there was nothing on earth more eminent and more august than their dignity']; and this is because, de Vattel argues, '*la Dignité, la Majesté réside origiment dans le Corps de l'Etat; celle du Souverain lui vient de ce qu'il réprésente sa Nation*' ['the dignity, the majesty, resides originally in the body of the state; that of the sovereign is derived from his representing the nation'; my translation].

35 According to Giesey, the mannequins were adopted for practical reasons, that is to avoid exposing a rotting corpse to the public and to allow the funeral rituals to be carried out in complete calm. This explanation, however, as Ginzburg pointed out, is not convincing at all. For other symbols and objects could be used in place of the wooden or wax doubles and effigies, such as the catafalque or the coffin covered with a pall – alternatives that had already been accepted by tradition.

36 Ginzburg, *Wooden Eyes*, 66; emphasis added.

37 Agamben, *Homo Sacer*, 98.

38 Giesey, *The Royal Funeral Ceremony*, viii.

39 Agamben, *Homo Sacer*, 101.

40 Ibid., 100.

41 Ginzburg, *Wooden Eyes*, 65.

42 See Jean-Claude Richard, 'Enée, Romulus, César et les funérailles impériales (Dion Cassius, 56, 34, 2; Tacite, *Annales*, 4, 9, 3)', *Mélanges de l'École française de Rome* 78, no. 1 (1966): 67–78.

43 *Historia Augusta* 19, 1: 'Let the memory of the murderer and the gladiator [Commodus] be utterly wiped away. Let the statues of the murderer and the gladiator be overthrown. Let the memory of the foul gladiator be utterly wiped away. Cast the gladiator into the charnel-house.'

44 Agamben, *Homo Sacer*, 94.

45 Kantorowicz, *The King's Two Bodies*, 502.

46 Giesey, *The Royal Funeral Ceremony*, 177ff.

Notes

47 Kantorowicz, *The King's Two Bodies*, 316.

48 Edward Coke cited in Kantorowicz, *The King's Two Bodies*, 317–18.

49 Ibid., 330.

50 Hobbes, *Leviathan*, 155–6, emphasis added.

51 Ibid., 154.

52 See André Magdelain, *Recherches sur l'"imperium": la loi curate et les auspices d'investiture* (Paris: Presses Universitaires de France, 1968); Rafael Domingo, *Teoría de la 'auctoritas'* (Pamplona: Ediciones Universidad de Navarra, 1987), 47–51.

53 See André Magdelain, 'Auspicia ad patres redeunt', in *Jus imperium auctoritas: Études de droit romain* (Rome: École française de Rome, 2015), 356.

54 Ibid., 346.

55 It is worth noting that 'the continuity is ensured by *the absence of hiatus* – and *not by the passage from hand to hand* – of a precious deposit [of power] entrusted once for all to the [city] founder' (Magdelain, 'Préface', in *Jus imperium auctoritas*, xxii, emphasis added).

56 See Livy, i, 17.6: *quinque dierum spatio finiebatur imperium ac per omnes in orbem ibat; annuumque intervallum regni fuit. Id ab re, quod nunc quoque tenet nomen, interregnum appellatum* ['Their power was limited to five days, and they exercised it in rotation. This break in the monarchy lasted for a year, and it was called by the name it still bears – that of "interregnum"']; and Dionysius of Halicarnassus, *Roman Antiquities* ii, 57.2: Ἐκεῖνοι δ' οὐχ ἅμα πάντες ἐβασίλευον, ἀλλ' ἐκ διαδοχῆς ἡμέρας πέντε ἕκαστος, ἐν αἷς τάς τε ῥάβδους εἶχε καὶ τὰ λοιπὰ τῆς βασιλικῆς ἐξουσίας σύμβολα ['They did not all reign together, but successively, each for five days, during which time they had both the rods and the other insignia of the royal power']. See also Theodor Mommsen, *Römisches Staatsrecht* (Leipzig: Verlag von S. Hirzel, 1874), vol 2: 8.

57 Magdelain, 'Cinq jours épagomènes à Rome?', in *Jus imperium auctoritas*, 280. For a good discussion, which, however, does not engage with the symbolism and function of the number five, see Aleksandr Koptev, 'The Five-Day Interregnum in The Roman Republic', *Classical Quarterly* 66, no. 1 (2016): 205–21.

58 See also Magdelain, 'Cinq jours épagomènes à Rome?' 280.

59 See, for example, Mircea Eliade, *The Myth of the Eternal Return or, Cosmos and History* (Princeton: Princeton University Press, 1974), 51–2. See also Magdelain, 'Cinq jours épagomènes à Rome?' 290–2.

60 Eliade, *The Myth of the Eternal Return*, 51–2.

61 Varro, *De lingua latina* vi, 13: *Terminalia, quod is dies anni extremus constitutus: duodecimus enim mensis fuit Februarius et cum intercalatur inferiores quinque dies*

duodecimo demuntur mense ['The Festival of Terminus, because this day is set as the last day of the year; for the twelfth month was February, and when the extra month is inserted the last five days are taken off the twelfth month'].

62 Ibid. It is worth noting that Terminalia was also a festival in honour of Terminus, the god of boundaries and limits. In this sense, Terminalia had a twofold function: spatial and temporal. Such festivals were 'situated at the two levels of the sky and of the earth; festivals of limits and limits of festivals: *sacrorum finis*'. Magdelain, 'Cinq jours épagomènes à Rome?' 302.

63 Ibid., 299. Magdelain, *Recherches sur l'"imperium"*, 32.

64 As Georges Dumézil put it in his *La Religion romaine archaïque* (Paris: Payot, 1974), 337: *Tout passage suppose deux lieux, deux états, celui qu'on quitte, celui où l'on pénètre* ['every passage presupposes two places, two states, the one that is left and the one that is entered'; my translation].

65 For a detailed discussion, see Edoardo Bianchi, *Il rex sacrorum a Roma e nell'Italia antica* (Milan: Vita e Pensiero, 2010).

66 According to Momigliano, these tasks were eventually taken over by other *flamines*. See Arnaldo Momigliano, *Quarto contributo alla storia degli studi classici e del mondo antico* (Rome: Edizioni di Storia e Letteratura, 1969), 400–2. This argument is in line with Dionysius of Halicarnassus's account; see his *Roman Antiquities* iv, 72–5.

67 See Magdelain, 'Cinq jours épagomènes à Rome?'; Bianchi, *Il rex sacrorum a Roma e nell'Italia antica*.

68 Festus, *De verborum significatu*, xiv, 198: *Ordo sacerdotum aestimatur deorum ordine, ut deus maximus quisque*. Maximus videtur Rex, *dein Dialis, post hunc Martialis, quarto loco Quirinalis, quinto pontifex maximus. Itaque in soliis Rex supra omnis accumbat licet; Dialis supra Martialem, et Quirinalem; Martialis supra proximum; omnes item supra pontificem. Rex, quia potentissimus: Dialis, quia universi mundi sacerdos, qui appellatur Dium; Martialis, quod Mars conditoris urbis parens; Quirinalis, socio imperii Romani Curibus ascito Quirino; pontifex maximus, quod iudex atque arbiter habetur rerum divinarum humanarumque*; emphasis added.

69 Livy, ii, 2: '*et quia quaedam publica sacra per ipsos reges factitata erant, necubi regum desiderium esset, regem sacrificolum creant. Id sacerdotium pontifici subiecere, ne additus nomini honos aliquid libertati, cuius tunc prima erat cura, officeret*' ['And because certain public functions had hitherto been executed by the kings themselves, a "king for sacrifices" was created, so that there should be no want of such kings. And lest the title added to the name might threaten

liberty, which was their first care, they made this office subordinate to that of Pontifex (*sc.* Maximus)].' See also Plutarch, *Roman Questions*, trans. Frank Cole Babbitt (Cambridge, MA: Harvard University Press, 1962), 63: 'Why is the so-called *rex sacrorum*, that is to say "king of the sacred rites," forbidden to hold office or to address the people? Is it because in early times the kings performed the greater part of the most important rites, and themselves offered the sacrifices with the assistance of the priests? But when they did not practise moderation, but were arrogant and oppressive, most of the Greek states took away their authority, and left to them only the offering of sacrifice to the gods; but the Romans expelled their kings altogether, and to offer the sacrifices they appointed another, whom they did not allow to hold office or to address the people, so that in their sacred rites only they might seem to be subject to a king, and to tolerate a kingship only on the gods' account.'

70   See, for example, Theodor Mommsen, *The History of Rome* [1862], vol. I, trans. William P. Dickson (Cambridge: Cambridge University Press, 2009), 255–6: 'The exasperation of the people is attested by the formal vow which they made man by man for themselves and for their posterity that thenceforth they would not tolerate a king; by the blind hatred with which the name of king ever afterwards was regarded in Rome; and above all by the enactment that the "king for sacrifice" (*rex sacrorum*) – whom they considered it their duty to create that the gods might not miss their accustomed mediator – should be disqualified from holding any farther office, so that this official was at once the first in rank and the least in power of all the Roman magistrates.' Mommsen's position is in line with Livy ii, 2 and with Dionysius of Halicarnassus, *Roman Antiquities* v, 1. For a comparison between *rex sacrorum* and *archōn basileus*, see the classical study by De Sanctis, *Storia dei romani: la conquista del primato in Italia*, vol. 1 (Turin: Fratelli Bocca editori, 1907), 401–4.

71   Plutarch, *Roman Questions* 63: 'There is a sacrifice traditionally performed in the forum at the place called Comitium, and, when the rex has performed this, he flees from the forum as fast as he can.'

72   Ovid, *Fasti*, ii, 685: '*Nunc mihi dicenda est regis fuga. Traxit ab illa sextus ab extremo nomina mense dies. Ultima Tarquinius Romanæ gentis habebat regna, vir iniustus, fortis ad arma tamen.*' See Magdelain's masterful discussion in 'Cinq jours épagomènes à Rome?'. See also Elmer T. Merrill, 'The Roman Calendar and the Regifugium', *Classical Philology* 19, no. 1 (1924), 35: 'We certainly have to do here with a very antique ceremony, which had become a mere piece of inert ritual so long before what we may call historical times that all remembrance of its origin and meaning had utterly vanished.'

202 *Notes*

73 'In fact, the last five days of February, after Terminalia, do not belong neither to this month nor to the year gone by. They do not belong to the following year either, which, according to a consolidated tradition inscribed in the numbering from *Quinctilis* to *December*, does not begin until the calends of March. *They are supernumerary between the two years*' (Magdelain, 'Cinq jours épagomènes à Rome?', 288, emphasis added). On the relevance of the annual cycle for the Romans, see Mircea Eliade, *A History of Religious Ideas. II. From Gautama Buddha to the Triumph of Christianity* (Chicago and London: University of Chicago Press, 1982), 113–14: 'For the Romans, as for rural societies in general, the ideal norm was manifested in the regularity of the annual cycle, in the orderly succession of the seasons. Every radical innovation constituted an attack on the norm; in the last analysis, *it involved the danger of a return to chaos*'; emphasis added.

74 Magdelain, 'Cinq jours épagomènes à Rome?' 296–7.

75 Eliade, *The Myth of the Eternal Return*, 54, emphasis added.

76 Ibid.

77 For a general discussion, see James G. Frazer, *The Golden Bough: A Study in Magic and Religion* (London: Macmillan, 1941), 264–83.

78 Eliade, *The Myth of the Eternal Return*, 55.

79 See James G. Frazer, *The Scapegoat* (London: Macmillan, 1913). See also, by the same author, *Lectures on the Early History of the Kingship* (London: Macmillan, 1905): 191–2: 'People feared that if they allowed the man-god to die of sickness or old age, his divine spirit might share the weakness of its bodily tabernacle, or perhaps perish altogether, thereby entailing the most serious dangers on the whole body of his worshippers who looked to him as their stay and support. Whereas, by putting him to death while he was yet in full vigour of body and mind, they hoped to catch his sacred spirit uncorrupted by decay and to transfer it in that state to his successor. Hence it has been customary in some countries, first, to require that kings should be of unblemished body and unimpaired mind, and second, to kill them as soon as they begin to break up through age and infirmity. A more stringent application of these principles led in other places to a practice of allowing the divine king or human god to live and reign only for a fixed period, after which he was inexorably put to death. The time of grace granted to limited monarchs of this sort has varied from several years to one year or even less. ... I conjecture that the King of the Wood at Nemi formerly reigned for a fixed period only, probably for a year, and that he had to slay himself or be slain at a great festival when his term of office was up.' It is important to note that, according to Frazer, the duration of the king's reign *mirrored the annual cycle*.

Notes 203

80 Merrill, 'The Roman Calendar and the *Regifugium*', 35–6.

81 Frazer, *Lectures on the Early History of the Kingship*, 282.

82 See Frazer, *The Golden Bough*, 283–9. On Mesopotamian kingship, see René Labat, *Le Caractère religieux de la royauté assyro-babylonienne* (Paris: Adrien-Maisonneuve, 1939), 98ff.; Henri Frankfort, *Kingship and the Gods: A Study of Ancient Near Eastern Religion as the Integration of Society and Nature* (Chicago: University of Chicago Press, 1948), 264: 'As the representative of the people, the king was threatened by every evil omen of importance. But his person was immensely precious because his election by the gods constituted a pledge of their support. Hence, when disaster seemed imminent, he was, as it were, temporarily withdrawn from his function; and a substitute was exposed to the danger or was sacrificed as the victim the supernatural powers seemed to require.'

83 There are at least two indications that support this thesis. First, and in general terms, many examples of royal substitutes 'show clearly that it is especially the divine or magical functions of the king which are transferred to his temporal substitute' (Frazer, *The Golden Bough*, 288). In this sense, precisely because they maintained the mediatory character of sovereignty ('Ministers of Agriculture' are defined by Frazer) and because they were intermediaries between nature and culture, they were exposed to the power of cyclicity, contingency and sacrifice. *Rex sacrorum* is no exception, since he, too, possessed divinatory and regulatory functions (see Macrobius, *Saturnalia* i, 15.9). Second, and more specifically, this interpretation allows us to shed light on the unexplained presence of the Salii (the 'leaping priests') during the festival of Regifugium or Fugalia (see Festus, *De verborum significatu*, 346 L). It is known that during the archaic period this ancient priestly order used to celebrate an annual ritual that closely recalls rites of purification and of passage from the old year to the new, although it has been interpreted in quite different ways. They would take oval shields (*ancilia*) out of the Temple of Mars and carry them in solemn precession (*ancilia movere*), then return them to the temple (*ancilia condere*). Even more important (though not entirely clear) is the link between this rite and the Mamuralia or Sacrum Mamurio ('The Festival for Mamurius'), a feast that ended the year and in which a scapegoat was beaten and dragged outside of the city walls. In their ritual hymn (*carmen saliare*, 'the song of the Salii'), the Salii invoked this obscure figure. Consequently, there would seem to be a relationship between the end-of-year rituals of purification and the propitiatory sacrifices that the Salii might have attended. On this, see vol. 5 of Hermann Usener's *Kleine Schriften*, which is entitled *Arbeiten zur Religionsgeschichte* (Leipzig und Berlin: B.G. Teubner, 1913), 122ff.

204   *Notes*

84   Frankfort, *Kingship and the Gods*, 262.

85   I intend to develop these theses at length in a future monograph.

86   Frazer, *Lectures on the Early History of the Kingship*, 280.

87   Ibid., 290.

88   Arthur M. Hocart, *Kingship* (London: Watts & Co., 1941), 24, emphasis added.

89   Frazer, *The Golden Bough*, 265.

90   Eliade, *The Myth of the Eternal Return*, 62.

91   Frazer, *The Golden Bough*, 278.

92   See, for example, Eric Voegelin, *The New Science of Politics: An Introduction* [1952] (Chicago and London: University of Chicago Press, 1987), 40–1: 'When articulation expands throughout society, the representative will also expand … Articulation, thus, is the condition of representation.'

93   Frazer, *Lectures on the Early History of the Kingship*, 30. Dionysius of Halicarnassus, *Roman Antiquities* iv, 74: 'For [the] principle by which the same person both rules and is ruled in turn and surrenders his authority before his mind has been corrupted restrains arrogant dispositions and does not permit men's natures to grow intoxicated with power. If we establish these regulations we should be able to enjoy all the benefits that flow from monarchy and at the same time to be rid of the evils that attend it. But to the end that the name, too, of the kingly power, which is traditional with us and made its way into our commonwealth with favourable auguries that manifested the approbation of the gods, may be preserved for form's sake, let there always be appointed a king of sacred rites, who shall enjoy the honour for life exempt from all military and civil duties and, like the "king" at Athens, exercising this single function, the superintendence of the sacrifices, and no other.'

94   Thomas Hobbes, *The Elements of Law: Natural and Politic* [1640] (London: Routledge, 2013), 93.

95   Thomas Hobbes, *De cive* [1642] (Oxford: Oxford University Press, 1983), 24.

96   For a detailed discussion, see Chapter 2.

Chapter 2

1   Michel Foucault, *The Order of Things: An Archaeology of the Human Sciences* [1966], trans. Alan M. Sheridan Smith (New York: Vintage Books, 1994), xxii.

2   Michel Foucault, *Madness and Civilization: A History of Insanity in the Age of Reason* [1961], trans. Richard Howard (New York: Vintage Books, 1988), 288.

Notes 205

3   Michel Foucault, *The Archaeology of Knowledge* [1969], trans. Alan M. Sheridan Smith (New York: Vintage Books, 2010), 193–4.

4   See, most notably, Carl Schmitt, *Theodor Däublers 'Nordlicht': Drei Studien über die Elemente, den Geist und die aktualität des Werkes* [1916] (Berlin: Duncker & Humblot, 1991); Walter Benjamin, *The Origin of German Tragic Drama* [1963], trans. John Osborne (London: Verso, 2003); Foucault, *The Order of Things*; Theodor Adorno, *Aesthetic Theory* [1970], trans. Robert Hullot-Kentor (London: Continuum, 2002). For a more historical account, see Erwin Panofsky, *Perspective as Symbolic Form* [1927], trans. Christopher S. Wood (New York: Zone Books, 1991); Ernst H. Gombrich, *Art and Illusion: A Study in the Psychology of Pictorial Representation* (London: Phaidon, 1960); Martin Jay, 'Scopic Regimes of Modernity', in *Vision and Visuality*, ed. Hal Foster (Seattle: Bay Press, 1988), 3–23; Carlo Ginzburg, *Wooden Eyes: Nine Reflections on Distance*, trans. Martin Ryle and Kate Soper (New York: Columbia University Press, 2001). For a more recent discussion of the relationship between politics and spatiality, see John G. Ruggie, 'Territoriality and Beyond: Problematizing Modernity in International Relations', *International Organization* 47, no. 1 (1993): 139–74; Michael Biggs, 'Putting the State on the Map: Cartography, Territory, and European State Formation', *Comparative Studies in Society and History* 41, no. 2 (1999): 374–411; John Pickles, *A History of Spaces: Cartographic Reason, Mapping, and the Geo-Coded World* (New York: Routledge, 2004); Jens Bartelson, *Sovereignty as Symbolic Form* (London and New York: Routledge, 2014).

5   See, for instance, John Milbank, Catherine Pickstock and Graham Ward, eds., *Radical Orthodoxy* (London and New York: Routledge, 1999).

6   Pavel Florensky, 'The Church Ritual as a Synthesis of the Arts' [1922], in *Beyond Vision: Essays on the Perception of Art* (London: Reaktion Books, 2002), 106.

7   Ibid., 104.

8   Carl Schmitt, *Land and Sea* [1954], trans. Simona Draghici (Washington, DC: Plutarch Press, 1997), 36.

9   Carl Gustav Jung, *The Collected Works of C.G. Jung, Volume 1: Psychiatric Studies*, ed. Herbert Read, Michael Fordham and Gerhard Adler, trans. R.F.C. Hull (New York: Routledge, 1970), 100.

10   Michel de Certeau, *The Practice of Everyday Life*, trans. Steven F. Rendall (Los Angeles: University of California Press, 1984), ix.

11   Cf. Giorgio Vasari, *The Lives of the Artists* [1568], trans. Julia Conaway Bondanella and Peter Bondanella (New York: Oxford University Press, 1998), 57. In line with Vasari, in this chapter I use the terms 'modern' and 'modernity'

in their literal and etymological sense. When Vasari, for example, writes that Masaccio 'gave birth to that *modern style* which has been followed from those times down to our own day by all our artists', by 'modern' he meant not only the Latin postclassical *modernus*, which was a derivative of the adverb *modo* ('now', in one of its senses; and hence equivalent with *hodiernus*), but also 'belonging to a *modus*', that is to a measure or form; for him *modernus* was reminiscent of both these words. Hence it designated something that is contemporary and pushed the limits, perfected the forms and renewed the canons (*modi*) of representing.

12 The first four decades of the life of Tommaso di Cristoforo Fini, known as Masolino, are shrouded in mystery. Even his place of birth is uncertain. In a pioneering monograph dedicated to Masolino's work, Pietro Toesca writes: 'He was born in 1383; in 1424, he registered in the Guild of Apothecaries and worked in Empoli for the Fellowship of the Holy Cross; in 1427, he was in Hungary where he worked for Pippo Spano, the Hospodar of Temesvár, the adventurous Florentine merchant confidant of Emperor Sigismund. Masolino probably died in 1447' (*Masolino da Panicale* (Bergamo: Istituto italiano d'arti grafiche, 1908), 11). We do not know with certainty whether Masolino died in 1440 or 1447; see Paul Joannides, *Masaccio and Masolino: A Complete Catalogue* (London: Phaidon, 1993), 34: 'The record in the Florentine *libro dei morti* [book of the dead] of a Maso di Cristofano in either 1440 or 1447 may or may not refer to Masolino, but of the two dates the earlier is more likely.'

13 Vasari, *The Lives of the Artists*, 106.

14 Joannides, *Masaccio and Masolino*, 7.

15 Toesca, *Masolino*, 2.

16 Joannides, *Masaccio and Masolino*, 61.

17 For a discussion, see the magisterial work of Roberto Longhi, 'Masolino and Masaccio', in *Three Studies*, trans. David Tabbat and David Jacobson (New York: Stanley Moss-Sheep Meadow Book, 1995), 1–91. Cf. also Ornella Casazza, *Masaccio and the Brancacci Chapel* (Siena: Scala, 1990).

18 Vasari, *The Lives of the Artists*, 105.

19 In discussing the frescoes in San Clemente – which, according to him, show qualities that are inferior to the Brancacci Chapel frescoes (in terms of 'the science of composition and narrative, the grandeur of the landscape, the art of perspective') – Vasari comes to believe that Masaccio painted the former. See Toesca, *Masolino*, 67.

20 Vasari, *The Lives of the Artists*, 102, emphasis added.

21 Ibid., 101.

22 Ibid., 102.

23 Ibid., 57, emphasis added.

24 Ibid., 104.

25 Toesca, *Masolino*, 67. See also August Schmarsow, *Masaccio Studien* (Kassel: T.G. Fisher, 1895), 76.

26 It is not by chance that Alberti, in his very influential work on perspective, *De pictura* (1435), recognizes in Brunelleschi, 'in our great friend the sculptor Donatello', and in Masaccio 'a genius for every laudable enterprise in no way inferior to any of the ancients who gave fame in this arts'. Masolino, it goes without saying, is not even mentioned. See Leon Battista Alberti, *On Painting* (London: Penguin, 2004), 34.

27 Vasari, *The Lives of the Artists*, 105.

28 Joannides, *Masaccio and Masolino*, 417.

29 Ibid., 418.

30 Ibid., emphasis added.

31 Ibid.

32 Ibid., emphasis added.

33 Ibid., emphasis added.

34 Ibid., 419.

35 Toesca, *Masolino*, 70.

36 Vasari, *The Lives of the Artists*, 105.

37 Pavel Florensky, 'Reverse Perspective', in *Beyond Vision*, 239.

38 The Bible and the 'Church' in St Jerome's hands, as well as St John's cross and column, are symbols and not mere simulacra – that is naturalistic representation of objects.

39 From a historical and ecclesiastical standpoint, the Colonna Altarpiece is extremely relevant. In 1417 the election of Pope Martin V had ended the Western Schism and restored Rome as official apostolic seat. The pope, once returned back to the Eternal City, proclaimed a Jubilee in 1423 in order to bring it to its former glory. It is in this climate that the work was probably commissioned.

40 Florensky, 'Reverse Perspective', 208–9 and 216.

41 On this point it is worth citing Bernard Berenson's critical remarks on naturalism: 'What is a Naturalist? I venture upon the following definition: A man with a native gift for science who has taken to art. His purpose is not to extract the material and spiritual significance of objects, thus communicating them to us more rapidly and intensely than we should perceive them ourselves, and thereby giving us a sense of heightened vitality; his purpose is research, and his

communication consists in nothing but facts ... What the scientist who paints – the naturalist, that is to say – attempts to do is not to give us what art alone can give us, the life-enhancing qualities of objects, but a reproduction of them as they are. If he succeeded, he would give us the exact visual impression of the objects themselves; but art ... must give us not the mere reproductions of things but a quickened sense of capacity for realizing them' (Bernard Berenson, *The Italian Painters of the Renaissance*, vol. 2: *Florentine and Central Italian Schools* (London and New York: Phaidon, 1968), 18).

42 Florensky, 'Reverse Perspective', 218 and 216.

43 By linear perspective I refer to the 'mathematical system for creating the illusion of space and distance on a flat surface'. This definition is consistent with Leon Battista Alberti's intentions. However, linear perspective cannot be considered a mere artistic technique because, as I have tried to show, it presupposes a specific ontological vision. In the words of Alberti [emphasis added]: 'No one will deny that things which are not visible do not concern the painter, *for he strives to represent [imitar] only the things that are seen.*' The entire passage reads: '*Però che quelle cose che non sono comprese dall'occhio, non è alcuno che non confessi che elle non hanno niente che fare col Pittore. Conciossiachè il Pittore si affatica di imitar solamente quelle cose, che mediante la luce si possano vedere.*' All the quotations here come from Alberti, *On Painting*, 37. This 'scopic regime' is the hidden ontology of this new discourse of representation.

44 Florensky, *Reverse Perspective*, 264, emphasis in original.

45 Carl Schmitt, *Constitutional Theory* [1928], trans. Jeffrey Seitzer (Durham and London: Duke University Press, 2008), 239.

46 Ibid., 240.

47 Ibid., 240–1.

48 Ibid., 240.

49 Ibid., 242.

50 Ibid.

51 Ibid., 243.

52 Ibid., 247.

53 Thomas Hobbes, *The Leviathan or, The Matter, Form, and Power of a Common-Wealth Ecclesiastical and Civil* (London: Andrew Crooke, 1651), 87. For an in-depth discussion of Hobbes's doctrine of representation, see Chapter 1 in this volume.

54 On the influence of geometry on Hobbes's thought, see Johan Tralau, 'Leviathan, the Beast of Myth: Medusa, Dionysos, and the Riddle of Hobbes's Sovereign

Notes

Monster', in *The Cambridge Companion to Hobbes's Leviathan*, ed. Patricia Springborg (Cambridge: Cambridge University Press, 2007), 61–81.

55 Thomas Hobbes, 'Concerning Government and Society', in *English Works*, vol. 2, ed. Sir William Molesworth (London: John Bohn, 1841), iv.

56 Ibid.

57 Thomas Hobbes, 'Concerning Body', in *English Works*, vol. 1, ed. Sir William Molesworth (London: John Bohn, 1839), 10.

58 Ibid., 5.

59 Ibid., 4.

60 Ibid., 102, emphasis in original.

61 Martin Heidegger, *Bemerkungen zu Kunst – Plastik – Raum* (St. Gallen: Erker Verlag, 1996), 11.

62 Hobbes, 'Concerning Body', 102.

63 Ibid.

64 Ibid., 94.

65 Ibid., 405.

66 Frederick Copleston, *A History of Philosophy, Volume V. British Philosophy: Hobbes to Hume* (London: Bloomsbury, 2010), 25.

67 For Hobbes, *ceteris paribus*, imagination 'is nothing else but sense decaying, or weakened, by the absence of the object' (Hobbes, 'Concerning Body', 396).

68 Ibid., 448.

69 Ibid., 93.

70 It is known that, during his stay in Paris, Hobbes conducted intense visual experiments with a perspective glass, which was developed by the French mathematician Jean-François Nicéron (1613–46). The purpose of these experiments was to demonstrate the possibility of developing a visual unity in the plurality of subjective points of view, or 'to create a new image formed out of fragments of a different image ... an analogy for a higher state of awareness'. Here we encounter, once more, one of Hobbes's central concerns in the *Leviathan*: representation – that is how to 'transmute' the multitude of modern subjects (and their individual perspectives) into a new unity-in-plurality. On this, see Horst Bredekamp, 'Thomas Hobbes's Visual Strategies', in *The Cambridge Companion to Hobbes's Leviathan*, 42ff.

71 Hobbes, 'Concerning Body', 99, emphasis added.

72 Ibid., 98–100.

73 Ibid., 97.

74 Cf. Carl Schmitt, *The Leviathan in the State Theory of Thomas Hobbes: Meaning and Failure of a Political Symbol* [1938], trans. George Schwab and Herna

210 *Notes*

Hilfstein (Chicago: University of Chicago Press, 1996), 32. Schmitt's concept of representation originates here. As he writes in one of his first books, 'The state is not a construction made by people but, on the contrary, it is the state that transforms human beings into a construction ... because the sum of a hundred thousand individuals cannot elevate itself above the nature of what is summed' (Carl Schmitt, *Der Wert des Staates und die Bedeutung des Einzelnen* (Tübingen: Mohr), 1914, 93, 30).

75 Hobbes, *Leviathan*, 82, emphasis added.

76 Ibid., 137.

77 Schmitt, *The Leviathan*, 32.

78 Pavel Florensky cited in Victor Bychkov, *The Aesthetic Face of Being: Art in the Theology of Pavel Florensky*, trans. Richard Pevear and Larissa Volokhonsky (Crestwood, NY: St. Vladimir's Seminary Press, 1997), 70.

79 Carl Schmitt, *Roman Catholicism and Political Form* [1923], trans. Gary L. Ulmen (Westport, CT: Greenwood Press, 1996), 21.

80 Schmitt, *The Leviathan*, 34.

81 See Michel de Certeau, 'The Gaze Nicholas of Cusa', *Diacritics* 17, no. 3 (1987): 22: 'A property (or *perfectio*) is all the *more true* to the extent that it *disappears*; the more it escapes from view (that of the eyes, then even that of the intelligence), the more it approaches the "true", in such a way that at the extreme it is in a blind dazzling of the eyes of the body and of reason, in a point where the visible vanishes, that it can be the object of a *true telling* identical to a non-seeing or to a *believing*.'

82 Bredekamp, 'Thomas Hobbes's Visual Strategies', 40.

83 Cf. Florensky, 'Reverse Perspective', 262.

84 Ibid.

85 Ibid., 263.

86 Schmitt, *The Leviathan in the State Theory of Thomas Hobbes*, 33.

87 Martin Heidegger, 'The Age of the World Picture' [1950], in *Off the Beaten Track*, trans. Julian Young and Kenneth Haynes (Cambridge: Cambridge University Press, 2002), 66, emphasis added.

88 Interestingly, there is another version of *The Ideal City*: it is located in the Walters Art Museum in Baltimore and attributed to the same painter but, unlike the other, contains some human figures strolling through the centre of a square. However – and this is important for my argument – it has been demonstrated that the authenticity of the figures is questionable, as *they were painted over the final layer of the architectural scene*. See Richard Krautheimer, 'Le tavole

Notes   211

di Urbino, Berlino e Baltimora riesaminate', in *Rinascimento: da Brunelleschi a Michelangelo. La rappresentazione dell'architettura*, ed. Henry A. Millon and Vittorio Magnago Lampugnani (Milan: Bompiani, 1994), 238.

89   Martin Heidegger, 'The Question of Being', in *Philosophical and Political Writings*, ed. Manfred Stassen, trans. William Kluback and Jean T. Wilde (New York and London: Continuum, 2003), 128, emphasis added.

90   Ibid., 129.

91   Hobbes, *Concerning Body*, 10.

92   Cf. Florensky, *Reverse Perspective*, 209–10.

93   In Heidegger's own formulation, '*Warum ist überhaupt Seiendes und nicht vielmehr Nichts?*' Cf. Martin Heidegger, 'Was ist Metaphysik? [1929]', in *Wegmarken* (GA9), ed. Friedrich-Wilhelm von Herrmann (Frankfurt am Main: Vittorio Klostermann, 1976), 122.

Chapter 3

1   Cf. Max Weber, *The Methodology of the Social Sciences*, trans. Edward A. Shils (Glencoe, IL: Free Press, 1949), 55 and 112; Carl Schmitt, 'The Age of Neutralizations and Depoliticizations', in *The Concept of the Political* [1932], ed. George Schwab, trans. Matthias Konzen and John P. McCormick (Chicago, IL: The University Chicago Press, 2007), 82–9.

2   This is the guiding idea of the seminal works of Gary L. Ulmen, 'The Sociology of the State: Carl Schmitt and Max Weber', *State, Culture, and Society* 1 (1985): 3–57; and *Politischer Mehrwert: Eine Studie über Max Weber und Carl Schmitt* (Weinheim: VCH Acta humaniora, 1991). For a similar interpretation, which explores the Weber–Schmitt relation within the larger frame of the crisis of modernity, see Carlo Galli, *Genealogia della politica: Carl Schmitt e la crisi del pensiero politico moderno* (Bologna: il Mulino, 1996), 77–122.

3   See Catherine Colliot-Thélène, 'Carl Schmitt versus Max Weber: Juridical Rationality and Economic Rationality', in *The Challenge of Carl Schmitt*, ed. Chantal Mouffe (London: Verso, 1999), 142; Jürgen Habermas, 'Discussion on Value Freedom and Objectivity', in *Max Weber and Sociology Today*, ed. Otto Stammer (Oxford: Basil Blackwell, 1971), 66.

4   For an overview, see Kjell Engelbrekt, 'What Carl Schmitt Picked Up in Weber's Seminar: A Historical Controversy Revisited', *The European Legacy* 14, no. 6 (2009): 667–84.

5   See, for example, Ernst Topitsch, 'Max Weber and Sociology Today', in *Max Weber and Sociology Today*, 19.

6   See György Lukács, *The Destruction of Reason*, trans. Peter R. Palmer (London: Merlin Press, 1980), 652–61.

7   Colliot-Thélène, 'Carl Schmitt versus Max Weber', 138–41. I follow the analytical distinction developed by Colliot-Thélène but disagree with her conclusions. First, it is an oversimplification to describe Weber as an 'economist'. Second, it is misleading to stigmatize Weber's theory of rationalization as a teleological and irreversible process. Finally, as we shall see, if Schmitt, unlike Weber, openly fights against 'disenchantment', this is precisely because he 'ideologizes' politics and law in a way that would have been too one-sided for Weber. On Weber's analysis of rationalization, see the solid work of Johannes Weiss, 'On the Irreversibility of Western Rationalization and Max Weber's Alleged Fatalism', in *Max Weber, Rationality and Modernity*, ed. Sam Whimster and Scott Lash (London: Allen & Unwin, 1987), 154–63.

8   The basis of the essay is a lecture that Schmitt delivered in a seminar organized by his friend Ernst Forsthoff in the town of Ebrach on 23 October 1959. Along with Schmitt, other well-known scholars attended the meeting, including Joachim Ritter, Julien Freund, Reinhart Koselleck, Arnold Gehlen and Ernst-Wolfgang Böckenförde. The original theme of the seminar can be gleaned from its title: 'The Dissolution of the Unity of Science'; see Dorothee Mußgnug, Reinhard Mußgnug and Angela Reinthal, eds., *Ernst Forsthoff – Carl Schmitt. Briefwechsel 1926–1974* (Berlin: Akademie Verlag, 2007), 149. After Forsthoff's talk on 'Virtue and Value in the Theory of the State' (*Tugend und Wert in der Staatslehre*), the debate shifted on the topic of 'values'. Schmitt's contribution was first printed in a volume 'not for sale' dedicated to those who attended the seminar in Ebrach; see Carl Schmitt, *Die Tyrannei der Werte. Überlegungen eines Juristen zur Wert-Philosophie*, 200 copies (Stuttgart: Kohlhammer, 1960). A shorter German version was published, without Schmitt's approval, in the *Frankfurter Allgemeine Zeitung* 146 (27 June 1964). For this reason, the 'unaltered' (*unverändert*) document, with a new introduction, was included in a Festschrift in honour of Forsthoff's sixty-fifth birthday; see Carl Schmitt, 'Die Tyrannei der Werte', in *Säkularisation und Utopie. Ebracher Studien. Ernst Forsthoff zum 65 Geburstag*, ed. Sergius Buve (Stuttgart: Kohlhammer, 1967), 37–62. Schmitt borrows the expression 'tyranny of values' from Nicolai Hartmann's *Ethics*: 'Every value – when once it has gained power over a person – has the tendency to set itself up as sole tyrant of the whole human ethos, and indeed at the expense of other values,

Notes   213

even of such as are not inherently opposed to it' (Nicolai Hartmann, *Ethics*, vol.
2: *Moral values* [1926], trans. Stanton Coit (London: Allen and Unwin, 1932),
423). I have rendered the German word *Werte* as 'values' (and not as 'valours')
to respect Schmitt's intention. In a public interview given on 9 November 1982
(one of his last), Schmitt argued: 'The essay [*The Tyranny of Values*] focuses on
the conflict of values. I believe that value is a concept that leads inescapably to
economization. What is the highest value? An answer can be provided only if you
have already correctly economized. This is my thesis. These days even the newly
elected Pope John Paul II speaks of values even though he doesn't know what he
is talking about when he cites German philosophers such as Max Scheler. It is
so sad and I feel very sorry for this. What should we do? This is very dangerous'
(Carl Schmitt, *Un giurista davanti a se stesso: Saggi e interviste* (Vicenza: Neri
Pozza, 2005), 177–8).

9   Cf. Carl Schmitt, *Die Tyrannei der Werte* [1967], 3rd edn, rev. (Berlin: Duncker &
     Humblot, 2011), 42, where he acknowledges '*Webers intellektuelle Redlichkeit*'.

10   See the inaugural lecture delivered by Max Weber in May 1895 at Freiburg
     University: 'The Nation State and Economic Policy', in *Weber: Political Writings*,
     ed. Peter Lassman and Ronald Speirs (Cambridge: Cambridge University Press,
     2007), 27. On the different meanings of the Weberian notion of 'responsibility',
     see Guenther Roth, 'Max Weber's Ethics and the Peace Movement Today', *Theory
     and Society* 13, no. 4 (1984): 491–511.

11   For an in-depth discussion, see Chapter 4 in this volume.

12   Habermas, 'Discussion on Value Freedom and Objectivity', 66.

13   Lukács, *The Destruction of Reason*, 652. On Weber and Lukács, see Mary Gluck,
     Georg Lukács and His Generation, 1900–1918 (Cambridge, MA: Harvard
     University Press, 1985); and Marianne Weber, *Max Weber: A Biography* (New
     Brunswick, NJ: Transaction, 1988), 465–6.

14   See Meyer Schapiro, 'A Note on Max Weber's Politics', *Politics* 2, no. 2 (1945):
     44–8. For a defence, see Hans H. Gerth, 'Max Weber's Politics: A Rejoinder',
     Politics 3, no. 4 (1945): 119–20.

15   Leo Strauss, *Natural Right and History* (Chicago, IL: The University of Chicago
     Press, 1953), 42.

16   Reinhard Bendix and Guenther Roth, *Scholarship and Partisanship: Essays on
     Max Weber* (Berkeley, CA: University of California Press, 1971), 55.

17   Wolfgang J. Mommsen, *Max Weber and German Politics, 1890–1920*, trans.
     Michael S. Steinberg (Chicago, IL: The University of Chicago Press, 1984).

18   Ibid., 449.

19 Ibid., 382–3.

20 Ibid., xvii. It is not my intention to criticize Mommsen. Moreover, in the preface to the English edition, he acknowledges some of the limitations of his work: 'This book was written in a political climate of a rather specific kind, colored by the determination of a whole generation of Germans to make democracy work after all. Those historians who began their academic work in the 1950s were especially influenced by the West European and American examples; "reeducation" had left an intellectual mark on many of them. ... These historians tended to adopt a fundamentalist conception of democracy, which emphasized its base in the inalienable rights of natural law. ... The writing of this book was strongly influenced by this trend, and it undoubtedly owes some of its strengths, but possibly also some of its shortcomings, to the singular intellectual constellation that existed in the Federal Republic of Germany in the 1950s' (ibid., vii).

21 See, for example, Max Weber, 'Roscher and Knies and the Logical Problems of Historical Economics', in *Collected Methodological Writings*, ed. Hans Henrik Bruun and Sam Whimster, trans. Hans Henrik Bruun (New York: Routledge, 2012), 3–94. On the formal and substantive unity of Weber's work, see Sheldon S. Wolin, 'Max Weber: Legitimation, Method, and the Politics of Theory', *Political Theory* 9, no. 3 (1981): 401–24.

22 Max Weber, 'Critical Studies in the Logic of the Cultural Sciences', in *Collected Methodological Writings*, 140.

23 Schmitt, *Un giurista davanti a se stesso*, 34. See also Carl Schmitt, *Political Romanticism* [1919], trans. Guy Oakes (Cambridge, MA: MIT Press, 1985), 52: 'Modern philosophy is governed by a schism between thought and being, concept and reality, mind and nature, subject and object, that was not eliminated even by Kant's transcendental solution.'

24 John P. McCormick, 'Transcending Weber's Categories of Modernity? The Early Lukács and Schmitt on the Rationalization Thesis', *New German Critique* 75 (1998): 174. See also John P. McCormick, *Carl Schmitt's Critique of Liberalism* (Cambridge: Cambridge University Press, 1997), 31–82.

25 Cf. McCormick, 'Transcending Weber's Categories of Modernity?', 175–6.

26 Schmitt, *Die Tyrannei der Werte*, 42, emphasis added.

27 On this, see Ulmen, 'The Sociology of the State', 5.

28 Carl Schmitt, 'The Question of Legality' [1950], in *State, Movement, People. The Triadic Structure of the Political Unity*, ed. Simona Draghici (Corvellis, OR: Plutarch Press, 2001), 62.

Notes 215

29 Carl Schmitt, *Glossarium. Aufzeichnungen der Jahre 1947–1951* (Berlin: Duncker & Humblot, 1991), 113.

30 For an attempt to reconstruct the relationship between Weber and Schmitt, see McCormick, *Carl Schmitt's Critique of Liberalism*, 206–12.

31 Karl Löwith, 'The Occasional Decisionism of Carl Schmitt' [1935], in *Heidegger and European Nihilism*, ed. Richard Wolin, trans. Gary Steiner (New York: Columbia University Press, 1998), 144.

32 Schmitt, *Die Tyrannei der Werte*, 44–6.

33 In this short genealogical reconstruction of the concept of value, I take into account only those authors and works that are relevant for contextualizing Weber's and Schmitt's positions. For further discussion, see the entries 'valŏur' and 'valūe' in *Middle English Dictionary*, ed. Robert E. Lewis (Ann Arbour, MI: The University of Michigan Press, 1997), 501–3; *The Oxford English Dictionary*, vol. XIX, ed. John A. Simpson and Edmund S.C. Weiner (Oxford: Clarendon Press, 1989), 414–18; *Dictionnaire de l'ancienne langue française*, vol. X, ed. Frédéric Godefroy (New York: Krauss, 1961), 828–9; and the entry 'Wert' in *Historisches Wörterbuch der Philosophie*, Band XII, ed. Joachim Ritter and Rudolf Eisler (Basel: Schwabe, 2004), 556–91. For a good overview, see Franco Volpi, afterword to *La tirannia dei valori*, by Carl Schmitt (Milan: Adelphi, 2008), which I partially follow here.

34 José Ortega y Gasset, *Introducción a una estimative: Que son los valores?* [1923] (Madrid: Ediciones Encuentro, 2004), 11.

35 Max Weber, '"Objectivity" in Social Science and Social Policy', in *The Methodology of the Social Sciences*, 107. On Weber's reservations concerning the term 'value', see his letters to Marianne Weber and Heinrich Rickert, and the so-called Nervi's Fragment in Weber, *Collected Methodological Writings*, 374–5 and 413–14.

36 Schmitt, *Die Tyrannei der Werte*, 37. Schmitt borrows this idea from Martin Heidegger, 'Nietzsche's Word: "God Is Dead"' [1943], in *Off the Beaten Track*, ed. and trans. Julian Young and Kenneth Haynes (Cambridge: Cambridge University Press, 2002), 170. In fact Heidegger's influence on Schmitt's 'critique of values' is profound.

37 Plato, *Republic* 6, 508e1–2 (here from vol. 2 of James Adam's classic edition) (Cambridge: Cambridge University Press, 1902), 60.

38 Aristotle, *Politics* 1252ᵃ1–2 (here from the edition of Franz Susemihl and Robert D. Hicks) (London: Macmillan, 1894), 138.

39 Aristotle, *Ethica Nicomacheia* 1095ᵃ26–7 (here from John Burnet's edition) (London: Methuen, 1900), 9.

216 *Notes*

40 Thomas Aquinas, *Summa contra gentiles* (Turin: Marietti, 1862), 236.

41 Plotinus, *The Enneads*, trans. Stephen MacKenna (London: Faber and Faber, 1956), 620.

42 Thomas Hobbes, *Leviathan: A Critical Edition* [1651], vol. 2, ed. G.A.J. Rogers and Karl Schuhmann (London and New York: Continuum, 2005), 144. It is worth noting that in Hobbes's system there are no clear signs of the transition from 'the Good' (understood as an 'objective' fulcrum on which one could establish the Commonwealth) to 'value' (understood as an expression of 'free' subjectivities). As he writes, 'I observe the Diseases of a Common-wealth, that proceed from the poyson of seditious doctrines; whereof one is, That every private man is Judge of Good and Evil actions' (ibid., 255).

43 Cf. the Latin edition of 1668, Thomas Hobbes, *Leviathan. Sive de materia, forma, et postestate civitatis ecclesiasticæ et civilis* (Aalen: Scientia, 1961), 137.

44 Cf. Volpi, afterword to *La tirannia dei valori*, 82.

45 Immanuel Kant, *The Metaphysics of Morals* [1797], trans. Mary Gregor (Cambridge: Cambridge University Press, 1996), 230.

46 Ibid., 231.

47 Schmitt, *Die Tyrannei der Werte*, 12–14.

48 Friedrich Nietzsche, *The Will to Power*, trans. Walter Kaufmann and R.J. Hollingdale (New York: Vintage, 1968), 7.

49 Heidegger, 'Nietzsche's Word: "God Is Dead"', 169.

50 Nietzsche, *The Will to Power*, 9.

51 Ibid., 7.

52 Friedrich Nietzsche, *Untimely Meditations* [1873–76], trans. R.J. Hollingdale (Cambridge: Cambridge University Press, 2007), 78.

53 Friedrich Nietzsche, *Beyond Good and Evil*, trans. Judith Norman (Cambridge: Cambridge University Press, [1886] 2002), 21.

54 Heinrich Rickert, *The Limits of Concept Formation in Natural Science* [1902], trans. Guy Oakes (Cambridge: Cambridge University Press, 1986), 215–16.

55 Ibid., 223, emphasis added.

56 For a critical discussion, see Guy Oakes, *Weber and Rickert: Concept Formation in the Cultural Sciences* (Cambridge, MA: MIT Press, 1988).

57 It is worth citing a long passage from the 'Nervi fragment' in which Weber's intellectual distance from Rickert is evident: 'As soon as one tries to look for something different, something *objective*, behind the *fact* that, in any given instance, historical interest will be limited and graduated, one enters in the domain of *norms*; that is to say: one is then looking for a principle from which it

Notes

217

would be possible to deduce not only *what* should, once and for all, be the object of our interest, but [also] to what *degree* we sh[ould] graduate our interest in the various el[ements] of reality. Precisely that is in fact the meaning – translated into everyday terms – of the "value metaphysics" with which R[ickert] concludes. Here it must suffice to express doubts as to the possibility of grasping the *substance* of such norms, and simply to add that such doubts might be consistent with the view that the "absolute validity" of certain "values" (what we would call "interests") could be taken to be more than simply a *limiting* concept. The *logical* possibility of a "formal ethics" at least shows us that the *concept* of *norms* [covering] the infinite multiplicity of the object of these norms does not in itself guarantee that [such norms] can be formulated in *substance*' (Max Weber, 'Note marked "Rickerts 'Werthe'" (Rickert's "Values") (The "Nervi Fragment"), *c*.1902/1903', in his *Collected Methodological Writings*, 413–14, emphasis in original). For a discussion, see Hans Henrik Bruun, 'Weber on Rickert: From Value Relation to Ideal Type', *Max Weber Studies* 1, no. 2 (2001): 138–60.

58   Max Weber, 'Letter to Robert Wilbrandt, 2 April 1913', in *Collected Methodological Writings*, 406.

59   Cf. Weber, '"Objectivity" in Social Science and Social Policy', 103; 'The Meaning of "Value Freedom" in the Sociological and Economic Sciences', in *Collected Methodological Writings*, 314; and 'Science as a Profession and Vocation', in *Collected Methodological Writings*, 348.

60   Karl Löwith, 'Die Entzauberung der Welt durch Wissenschaft', *Merkur* 18 (1964): 509.

61   Regis A. Factor and Stephen P. Turner, 'The Limits of Reason and Some Limitations of Weber's Morality', *Human Studies* 2, no. 3 (1979): 304, emphasis added.

62   Ibid.

63   Max Weber, 'Science as a Vocation', in *From Max Weber: Essays in Sociology*, ed. Hans H. Gerth and Charles Wright Mills (New York: Oxford University Press, 1946), 147.

64   Ibid., 143.

65   Herbert Simon, *Reason in Human Affairs* (Stanford, CA: Stanford University Press, 1983), 5–7. For a similar view, see Carl Gustav Hempel, *Aspects of Scientific Explanation and Other Essays in the Philosophy of Science* (New York: Free Press, 1965), 81–96.

66   Nietzsche, *Beyond Good and Evil*, 13, emphasis in original.

67   Strauss, *Natural Right and History*, 42.

218   *Notes*

68 Ibid., 48, emphasis added.

69 It goes without saying that Strauss's interpretation is value-related and not universal. It is not a coincidence that Strauss uses examples of ideal-types in the Western ethical tradition (prostitution, bravery, nobility of spirit etc.) when he sets out to develop his own 'objective criticism' of Weber's position (cf. ibid., 53–4). In this regard, and to clarify the question of 'rationality' and its alleged objective foundation, it is worth quoting a passage from Heidegger's work: 'The [ratio] is by no means a just judge. It unscrupulously pushes everything not in conformity with it into the presumable swamp of the irrational, which it itself has staked out. Reason and its conceptions are only one kind of thinking and are by no means determined by themselves but by that which has been called thinking, to think in the manner of the ratio. That its dominance arises as rationalization of all categories, as establishing norms, as leveling in the course of the unfolding of European nihilism, provides food for thought, just as do the concomitant attempts at flight into irrational' (Martin Heidegger, 'The Question of Being' [1955], in his *Philosophical and Political Writings*, ed. Manfred Strassen (New York: Continuum, 2003), 122–3).

70 Weber, 'Science as a Vocation', 143.

71 Friedrich Nietzsche, *On the Genealogy of Morality* [1887], trans. Carol Diethe (Cambridge: Cambridge University Press, 2007), 119, emphasis in original.

72 Löwith, 'Die Entzauberung der Welt durch Wissenschaft', 509–10.

73 Karl Löwith, *Max Weber and Karl Marx* [1932] (London: Routledge, 1993), 76, emphasis added.

74 Weber, 'Science as a Profession and Vocation', 348.

75 Wilhelm Windelband, *An Introduction to Philosophy* [1914], trans. Joseph McCabe (London: T. Fisher Unwin, 1921), 326.

76 Löwith, *Max Weber and Karl Marx*, 18.

77 Weber, *The Methodology of the Social Sciences*, 57.

78 Rickert, *The Limits of Concept Formation*, 220.

79 Weber, *The Methodology of the Social Sciences*, 152.

80 Weber, 'Fragment on Formal Ethics', in *Collected Methodological Writings*, 421–2.

81 Max Weber, *Gesammelte Aufsätze zur Wissenschaftslehre* (Tübingen: J.C.B. Mohr/ Paul Siebeck, 1922), 468.

82 Schmitt, *Die Tyrannei der Werte*, 41.

83 Ibid., 45 and 39.

84 Max Scheler, *Formalism in Ethics and Non-Formal Ethics of Values: A New Attempt toward the Foundation of an Ethical Personalism* [1913–16], trans. Manfred S. Frings and Roger L. Funk (Evanston, IL: Northwestern University Press, 1973), 6.

Notes

85 Ibid., xxiv.

86 Schmitt, *Die Tyrannei der Werte*, 42.

87 Ibid., 46.

88 Cf. Weber, *Gesammelte Aufsätze zur Wissenschaftslehre*, 246: 'nur das formale Element gemeinsam, daß ihr Sinn darauf geht, uns eben die möglichen »Standpunkte« und »Angriffspunkte« der »Wertung« aufzudecken.' In the English editions of Weber's writings, the expression 'Angriffspunkte' is translated either as 'evaluative approaches' (Weber, *The Methodology of the Social Sciences*, 144) or as 'points of application' (Weber, *Collected Methodological Writings*, 157).

89 Weber, *The Methodology of the Social Sciences*, 121 and 124.

90 Isaiah Berlin, 'The Originality of Machiavelli', in *Against the Current: Essays in the History of Ideas*, ed. Henry Hardy (New York: Free Press, 2001), 74.

91 Cf. Weber, 'Parliament and Government in Germany under a New Political Order' [1918], in *Weber: Political Writings*, 219.

92 Schmitt, *The Concept of the Political*, 33.

93 Weber, *The Methodology of the Social Sciences*, 17–18, emphasis added.

94 Carl Schmitt, *Der Wert des Staates und die Bedeutung des Einzelnen* (Tübingen: Mohr, 1914), 4.

95 Ibid., 93, emphasis added.

96 Carl Schmitt, *The Crisis of Parliamentary Democracy* [1923], trans. Ellen Kennedy (Cambridge and London: MIT Press, 1988), 6.

97 Carl Schmitt, 'Ethic of State and Pluralistic State' [1930], in *The Challenge of Carl Schmitt*, ed. Chantal Mouffe (London: Verso, 1999), 203.

98 Löwith, 'The Occasional Decisionism of Carl Schmitt', 166.

99 On this, see Galli, *Genealogia della politica*.

100 Löwith, 'The Occasional Decisionism of Carl Schmitt', 153.

101 Weber, 'The Meaning of "Value Freedom" in the Sociological and Economic Sciences', 315.

102 Schmitt, *Die Tyrannei der Werte*, 54 (for all the quotations in this paragraph).

103 Jacob Taubes, *The Political Theology of Paul*, trans. Dana Hollander (Stanford, CA: Stanford University Press, 2004), 109.

104 Schmitt, *Der Wert des Staates und die Bedeutung des Einzelnen*, 108.

105 Theodor Däubler, *Hymne an Italien* [1916] (Leipzig: Insel-Verlag, 1919), 65: 'Der Feind ist unsre eigne Frage als Gestalt./Und er wird uns, wir ihn zum selben Ende hetzen./Doch aus der Volksbesonnenheit kommt Gewalt./Auf Vorgebirgen treffen sich verwandte Ahnen/Und bleiben stumm, wenn Flut an Flut zerprallt.'

220 *Notes*

Chapter 4

1 Carl Schmitt, *Der Begriff des Politischen. Text von 1932 mit einem Vorwort und drei Corollarien* [1932] (Berlin: Duncker & Humblot, 1963), 15. All translations from this work are mine.

2 As Schmitt puts it: 'What is said here serves only to "theoretically frame an incommensurable [*unermeßliches*] problem"' (ibid., 9).

3 See Carl Schmitt, *Glossarium: Aufzeichnungen der Jahre 1947–1951* (Berlin: Duncker & Humblot, 1991), 169.

4 Kenneth Waltz, *Man, the State and War: A Theoretical Analysis* [1959] (New York: Columbia University Press, 2001), 12.

5 Schmitt, *Der Begriff des Politischen*, 121: 'Wenn Hobbes von der *Natur* im Sinne von *Physis* spricht, denkt er antik, insofern ed die Kostanz der Arten unterstellt. Er denkt vor-evolutionistisch, vor-darwinistisch.'

6 Waltz, *Man, the State and War*, 224–5.

7 Carl Schmitt, 'The Age of Neutralizations and Depoliticizations' [1929], in *The Concept of the Political*, trans. Matthias Konzett and John P. McCormick (Chicago and London: The University of Chicago Press, 2007), 87.

8 Karl Löwith, *Meaning in History* (Chicago and London: University of Chicago Press, 1949), 4.

9 Thucydides, *The Peloponnesian War*, trans. Martin Hammond (New York: Oxford University Press, 2009), 12.

10 Schmitt, *Der Begriff des Politischen*, 64. Waltz distinguishes between permissive and efficient causes (see his *Man, the State and War*, 232). However, his analysis is completely devoid of Aristotle's conception of the four causes and of Weber's method of 'causal imputation'. See Max Weber, 'Critical Studies in the Logic of the Cultural Sciences' [1906], in *Collected Methodological Writings*, ed. Hans Henrik Bruun and Sam Whimster, trans. Hans Henrik Bruun (London and New York: Routledge, 2012), 139–84.

11 René Girard, *I See Satan Fall Like Lightning*, trans. James G. Williams (Maryknoll, NY: Orbis Books, 2001), 11.

12 René Girard, *Things Hidden since the Foundation of the World*, trans. Stephen Bann and Michael Metteer (Stanford, CA: Stanford University Press, 1987), 299–305.

13 René Girard, *Violence and the Sacred*, trans. Patrick Gregory (Baltimore, MD: The Johns Hopkins University Press, 1977), 145.

14 See Girard, *Things Hidden since the Foundation of the World*, 304: 'In the first place, … the mimetic rivals quarrel over an object, and the value of the object

Notes

221

increases by virtue of the greedy rivalry it inspires. This becomes detached from the object and comes to rest upon the obstacle that the adversaries constitute for one another.'

15 See Girard, *Violence and the Sacred*, 145: 'The statement that violence is "instinctive" adds nothing to our understanding of this strange and startling relationship; on the contrary, it only clouds the issue.' See also Jean-Pierre Dupuy, 'Mimésis et morphogénèse', in *René Girard et le problème du Mal*, ed. Michel Deguy and Jean-Pierre Dupuy (Paris: Grasset, 1982), 225–78; and Wolfgang Palaver, *René Girard's Mimetic Theory*, trans. Gabriel Borrud (East Lansing, MI: Michigan State University Press, 2013), 35.

16 See, for example, Leo Strauss's letter of 4 September 1932 to Carl Schmitt: 'The ultimate foundation of the Right is the principle of the natural evil of man; because man is by nature evil, he therefore needs *dominion*' (in Heinrich Meier, *Carl Schmitt and Leo Strauss: The Hidden Dialogue*, trans. J. Harvey Lomax (Chicago and London: The University of Chicago Press, 2006), 125).

17 Schmitt, *Der Begriff des Politischen*, 64.

18 Ibid., 121.

19 Carl Schmitt, *Ex Captivitate Salus. Erfahrungen der Zeit 1945/47* (Köln: Greven, 1950), 89–90.

20 Schmitt, *Der Begriff des Politischen*, 38.

21 René Girard, 'Mimesis and Violence', in *The Girard Reader*, ed. James G. Williams (New York: The Crossroad Publishing Company, 1996), 12.

22 Cf. Hans J. Morgenthau, *Scientific Man vs. Power Politics* (London: Latimer House Limited, 1947), 165. See also Alexandre Kojève, *Introduction to the Reading of Hegel*, trans. James H. Nichols, Jr. (Ithaca and London: Cornell University Press, 1969), 139: 'Only Man creates and destroys *essentially*. Therefore, the natural reality implies Time only if it implies a human reality. Now, man essentially creates and destroys in terms of the idea that he forms of the Future. And the idea of the Future appears in the real present in the form of a Desire directed toward another Desire – that is, in the form of a Desire for social *Recognition*. Now, Action that arises from *this* Desire engenders History.'

23 See Dupuy, 'Mimésis et morphogénèse', 233.

24 Schmitt, *Der Begriff des Politischen*, 38.

25 Ibid., 9.

26 See Augustine, *De natura boni, contra Manichaeos*, chs. 3–18.

27 See René Girard, *Quand ces choses commenceront ... Entretiens avec Michel Treguer* (Paris: Arléa, 1994), 196.

222 *Notes*

28 Dupuy, 'Mimésis et Morphogénèse', 232.

29 René Girard, 'The Goodness of Mimetic Desire', in *The Girard Reader*, 63. Palaver, *René Girard's Mimetic Theory*, 91.

30 Reinhold Niebuhr, *Christianity and Power Politics* (New York: Charles Scribner's Sons, 1940), 157.

31 Carl Schmitt, *Political Theology: Four Chapters on the Concept of Sovereignty* [1922], trans. George Schwab (Cambridge, MA: MIT Press, 1985), 57. See also Schmitt's discussion of 'original sin', in *Roman Catholicism and Political Form* [1923], trans. Gary L. Ulmen (Westport, CT: Greenwood Press, 1996), 7–9.

32 *'Item quia peccatum vel iniquitas non est appetitio naturarum malarum sed desertio meliorum, sic in Scripturis invenitur scriptum: "Omnis creatura Dei bona est". Ac per hoc et omne lignum quod in paradiso Deus plantavit, utique bonum est. Non ergo malam naturam homo appetivit cum arborem vetitam tetigit; sed id quod melius erat deserendo, factum malum ipse commisit'* (Augustine, *De natura boni*, ch. 34; emphasis added; all translations from this work are mine).

33 Ibid., ch. 7: 'To his most excellent creatures, that is, to rational spirits, God has granted the opportunity not to be corrupted if they do not wish to be – that is, if they remain obedient under the Lord their God and remain attached in this way to his incorruptible beauty'
(*Creaturis autem praestantissimis, hoc est rationabilibus spiritibus, hoc praestitit Deus ut si nolint, corrumpi non possint, id est si obedientiam conservaverint sub Domino Deo suo ac sic incorruptibili pulchritudini eius adhaeserint*).

34 Girard, 'The Goodness of Mimetic Desire', 64.

35 Schmitt, *Der Begriff des Politischen*, 38: 'Das Politische ... bezeichnet kein eigenes Sachgebiet, sondern nur den *Intensitätsgrad* einer Assoziation oder Dissoziation von Menschen.'

36 Carl Schmitt, *Theorie des Partisanen: Zwischenbemerkung zum Begriff des Politischen* [1963] (Berlin: Duncker & Humblot, 1975), 85.

37 Schmitt, *Der Begriff des Politischen*, 54, emphasis added.

38 See Carlo Galli, 'Carl Schmitt and the Global Age', *New Centennial Review* 10, no. 2 (2010): 2.

39 The influence of Augustine on Schmitt is significant, yet difficult to decipher. Schmitt often cites Augustine, but in an unsystematic way. In his polemic with Schmitt, Erik Peterson referred to Schmitt as the 'new Eusebius', and criticized him and his politicization of religion from an Augustinian standpoint. Schmitt, however, in his response to Peterson, argued that it is precisely in Augustine's work – namely in chapter 30 of *Civitas Dei*, Book 3 – that the problem of the

Notes 223

political emerges more clearly, thus tarnishing the purity of the 'theological'; see Carl Schmitt, *Political Theology II. The Myth of the Closure of Any Political Theology* [1970], trans. Michael Hoelzl and Graham Ward (Cambridge: Polity Press, 2010), 98–102. In short, the theological roots of Schmitt's thought are difficult to ascertain. On this, see William S. Durden, 'Public and Private Responsibility: Christianity and Politics in Carl Schmitt's *The Concept of the Political*', *Christianity & Literature* 60, no. 4 (2011): 561–79 and Mika Ojakangas, '*Potentia absoluta et potentia ordinata Dei*: On the Theological Origins of Carl Schmitt's Theory of Constitution', *Continental Philosophy Review* 45, no. 4 (2012): 505–17. In this chapter, however, I do not intend to explore the origins of Schmitt's political theology but rather his *theodicy*, that is the hidden assumptions of his conception of evil. In my view, there is a structural (and not substantive) analogy between Schmitt's and Augustine's thinking on the matter of theodicy. It goes without saying that this does not mean that they share a similar theology of peace and order; rather, Schmitt recovers the structure of Augustinian theodicy and applies it to a world completely immanentized and nihilistic or, as he puts it, to a world 'in need of salvation'.

40 *Proinde cum quaeritur unde sit malum, prius quaerendum est quid sit malum; quod nihil aliud est quam corruptio vel modi, vel speciei, vel ordinis naturalis. Mala itaque natura dicitur quae corrupta est: nam incorrupta utique bona est. Sed etiam ipsa corrupta, in quantum natura est, bona est; in quantum corrupta est, mala est* (Augustine, *De natura boni*, ch. 4, emphasis added).

41 This is how Schmitt describes the problem of stasis: 'The One – *to Hen* – is always in uproar – *stasiazon* – against itself – *pros heauton*' (Schmitt, *Political Theology II*, 122).

42 *Corruptio autem si omnem modum, omnem speciem, omnem ordinem rebus corruptibilibus auferat, nulla natura remanebit. Ac per hoc omnis natura quae corrumpi non potest summum bonum est, sicut Deus est. Omnis autem natura quae corrumpi potest, etiam ipsa aliquod bonum est: non enim posset ei nocere corruptio nisi adimendo et minuendo quod bonum est* (Augustine, *De natura boni*, ch. 6).

43 Schmitt, *Political Theology II*, 124.

44 For an in-depth discussion of Girard's understating of this concept, see Chapter 7 in this volume.

45 See Girard, *Things Hidden since the Foundation of the World*, 90; Palaver, *René Girard's Mimetic Theory*, 122–4; and, above all, Frans de Waal, *Good Natured: The Origins of Right and Wrong in Humans and Other Animals* (Cambridge, MA: Harvard University Press, 1996), 71–3.

46 Girard, *Things Hidden since the Foundation of the World*, 3.

47 René Girard, *Battling to the End: Conversations with Benoît Chantre*, trans. Mary Baker (East Lansing, MI: Michigan State University Press, 2010), 62.

48 Girard, *Things Hidden since the Foundation of the World*, 28–9.

49 Ibid., 37.

50 For a discussion, see, among others, Giorgio Agamben, *Homo Sacer: Sovereign Power and Bare Life*, trans. Daniel Heller-Roazen (Stanford, CA: Stanford University Press, 1998), 75–80.

51 See Girard, *Violence and the Sacred*, 115.

52 Girard, *Battling to the End*, ix.

53 Girard, *Things Hidden since the Foundation of the World*, 32.

54 Ibid., 53, emphasis added.

55 For a detailed account of these sacrificial practices, see Chapter 1 in this volume. See also James G. Frazer, *The Golden Bough: A Study in Magic and Religion*, abridged edition (London: Macmillan, 1941), 264–83.

56 Shakespeare, *Henry IV, Part 1* (Oxford: Oxford University Press, 1987), 271. It is not by chance that Shakespeare is one of Girard's favourite authors. The French scholar also published a study on the Bard titled *A Theatre of Envy: William Shakespeare* (New York: Oxford University Press, 1991).

57 With the notable exception of *Battling to the End*, most of Girard's work focuses on archaic religions and myths. On Schmitt's understanding of (political) modernity, see the magisterial work of Carlo Galli, *Genealogia della politica: Carl Schmitt e la crisi del pensiero politico moderno* (Bologna: il Mulino, 1996).

58 Cf. Carl Schmitt, *Der Nomos der Erde im Völkerrecht des Jus Publicum Europaeum* [1950] (Berlin: Duncker & Humblot, 1974), 13.

59 Carl Schmitt, *Der Wert des Staates und die Bedeutung des Einzelnen* (Tübingen: Mohr, 1914), 78–9; all translations from this work are mine.

60 Ibid., 85, emphasis added.

61 Girard, *Battling to the End*, 108.

62 Carl Schmitt, 'The Changing Structure of International Law', *Journal for Cultural Research* 20, no. 3 (2016): 310.

63 Carl Schmitt, *Constitutional Theory* [1928], trans. Jeffrey Seitzer (Durham and London: Duke University Press, 2008), 241.

64 Ibid., 243.

65 Girard, *Battling to the End*, xiii, xvi.

66 Ibid., xv.

67 René Girard, *Deceit, Desire and the Novel. Self and Other in Literary Structure* [1961], trans. Yvonne Freccero (Baltimore and London: The Johns Hopkins University Press, 1966), 286.

Notes

68 Girard, *Battling to the End*, xiv.

69 Cf. Palaver, *René Girard's Mimetic Theory*, 30.

70 Max Weber, 'Roscher and Knies and the Logical Problems of Historical Economics', in *Collected Methodological Writings*, 10.

71 Ibid., 5.

72 Charles S. Peirce, *Collected Papers of Charles Sanders Peirce: Elements of Logic*, ed. Charles Hartshorne and Paul Weiss (Cambridge, MA: Belknap Press of Harvard University Press, 1960), 496.

73 Schmitt, *Roman Catholicism and Political Form*, 10–21.

74 Schmitt, *Political Theology II*, 115.

75 See Chapter 5 in this volume. See also Carlo Galli, *Lo sguardo di Giano: Saggi su Carl Schmitt* (Bologna: il Mulino, 2008).

76 Carl Schmitt, 'Die Einheit der Welt' [1952], in *Staat, Großraum, Nomos: Arbeiten aus den Jahren 1916–1969*, ed. Günter Maschke (Berlin: Duncker & Humblot, 1995), 496–512.

77 Harold J. Berman, *Faith and Order: The Reconciliation of Law and Religion* (Cambridge: William B. Eerdmans Publishing, 2000), x.

78 Schmitt, 'The Age of Neutralizations and Depoliticizations', 94.

79 Carl Schmitt, *Land and Sea* [1954], trans. Simona Draghici (Corvallis, OR: Plutarch Press, 1997), 58.

80 Schmitt, 'The Age of Neutralizations and Depoliticizations', 94.

81 Schmitt, *Glossarium*, 110.

82 Schmitt, *Roman Catholicism and Political Form,* 17.

83 Schmitt, *Political Theology II*, 129.

84 See Schmitt, *Der Wert des Staates und die Bedeutung des Einzelnen*, 31; and Friedrich Nietzsche, *Beyond Good and Evil* [1886], trans. Judith Norman (Cambridge: Cambridge University Press, 2002), 21.

Chapter 5

1 Jürgen Habermas, 'Notes on Post-Secular Society', *New Perspectives Quarterly* 25, no. 4 (2008): 20.

2 For an in-depth discussion of the '(de)secularization debate', see the double special issue 'After Secularization', *Hedgehog Review* 8, no. 1/2 (2006).

3 Habermas, 'Notes on Post-Secular Society', 21.

4 Charles Taylor et al., *Multiculturalism: Examining the Politics of Recognition* (Princeton, NJ: Princeton University Press, 1994).

226   *Notes*

5   Jürgen Habermas and Joseph Ratzinger, *The Dialectics of Secularization: On Reason and Religion* (San Francisco, CA: Ignatius Press, 2006).

6   Habermas, 'Notes on Post-Secular Society', 29.

7   Ibid., 29. See also Jürgen Habermas, 'On the Relations between the Secular Liberal State and Religion', in *Political Theologies: Public Religion in a Post-Secular World*, ed. Hent de Vries and Lawrence E. Sullivan (New York: Fordham University Press, 2006), 251–60.

8   Habermas, 'Notes on Post-Secular Society', 28.

9   Ibid., 29.

10   For a discussion, see Chapter 1 in this volume.

11   For a discussion, see Sandro Mezzadra and Bret Neilson, *Border as Method, or, The Multiplication of Labor* (Durham, NC and London: Duke University Press, 2013).

12   It goes without saying that this problematic has been explored by many authors (e.g. Weber, Voegelin and Kantorowicz). However, as we shall see, Schmitt's work offers an original perspective on the problem of secularization.

13   *Republic*, Book 5, 462b; here in Tom Griffith's translation (Plato, *Republic* (Cambridge: Cambridge University Press, 2009), 160).

14   Ibid., Book 6, 500d (p. 205 in Griffin).

15   See Giorgio de Santillana, *The Origins of Scientific Thought: From Anaximander to Proclus, 600 B.C. to 500 A.D.* (Chicago, IL: University of Chicago Press, 1961).

16   Carlo Galli, *Political Spaces and Global War*, trans. Elisabeth Fay (Minneapolis: University of Minnesota Press, 2010), 9. See also Lewis Mumford, *The City in History: Its Origins, Its Transformation, and Its Prospects* (New York: Harcourt, 1989), 94–157.

17   See René Girard, *Violence and the Sacred*, trans. Patrick Gregory (Baltimore, MD: The Johns Hopkins University Press, 1977), 1–142.

18   Carl Schmitt, *Roman Catholicism and Political Form* [1923], trans. Gary L. Ulmen (Westport, CT: Greenwood Press, 1996), 19.

19   Carl Schmitt, 'The Visibility of the Church: A Scholastic Consideration', in *Roman Catholicism*, 51.

20   John 18:36.

21   As Schmitt puts it, 'Each time the forces of history cause a new breach, the surge of new energies brings new lands and new seas into the visual field of human awareness, the spaces of historical existence undergo a corresponding change. Hence, new criteria appear, alongside new dimensions of political and historical activity, new sciences, new social systems; nations are born or reborn.

Notes

227

This redeployment may be so profound and so sudden that it alters not only man's outlook, standards and criteria, but also the very contents of the notion of space. It is in that context that one may talk of a spatial revolution. Actually, all important changes in history more often than not imply a new perception of space. The true core of the global mutation, political, economic and cultural, lies in it' (Carl Schmitt, *Land and Sea* [1954], trans. Simona Draghici [Corvallis, OR: Plutarch Press, 1997], 29).

22 See Alexandre Koyré, *From the Closed World to the Infinite Universe* (Baltimore, MD: The Johns Hopkins University Press, 1957).

23 See Schmitt, *Land and Sea*, chapter 12. See also Galli, *Political Spaces*, 16–20.

24 Galli, *Political Spaces*, 17.

25 Carl Schmitt, *Carl Schmitt, Political Theology II. The Myth of the Closure of Any Political Theology* [1970], trans. Michael Hoelzl and Graham Ward (Cambridge: Polity Press, 2010), 114.

26 For a discussion, see Chapter 3 in this volume.

27 Carl Schmitt, 'The Age of Neutralizations and Depoliticizations' [1929], in *The Concept of the Political*, trans. Matthias Konzett and John P. McCormick (Chicago, IL: The University of Chicago Press, 2007), 89.

28 'Theologians, keep quiet on alien territory!'

29 Schmitt, *Political Theology II*, 114–15. See also Carl Schmitt, *The Nomos of the Earth in the International Law of the Jus Publicum Europaeum* [1950], trans. Gary L. Ulmen (New York: Telos Press, 2003), 121–6.

30 Cf. Gary L. Ulmen, 'Introduction', in Schmitt, *Roman Catholicism*, xvii.

31 Schmitt stresses the crucial difference that exists between the concept of *Repräsentation* (understood as 'public representation') and that of *Vertretung* (understood as 'private representation'). As he puts it, 'Representation is not a normative event, a process, and a procedure. It is, rather, something *existential*. To represent means to make an invisible being visible and present through a publicly present one … Representation can occur only in the *public* sphere. There is no representation that occurs in secret and between two people, and no representation that would be a "private matter." In this regard, all concepts and ideas are excluded that are essentially part of the spheres of the private, of private law, and of the merely economic … A parliament has representative character only so long as one believes that its actual activity lies in the public sphere' (Carl Schmitt, *Constitutional Theory* [1928], trans. Jeffrey Seitzer [Durham, NC and London: Duke University Press, 2008], 242–3).

32 See Schmitt, *Roman Catholicism*, 7–8.

228   *Notes*

33   Ibid., 21.

34   Carlo Galli, *Lo sguardo di Giano: Saggi su Carl Schmitt* (Bologna: il Mulino, 2008), 67; my translation. This point is missed by Habermas, who argues that his new post-secular genealogy 'renders futile the alternative presented by Carl Schmitt and Hans Blumenberg. In its political and spiritual forms, modernity is not a mere result of secularization' or 'a mere separation from the theological heritage to which it remains in opposition' (Habermas, 'A Post-Secular World Society?', 6).

35   As a matter of fact, modern political thought follows a monistic yet universalizing trajectory: the monarchic formula – 'one god, one king' – is initially replaced by the democratic one – 'one god, one people' – which, over time, translates into the idea of 'one god, one nation' and, finally, into the global motto 'one world, one humankind'.

36   See Carl Schmitt, *Political Theology: Four Chapters on the Concept of Sovereignty* [1922], trans. George Schwab (Cambridge, MA: MIT Press, 1985), 36. See also Thomas Hobbes, *Leviathan* [1651], ed. G.A.J. Rogers and Karl Schuhmann (London: Continuum, 2005), 256. In Hobbes's work, which, according to Schmitt, has conceptually 'completed' the Reformation, there is still openness to transcendence (even though this 'openness' to the sphere of the sacred is used instrumentally). On this, see Carl Schmitt, 'Die vollendete Reformation. Bemerkungen und Hinweise zu neuen Leviathan-Interpretationen', *Der Staat. Zeitschrift für Staatslehre, offentliches Recht und Verfassungsgeschichte* 4, no. 1 (1965): 51–69.

37   'In the struggle of opposing interests and coalitions, absolute monarchy made the decision and thereby created the unity of the state' (Schmitt, *Political Theology*, 48–9).

38   Ibid., 28 and 13.

39   Ibid., 21.

40   Ibid., 32.

41   Ibid., 13, emphasis added.

42   'In civitate constituta, legum naturæ interpretatio non a doctoribus et scriptoribus moralis philosopiæ dependent, sed ab authoritate civitatis. Doctrinæ quidem veræ esse possunt; sed authoritas, non veritas, facit legem.' Thomas Hobbes, *Leviathan, sive de materia, forma, et postestate civitatis ecclesiasticæ et civilis* [1668] (Aalen: Scientia, 1961), 202. 'The Interpretation of Lawes of Nature, in a Common-wealth, dependeth not on the books of Morall Philosophy. The

Authority of writers, without the Authority of the Common-wealth, maketh not their opinion Law, be they never so true.' Hobbes, *Leviathan*, 218.

43 Carl Schmitt, *Der Begriff des Politischen. Text von 1932 mit einem Vorwort und drei Corollarien* (Berlin: Duncker & Humblot, 1963), 122; all translations from this work are mine.

44 For a discussion, see Michael Marder, *Groundless Existence: The Political Ontology of Carl Schmitt* (New York: Continuum, 2010).

45 For a discussion, see Chapter 3 in this volume.

46 Carl Schmitt, 'Ethic of State and Pluralistic State' [1930], in *The Challenge of Carl Schmitt*, ed. Chantal Mouffe (London: Verso, 1999), 198.

47 Schmitt, 'Ethic of State', 203.

48 Schmitt, *The Concept of the Political*, 53.

49 Schmitt, 'Ethic of State', 196–7.

50 See Carl Schmitt, *State, Movement, People: The Triadic Structure of the Political Unity* [1933], trans. Simona Draghici (Corvallis, OR: Plutarch Press, 2001).

51 As Weber puts it, 'The right to use physical force is ascribed to other institutions or to individuals only to the extent to which the state permits it. The state is considered the sole source of the "right" to use violence' (Max Weber, 'Politics as a Vocation' [1919], in *From Max Weber: Essays in Sociology*, ed. and trans. Hans Heinrich Gerth and Charles Wright Mills [New York: Oxford University Press, 1946], 78).

52 Schmitt, *Der Begriff des Politischen*, 10.

53 Ibid., 11.

54 Schmitt, *Land and Sea*, 58.

55 See Carl Schmitt, 'Three Possibilities for a Christian Conception of History' [1950], *Telos*, trans. Mario Wenning, 147 (2009): 167–70.

56 See note 3 in this chapter.

57 Habermas, 'A Post-Secular World Society?', 9.

58 Ibid., 12.

59 Chantal Mouffe, 'Carl Schmitt and the Paradox of Liberal Democracy', in *The Challenge of Carl Schmitt*, 46.

60 Gerard Delanty, 'Habermas and Occidental Rationalism: The Politics of Identity, Social Learning and the Cultural Limits of Moral Universalism', *Sociological Theory* 15, no. 1 (1998), here 30.

61 Discussing the question of a European Constitution, Habermas had already argued in 1995: 'If in the same democratic political community various cultural, religious and ethnic forms of life are to exist among and with each other then the majority culture must be sufficiently detached from its traditional fusion with the *political*

230   *Notes*

culture shared by all citizens.' Jürgen Habermas, 'Remarks on Dieter Grimm's "Does Europe Need a Constitution?"', *European Law Journal* 1, no. 3 (1995): 306.

62 Schmitt, 'Ethic of State', 205.

63 For a similar critique, see Michael Reder, 'How Far Can Reason and Faith Be Distinguished?', in *An Awareness of What Is Missing. Faith and Reason in a Post-Secular Age*, ed. Jürgen Habermas et al. (Cambridge: Polity Press, 2010), 36–50.

64 See Albert O. Hirschman, *Exit, Voice and Loyalty* (Cambridge, MA: Harvard University Press, 1970).

65 Ernst-Wolfgang Böckenförde, 'The Rise of the State as a Process of Secularization', in *State, Society and Liberty: Studies in Political Theory and Constitutional Law*, trans. J. A. Underwood (New York: Berg, 1991), 44.

66 Jürgen Habermas, 'Prepolitical Foundations of the Democratic Constitutional State?', in Habermas and Ratzinger, *The Dialectics of Secularization*, 28.

67 Schmitt, 'Ethic of State', 207.

68 Ibid.

69 Ibid., 203.

70 Ibid., 201.

71 Karl Jaspers, *The Perennial Scope of Philosophy*, trans. Ralph Manheim (Hamden, CT: Archon Books, 1968), 94.

72 Carlo Galli, 'Introduzione', in *Multiculturalismo: ideologie e sfide*, ed. Carlo Galli (Bologna: il Mulino, 2006), 15; my translation.

73 Jaspers, *The Perennial Scope of Philosophy*, 180–1, emphasis added.

74 Mouffe, 'Carl Schmitt and the Paradox of Liberal Democracy', 51.

75 See, for example, Roberto Esposito, *A Philosophy for Europe: From the Outside*, trans. Zakiya Hanafi (Cambridge: Polity Press, 2018).

76 Mouffe, 'Carl Schmitt and the Paradox of Liberal Democracy', 51.

77 Aristotle, *Politics*, in *The Complete Works of Aristotle*, ed. Jonathan Barnes (Princeton, NJ: Princeton University Press, 1984), vol. 2, 1986 (= Book 1, 1252a).

78 Ibid., 2001 (= Book 2, 1261a).

79 Aristotle, *De intepretatione*, in *A New Aristotle Reader*, ed. J.L. Ackrill (Princeton, NJ: Princeton University Press, 1987), 14 (= ch. 4, 17a3–4).

80 Mouffe, 'Carl Schmitt and the Paradox of Liberal Democracy', 51.

81 Aldous Huxley, *The Perennial Philosophy* (London: Fontana Books, [1946] 1961), 9.

82 See Harold J. Berman, *Faith and Order: The Reconciliation of Law and Religion* (Atlanta, GA: Scholar Press, 1993); and more recently, Paolo Prodi, *Una storia*

della giustizia: Dal pluralismo dei fori al moderno dualismo tra coscienza e diritto (Bologna: il Mulino, 2000).

83 Schmitt, 'Ethic of State', 206.

84 Jaspers, *The Perennial Scope of Philosophy*, 182.

Chapter 6

1 Émile Durkheim, *The Elementary Forms of Religious Life* [1912], trans. Karen E. Fields (New York: Free Press, 1995), 34.

2 Ibid., 321 and 224.

3 Ibid., 322.

4 Ibid., 328.

5 Ibid.

6 Ibid., 327.

7 Claude Lévi-Strauss, *Totemism*, trans. Rodney Needham (Harmondsworth: Penguin Books, 1969), 170 (for both quotations).

8 Ibid.

9 See, Claude Lévi-Strauss, *Structural Anthropology*, trans. Claire Jacobson and Brooke Grundfest Schoepf (New York: Basic Books, 1963), 206–31.

10 Lévi-Strauss, *Totemism*, 175.

11 Mircea Eliade, *Patterns in Comparative Religion* [1949], trans. Rosemary Sheed (Lincoln and London: University of Nebraska Press, 1996), 2.

12 Ibid., 13.

13 Ibid., 5 and 13.

14 See Lévi-Strauss, *Structural Anthropology*, 21: 'If, as we believe to be the case, the unconscious activity of the mind consists in imposing forms upon content, and if these forms are fundamentally the same for all minds – ancient and modern, primitive and civilized (as the study of symbolic function, expressed in language, so strikingly indicates) – it is necessary and sufficient to grasp the unconscious structure underlying each institution and each custom in order to obtain a principle of interpretation valid for other institutions and other customs, provided, of course, that the analysis is carried far enough.'

15 Michel Foucault, 'Nietzsche, Genealogy, History', in *Aesthetics, Method, and Epistemology*, ed. James D. Faubion, trans. Robert Hurley (New York: The New Press, 1998), 370.

232   *Notes*

16 Giorgio Agamben, *The Signature of All Things: On Method*, trans. Luca D'Isanto and Kevin Attell (New York: Zone Books, 2009), 89.

17 Ibid., 110.

18 Ibid., 98.

19 René Girard with Pierpaolo Antonello and João Cezar de Castro Rocha, *Evolution and Conversion: Dialogues on the Origins of Culture* (London: Continuum, 2008), 98.

20 Carl Schmitt, 'The Age of Neutralizations and Depoliticizations' [1929], trans. Matthias Konzett and John P. McCormick, in *The Concept of the Political*, ed. George Schwab (Chicago, IL: The University of Chicago Press, 2007), 85.

21 Ludwig Wittgenstein, *Tractatus Logico-Philosophicus* [1921] (London: Routledge, 2001), 82 (= *Tractatus* 6.341).

22 Girard et al., *Evolution and Conversion*, 97.

23 René Girard, *Things Hidden since the Foundation of the World*, trans. S. Bann and M. Metteer (Stanford, CA: Stanford University Press, 1987), 94.

24 Ibid., 94–5, emphasis added.

25 Ibid., 102, emphasis added.

26 Ibid., 99.

27 Ibid., 226, emphasis added.

28 René Girard, *Battling to the End: Conversations with Benoît Chantre*, trans. Mary Baker (East Lansing: Michigan State University Press, 2010), ix, 21.

29 Giorgio Agamben, *Homo Sacer: Sovereign Power and Bare Life*, trans. Daniel Heller-Roazen (Stanford, CA: Stanford University Press, 1998), 73.

30 Ibid., 74.

31 Ibid., 182.

32 Giorgio Agamben, *The Sacrament of Language: An Archaeology of the Oath*, trans. Adam Kotsko (Stanford, CA: Stanford University Press, 2011), 13, 28.

33 Girard et al., *Evolution and Conversion*, 104, 107.

34 Agamben, *The Sacrament of Language*, 68–9.

35 Ibid., 71.

36 Giorgio Agamben, *The Use of Bodies*, trans. Adam Kotsko (Stanford, CA: Stanford University Press, 2016), 264.

37 Ibid., 208.

38 Agamben, *The Signature of All Things*, 92.

39 René Girard, *I See Satan Fall Like Lightning*, trans. James G. Williams (Maryknoll, NY: Orbis Books, 2001), 92, 97–9.

Notes 233

40 Giorgio Agamben, *The Kingdom and the Glory: For a Theological Genealogy of Economy and Government*, trans. Lorenzo Chiesa (Stanford, CA: Stanford University Press, 2011), 142–3, emphasis added and translation slightly modified.

41 Cf. Girard et al., *Evolution and Conversion*, 182–5; Agamben, *The Signature of All Things*, 68–70.

42 Carlo Ginzburg, *Clues, Myths and the Historical Method*, trans. John and Anne C. Tedeschi (Baltimore, MD: The Johns Hopkins University Press, 1989), 97–8.

43 Girard et al., *Evolution and Conversion*, 183.

44 Agamben, *The Signature of All Things*, 70.

45 The relationship between signified and signifier is based on intentionality, even when the purpose of an action is not 'shared' or 'consciously' pursued. Pavel Florensky has argued for this in the following manner: 'When we hear on the other side of a wall a noise in which we distinguish a certain articulation, we deduce that there are people *talking*. In this sense, we also affirm the conscious and finalized articulation of sounds. On the contrary, we "deny" a *human* origin to those sounds that are *not* finalized, or that are unintentional. Could those sounds come from a human being without having a purpose? Of course; but then they would lose their purely human character, thus becoming – despite coming *from* a human being – sounds of nature. Similarly, at the beginning of the nineteenth century, Boucher de Perthes unearthed fragments of flint in the quarry of Moulin-Quignon. The scientific discussion that ensued consisted in determining whether those "traces" were the work of *humans* or only random fragments. What does all this mean? If they were the work of humans, they would have built intentionally, with a purpose. Moreover: if they were built with a purpose, they would have a specific *use*, meaning that human beings lived there, in the quarry of Moulin-Quignon' (Pavel A. Florensky, *Il simbolo e la forma: Scritti di filosofia della scienza* [Turin: Bollati Boringhieri, 2007], 129; my translation).

46 This type of explanation is in fact called 'teleological'. See Carl G. Hempel and Paul Oppenheim, 'Studies in the Logic of Explanation', *Philosophy of Science* 15, no. 2 (April 1948): 135–75.

47 Max Weber, *Methodology of Social Sciences*, trans. Edward A. Shils and Henry A. Finch (Glencoe, IL: Free Press, 1949), 81, emphasis added.

48 See Girard et al., *Evolution and Conversion*, 98.

49 For a discussion, see Max Weber, 'Critical Studies in the Logic of the Cultural Sciences', trans. Hans H. Bruun, in *Collected Methodological Writings*, ed. Hans H. Bruun and Sam Whimster (London and New York: Routledge, 2012), 151–2.

50 Ginzburg, *Clues, Myths and the Historical Method*, xix.

51 Ibid., emphasis added.

52 For a critique, see also Chapter 4 in this volume.

53 Agamben, *The Use of Bodies*, 133.

54 Cf. Hempel and Oppenheim, 'Studies in the Logic of Explanation', 144.

55 Girard et al., *Evolution and Conversion*, 125.

56 See, for example, Agamben, *The Kingdom and the Glory*, 140–1: '[The] "gnostic" structure, which the theological *oikonomia* has transmitted to modern governmentality, reaches its apex in the paradigm of the government of the world that the great Western powers (in particular, the United States) try today to put into practice on both a local and a global scale. Independently of whether what is at stake is the breakup of preexisting constitutional forms or the imposition, through military occupation, of so-called democratic constitutional models on peoples for whom these models turn out to be unworkable, the basic point is that a country – and even the entire world – is being governed by remaining completely extraneous to it. The tourist, which is the radical reincarnation of the Christian *peregrinus in terra*, is the planetary figure of this irreducible extraneousness with regard to the world. In this sense, he is a figure whose "political" meaning is consubstantial with the prevailing governmental paradigm, just as the *peregrinus* was the figure that corresponded to the providential paradigm. In other words, the pilgrim and the tourist are the collateral effects of the same "economy" (in its theological and secularized versions).' Girard, too, believes that it is possible 'to proceed back beyond Western civilization itself and point straight to the real motor of the revelatory yet menacing dynamic that animates the whole of this civilization' (Girard, *Things Hidden since the Foundation of the World*, 138).

57 Agamben, *The Use of Bodies*, 111, emphasis added.

58 Agamben, *The Sacrament of Language*, 69.

59 Agamben, *The Signature of All Things*, 89.

60 For a discussion, see Antonio Cerella, 'Images of the World: Ontology and History in the Work of Foucault, Schmitt and Heidegger', in *Heidegger and the Global Age*, ed. Antonio Cerella and Louiza Odysseos (London and New York: Rowman and Littlefield International, 2017), 109–36.

61 See Henry Corbin, 'Mundus imaginalis ou l'imaginaire et l'imaginal', *Cahiers internationaux de symbolisme* 6 (1964): 3–26.

Notes 235

Chapter 7

1 See the International Convention on Maritime Search and Rescue (SAR), available at https://treaties.un.org/doc/publication/unts/volume%201405/volume-1405-i-23489-english.pdf (accessed 12 May 2018).

2 On this story, see Fulvio Vassallo, 'Ancora sotto accusa chi salva la vita in mare', available at http://www.meltingpot.org/Ancora-sotto-accusa-chi-salva-la-vita-in-mare.html#.VWSA-GTBzGd (accessed 12 May 2018). For a broader account of migration policy in Southern Europe, see Russell King and Daniela DeBono, 'Irregular Migration and the "Southern European Mode" of Migration', *Journal of Mediterranean Studies* 22, no. 1 (2013): 1–31; Daniela DeBono, '"Less than Human": The Detention of Irregular Immigrants in Malta', *Race and Class* 55, no. 2 (2013): 60–81.

3 Giorgio Agamben, *Means without End: Notes on Politics*, trans. Vincenzo Binetti and Cesare Casarino (Minneapolis and London: Minnesota University Press, 2000), 5.

4 The fact that 'migrants' often renounce their identity and documents (passports, IDs etc.) to get more chances to stay in a host country, thus inscribing themselves into the 'lap of sovereignty', shows the close relationship that exists today between freedom of movement and biopolitical subjection. For a critical discussion, see Sandro Mezzadra and Brett Neilson, *Border as Method, or, The Multiplication of Labor* (Durham, NC and London: Duke University Press, 2013), 142–50. See Nicholas De Genova and Natalie Peutz, eds., *The Deportation Regime: Sovereignty, Space, and the Freedom of Movement* (Durham, NC and London: Duke University Press, 2010).

5 Hannah Arendt, *The Origins of Totalitarianism* [1951] (New York: Harcourt Brace & Company, 1976), 284, emphasis added.

6 See Michael Dillon, 'The Scandal of the Refugee', in *Moral Spaces: Rethinking Ethics and World Politics*, ed. David Campbell and Michael J. Shapiro (Minneapolis: Minnesota University Press, 1999), 92–124.

7 As Agamben stated in an interview, 'those who are detained in these centers do not have any legal status assigned. *It is as if their physical existence had been separated from their legal status*' (Giorgio Agamben and Beppe Caccia, 'Nei campi dei senza nome', *Il Manifesto*, 3 November 1998, emphasis added).

8 Giorgio Agamben, *Homo Sacer: Sovereign Power and Bare Life*, trans. Daniel Heller-Roazen (Stanford, CA: Stanford University Press, 1998), 176, emphasis added.

236   *Notes*

9   For a good discussion, see Federico Rahola, *Zone definitivamente temporanee. I luoghi dell'umanità in eccesso* (Verona: Ombre Corte, 2003).

10   'A Top Pentagon Lawyer Faces a Senate Grilling on Torture', *Newsweek*, 5 April 2008. See also John Yoo, 'Commentary: Behind the "Torture Memos"', *UC Berkeley News*, 2 January 2005, available at https://www.berkeley.edu/news/ media/releases/2005/01/05_johnyoo.shtml (accessed 12 May 2018).

11   For an account of the so-called First Special Interrogation Plan, see the official log (kept by the US government) of Mohammed al-Qahtani's interrogation in Guantánamo, which is available at http://ccrjustice.org/home/get-involved/tools-resources/publications/publication-torture-mohammed-al-qahtani (accessed 12 May 2018).

12   Human Development Report (New York and Oxford: Oxford University Press, 1994), 23, emphasis added.

13   This is the crux of the 'responsibility to protect' doctrine: How can universal principles be concretized? By whom and where? As a matter of fact, 'humanitarian intervention' is constantly exposed to the risk of falling prey to universalist ideologies, power politics (e.g. the Israeli–Palestinian conflict), national interests (e.g. the civil war in Syria) and geo-political selectivity (e.g. the military intervention in Libya in 2011). For an overview, see James Pattison, *Humanitarian Intervention and the Responsibility to Protect: Who Should Intervene?* (Oxford: Oxford University Press, 2012); Aidan Hehir, *The Responsibility to Protect: Rhetoric, Reality and the Future of Humanitarian Intervention* (Basingstoke: Palgrave Macmillan, 2012).

14   Agamben, *Means without End*, 20.

15   Ibid.

16   Agamben, *Homo Sacer*, 9–10.

17   Agamben, *Means without End*, 39.

18   See in particular Giorgio Agamben, *State of Exception*, trans. Kevin Attell (Chicago, IL: University of Chicago Press, 2005).

19   Agamben, *Means without End*, 43.

20   In the last volume of the *Homo Sacer* project, Agamben has traced, genealogically, the structure of the exception back to 'first ontology' and to the 'event of language'. See Giorgio Agamben, *The Use of Bodies*, trans. Adam Kotsko (Stanford, CA: Stanford University Press, 2016), 111. In this regard, the present analysis distances itself from Agamben's, who in my view has not been able to clarify fully the genealogical relationship between ontology and history, between the individual (ontogeny) and the species (phylogeny), and between thinking and

Notes

237

action but has limited his speculations to a *formal* analogy that exists between the logic of inclusion–exclusion, the structure of language and (Western) politics. For a critical discussion, see Chapter 6 in this volume.

21 Acts of Apostles 6:5–8, 7:52–9.

22 As is well known, the term 'martyr' comes from the ancient Greek noun μάρτυς, 'witness' (pl. μάρτυρες). In early Christianity this description was applied to the apostles – those who witnessed the life and truth of Christ. During the period of Roman persecution, 'martyrs' (*martures*) were those who bore witness to their faith through the sacrifice of life, while those who had suffered persecution without losing their life where called 'confessors'. My interpretation of martyrdom here follows the work of Stefano Salzani, 'La città dei martiri: *bios* e *zoe aionios*', *Teologia politica* 3 (2007): 177–205.

23 Jacobi a Voragine, *Legenda aurea. Vulgo historia lombardica dicta* (Lipsiae: Impensis Librariae Arnoldianae, 1850), 49, my translation.

24 In my view, the perspective opened by René Girard in his *Violence and the Sacred* is not comprehensive enough and needs to be complemented. For in Girard's work sacrifice is always conceived of as an *expiatory* practice; even the crucifixion is, for him, a *universal form of expiation* – that is, the unveiling of the mechanism of the sacred. Sacrifice is a foundational practice because it discharges the tensions that cross human desires. And yet, as I will try to show, early Christian martyrdom is foundational precisely because it represents the fulcrum upon which the dialectical relationship between the visible and the invisible rests. Martyrdom is thought of as a short-circuit between these two worlds that makes possible, and exemplifies, *repraesentatio*. More importantly, it is because the martyr is *innocent* that she or he is sanctified and, consequently, able to open a sacral space and give life to a new political community. In other words, it is precisely through their innocent sacrifice that martyrs can become the 'columns' upon which Christian civilization is to be established.

25 The use of the crown to represent martyrdom and immortality symbolically is already attested in the epistle that narrates the martyrdom of Polycarp (AD 155?): '*Nam per tolerantiam devicto injusto praeside, sicque immortalitatis corona recepta*' (Thierry Ruinart, *Acta martyrum: opera ac studio collecta, selecta atque illustrata* [Ratisbonae: Josephi Manz, 1859], 90; all translations from this work are mine).

26 See Peter Brown, *The Cult of the Saints. Its Rise and Function in Latin Christianity* [1981] (Chicago, IL: Chicago University Press, 2015), 133, n. 16.

27 Ibid.

238   *Notes*

28   Ibid., 5–6.

29   Ibid., 7–9. See also Lewis Mumford, *The City in History* (New York: Harcourt, 1961), 243: 'Christian Rome found a new capital, the Heavenly City; and a new civic bond, the communication of the saints. Here was the invisible prototype of the new city.'

30   Jacques Le Goff, *À la recherche du temps sacré: Jacques de Voragine et la Légende dorée* (Paris: Perrin, 2011), 43, my translation.

31   For an overview, see David Cook, *Martyrdom in Islam* (Cambridge: Cambridge University Press, 2007).

32   Bernard Lewis and Buntzie Ellis Churchill, *Islam: The Religion and the People* (Upper Saddle River, NJ: Prentice Hall, 2009), 214.

33   Ruinart, *Acta martyrum*, 131.

34   Ibid.

35   Pavel Florensky, *Le porte regali: saggio sull'icona* (Milan: Adelphi, 1977), 51, my translation.

36   See Tertullian, *De pudicitia* (Paris: Alphonse Picard, 1906), 202 (the relevant passage is ch. 22.6). See also Godefridus J. C. Snoek, *Medieval Piety from Relics to Eucharist* (Köln: Brill, 1995), 175–6.

37   See also Ernst H. Kantorowicz, *The King's Two Bodies: A Study in Medieval Political Theology* [1957] (Princeton, NJ: Princeton University Press, 1997), 232–72.

38   Ernst H. Kantorowicz, '*Pro Patria Mori* in Medieval Political Thought', *The American Historical Review* 56, no. 3 (1951): 491.

39   Ibid., 487–8. See also Kantorowicz, *The King's Two Bodies*, 234–5.

40   In this chapter I am not trying to explain the *personal* and *psychological* motivations behind these actions (martyrdoms, suicide missions etc.); such motivations are, of course, unfathomable. My discussion tries only to frame theoretically the *political* and *ontological* background against which these complex phenomena take place. The relationship between these forms of violence and 'sovereignty' can be clarified by citing a very intense poem about 'martyrdom' published in December 2001 by Ayman Al-Skafi in the Weekly Magazine *Al-Istiqlal*. In it, the image of the *shahīd* is sublimated in symbols of nationalism and sovereignty (flag, territory, mythical origins etc.). The poem reads:

'Because I am a Palestinian
Because I am enamored of fate
And my fate is to have my blood

turned into songs
That sketch out the roads to freedom
My fate is to become a human bomb
Because I am a Palestinian.
[…]
Because I am a Palestinian
Because I bear the flag
And long for the memory of Hittin
I will place the parts of my body as bombs
In your hatred, in your origin
In your accursed fruit
And in spite of you, they will germinate
the most beautiful of flowers
They will germinate the most
beautiful Palestine
Because I am a Palestinian.'

41　Emily T. Yeh (2012), 'On "Terrorism" and the Politics of Naming', *Hot Spots, Cultural Anthropology website*, 8 April 2012, available at http://www.culanth. org/fieldsights/102-on-terrorism-and-the-politics-of-naming (accessed 12 May 2018).

42　See Mircea Eliade, *The Myth of the Eternal Return or, Cosmos and History*, trans. Willard R. Strask (Princeton, NJ: Princeton University Press, 1954), 10. For an archaeological account, see Richard Bradley, *The Idea of Order: The Circular Archetype in Prehistoric Europe* (Oxford: Oxford University Press, 2012), 3–45.

43　On Platonic, or rather Neoplatonist, influences on Augustine, see Robert Crouse, '*Paucis Mutatis Verbis*: St Augustine's Platonism', in *Augustine and His Critics*, ed. Robert Dodaro and George Lawless (London and New York: Routledge, 2000), 37–50.

44　Carl Schmitt, *Roman Catholicism and Political Form* [1923], trans. Gary L. Ulmen (Westport, CT: Greenwood Press, 1996), 56.

45　Giorgio Agamben, *The Kingdom and the Glory: For a Theological Genealogy of Economy and Government*, trans. Lorenzo Chiesa with Matteo Mandarini (Stanford, CA: Stanford University Press, 2007), 140.

46　Ibid., 141.

47　Ruinart, *Acta martyrum*, 131.

48 Thomas Hobbes, *Leviathan: A Critical Edition*, 2 vols, ed. G.A.J. Rogers and Karl Schuhmann (London and New York: Continuum, 2005), vol. 1, 20–5 (= Part 2, ch. 17).

49 As Yan Thomas has brilliantly shown, 'in Latin legal sources, the word *vita* refers either the fact of life or the way of life … The extravagant idea of an "institution of life" is rigorously unattested in any text'. See Yan Thomas, *La Mort du père. Sur le crime de parricide à Rome* (Paris: Albin Michel, 2017), 286, note 147; my translation. The politicization of life is one of the peculiar features of modernity.

50 For a discussion of the modern notion of 'space', see Chapter 2 in this volume.

51 Martin Heidegger, *The Question of Being*, trans. William Kluback and Jean T. Wilde (New York: Twayne Publishers, 1958), 57.

52 Michel Foucault, *The History of Sexuality. Vol. 1: An Introduction*, trans. Robert Hurley (New York: Pantheon Books, 1978), 139–40.

53 Carl Schmitt, *The Nomos of the Earth in the International Law of the Jus Publicum Europaeum* [1950], trans. Gary Ulmen (New York: Telos Press, 2003), 47.

54 See Carl Schmitt, 'The Changing Structure of International Law', trans. Antonio Cerella and Andrea Salvatore, *Journal for Cultural Research* 20, no. 3 (2016): 310–28.

55 Ibid., 335.

56 Agamben, *The Use of Bodies*, 263–79.

57 Ivan Illich, *The Rivers North of the Future: The Testament of Ivan Illich* (Toronto: Anansi Press, 2005).

Bibliography

Adorno, Theodor. *Aesthetic Theory* [1970]. Translated by Robert Hullot-Kentor. London: Continuum, 2002.

Agamben, Giorgio. *Homo Sacer: Sovereign Power and Bare Life*. Translated by Daniel Heller-Roazen. Stanford, CA: Stanford University Press, 1998.

Agamben, Giorgio. *The Kingdom and the Glory: For a Theological Genealogy of Economy and Government*. Translated by Lorenzo Chiesa. Stanford, CA: Stanford University Press, 2011.

Agamben, Giorgio. *Means without Ends: Notes on Politics*. Translated by Vincenzo Binetti and Cesare Casarino. Minneapolis and London: Minnesota University Press, 2000.

Agamben, Giorgio. *The Sacrament of Language: An Archaeology of the Oath*. Translated by Adam Kotsko. Stanford, CA: Stanford University Press, 2011.

Agamben, Giorgio. *The Signature of All Things: On Method*. Translated by Luca D'Isanto with Kevin Attell. New York: Zed Books, 2009.

Agamben, Giorgio. *State of Exception*. Traslated by Kevin Attell. Chicago, IL: University of Chicago Press, 2005.

Agamben, Giorgio. *The Use of Bodies*. Translated by Adam Kotsko. Stanford, CA: Stanford University Press, 2016.

Alberti, Leon Battista. *On Painting* [1435]. Translated by Cecil Grayson. London: Penguin, 2004.

Aquinas, Thomas. *Summa contra Gentiles*. Turin: Marietti, 1862.

Arendt, Hannah. *Between Past and Future: Six Exercises in Political Thought*. New York: Viking Press, 1961.

Arendt, Hannah. *The Origins of Totalitarianism* [1951]. New York: Harcourt Brace & Company, 1976.

Aristotle. 'De interpretatione'. In *A New Aristotle Reader*. Edited by John L. Ackrill. Princeton, NJ: Princeton University Press, 1987.

Aristotle. *Ηθικά Νικομάχεια*. Edited by John Burnet. London: Methuen, 1900.

Aristotle. 'Politics'. In *The Complete Works of Aristotle*, vol. II. Edited by Jonathan Barnes. Princeton, NJ: Princeton University Press, 1984.

242 *Bibliography*

Augustine of Hippo. *De natura boni, contra Manichaeos*. In *S. Aurelii Augustini Opera Omnia, editio latina*. Available at http://www.augustinus.it/latino/natura_bene/index.htm.

Bartelson, Jens. *Sovereignty as Symbolic Form*. London and New York: Routledge, 2014.

Bendix, Reinhard, and Guenther Roth. *Scholarship and Partisanship: Essays on Max Weber*. Berkeley, CA: University of California Press, 1971.

Benjamin, Walter. *The Origin of German Tragic Drama* [1963]. Translated by John Osborne. London: Verso, 2003.

Berenson, Bernard. *The Italian Painters of the Renaissance, Vol. 2: Florentine and Central Italian Schools*. London and New York: Phaidon, 1968.

Berlin, Isaiah. *Against the Current: Essays in the History of Ideas*. Edited by Henry Hardy. New York: The Free Press, 2001.

Berman, Harold J. *Faith and Order: The Reconciliation of Law and Religion*. Cambridge: William B. Eerdmans Publishing, 2000.

Bianchi, Edoardo. *Il* rex sacrorum *a Roma e nell'Italia antica*. Milan: Vita e Pensiero, 2010.

Biggs, Michael. 'Putting the State on the Map: Cartography, Territory, and European State Formation'. *Comparative Studies in Society and History* 41, no. 2 (1999): 374–411.

Böckenförde, Ernst-Wolfgang. *State, Society and Liberty: Studies in Political Theory and Constitutional Law*. Translated by J. A. Underwood. New York: Berg, 1991.

Bradley, Richard. *The Idea of Order: The Circular Archetype in Prehistoric Europe*. Oxford: Oxford University Press, 2012.

Brown, Peter. *The Cult of the Saints. Its Rise and Function in Latin Christianity* [1981]. Chicago, IL: Chicago University Press, 2015.

Bruun, Hans Henrik. 'Weber on Rickert: From Value Relation to Ideal Type'. *Max Weber Studies* 1, no. 2 (2001): 138–60.

Bychkov, Victor. *The Aesthetic Face of Being: Art in the Theology of Pavel Florensky*. Translated by Richard Pevear and Larissa Volokhonsky. Crestwood, NY: St. Vladimir's Seminary Press, 1997.

Casazza, Ornella. *Masaccio and the Brancacci Chapel*. Siena: Scala, 1990.

Cassirer, Ernst. *An Essay on Man: An Introduction to a Philosophy of Human Culture*. New Heaven and London: Yale University Press, 1944.

Cerella, Antonio. 'Images of the World: Ontology and History in the Work of Foucault, Schmitt and Heidegger'. In *Heidegger and the Global Age*. Edited by Antonio Cerella and Louiza Odysseos, 109–36. London and New York: Rowman and Littlefield International, 2017.

Bibliography

Colliot-Thélène, Catherine. 'Carl Schmitt versus Max Weber: Juridical Rationality and Economic Rationality'. In *The Challenge of Carl Schmitt*. Edited by Chantal Mouffe, 138–54. London: Verso, 1999.

Cook, David. *Martyrdom in Islam*. Cambridge: Cambridge University Press, 2007.

Copleston, Frederick. *A History of Philosophy, Volume V. British Philosophy: Hobbes to Hume* [1959]. London: Bloomsbury, 2010.

Corbin, Henry. 'Mundus imaginalis ou l'imaginaire et l'imaginal'. *Cahiers internationaux de symbolisme* 6 (1964): 3–26.

Croce, Benedetto. *La storia come pensiero e come azione* [1938]. Naples: Bibliopolis, 2002.

Crouse, Robert. '*Paucis Mutatis Verbis*: St Augustine's Platonism'. In *Augustine and His Critics*. Edited by Robert Dodaro and George Lawless, 37–50. London and New York: Routledge, 2000.

Danto, Arthur C. 'Letter to Posterity'. *The American Scholar*, 4 September 2012.

Däubler, Theodor. *Hymne an Italien* [1916]. Leipzig: Insel-Verlag, 1919.

DeBono, Daniela. '"Less than Human": The Detention of Irregular Immigrants in Malta'. *Race and Class* 55, no. 2 (2013): 60–81.

de Certeau, Michel. 'The Gaze Nicholas of Cusa'. *Diacritics* 17, no. 3 (1987): 2–38.

de Certeau, Michel. *The Practice of Everyday Life*. Translated by Steven F. Rendall. Los Angeles: University of California Press, 1984.

De Genova, Nicholas, and Natalie Peutz, eds. *The Deportation Regime: Sovereignty, Space, and the Freedom of Movement*. Durham and London: Duke University Press, 2010.

Deguy, Michel, and Jean-Pierre Dupuy, eds. *René Girard et le problème du Mal*. Paris: Grasset, 1982.

Delanty, Gerard. 'Habermas and Occidental Rationalism: The Politics of Identity, Social Learning and the Cultural Limits of Moral Universalism'. *Sociological Theory* 15, no. 1 (1998): 30–59.

De Sanctis, Gaetano. *Storia dei romani: La conquista del primato in Italia*, vol. I. Turin: Fratelli Bocca editori, 1907.

de Santillana, Giorgio. *The Origins of Scientific Thought: From Anaximander to Proclus, 600 B.C. to 500 A.D.* Chicago, IL: University of Chicago Press, 1961.

de Waal, Frans. *Good Natured: The Origins of Right and Wrong in Humans and Other Animals*. Cambridge, MA: Harvard University Press, 1996.

Dillon, Michael. 'The Scandal of the Refugee'. In *Moral Spaces: Rethinking Ethics and World Politics*. Edited by David Campbell and Michael J. Shapiro, 92–124. Minneapolis: Minnesota University Press, 1999.

Domingo, Rafael. *Teoría de la 'auctoritas'*. Pamplona: Ediciones Universidad de Navarra, 1987.

Dumézil, Georges. *La Religion romaine archaïque*. Paris: Payot, 1974.

Dupuy, Jean-Pierre. *Introduction aux sciences sociales: Logiques des phénomènes collectifs*. Paris: Ellipses, 1992.

Durden, William S. 'Public and Private Responsibility: Christianity and Politics in Carl Schmitt's *The Concept of the Political*'. *Christianity & Literature* 60, no. 4 (2011): 561–79.

Durkheim, Émile. *Hobbes à l'agrégation. Un cours d'Émile Durkheim suivi par Marcel Mauss*. Paris: Éditions de l'École des hautes etudes en sciences sociales, 2011.

Durkheim, Émile. *The Elementary Forms of Religious Life* [1912]. Translated by Karen E. Fields. New York: Free Press, 1995.

Eliade, Mircea. *A History of Religious Ideas, II: From Gautama Buddha to the Triumph of Christianity*. Chicago and London: University of Chicago Press, 1982.

Eliade, Mircea. *The Myth of the Eternal Return or, Cosmos and History*. Translated by Willard R. Strask. Princeton, NJ: Princeton University Press, 1954.

Eliade, Mircea. *Patterns in Comparative Religion* [1949]. Translated by Rosemary Sheed. Lincoln and London: University of Nebraska Press, 1996.

Engelbrekt, Kjell. 'What Carl Schmitt Picked Up in Weber's Seminar: A Historical Controversy Revisited'. *The European Legacy* 14, no. 6 (2009): 667–84.

Esposito, Roberto. *A Philosophy for Europe: From the Outside*. Translated by Zakiya Hanafi. Cambridge: Polity Press, 2018.

Factor, Regis A., and Stephen P. Turner. 'The Limits of Reason and Some Limitations of Weber's Morality'. *Human Studies* 2, no. 3 (1979): 301–34.

Florensky, Pavel. *Beyond Vision: Essays on the Perception of Art* [1922]. London: Reaktion Books, 2002.

Florensky, Pavel. *Il simbolo e la forma: Scritti di filosofia della scienza*. Turin: Bollati Boringhieri, 2007.

Florensky, Pavel. *Le porte regali: Saggio sull'icona*. Milan: Adelphi, 1977.

Foucault, Michel. *The Archaeology of Knowledge* [1969]. Translated by Alan M. Sheridan Smith. New York: Vintage Books, 2010.

Foucault, Michel. *The History of Sexuality. Vol. 1: An Introduction*. Translated by Robert Hurley. New York: Pantheon Books, 1978.

Foucault, Michel. *Madness and Civilization: A History of Insanity in the Age of Reason* [1961]. Translated by Richard Howard. New York: Vintage Books, 1988.

Foucault, Michel. 'Nietzsche, Genealogy, History'. In *Aesthetics, Method, and Epistemology*. Edited by James D. Faubion and translated by Robert Hurley, 369–91. New York: New Press, 1998.

Foucault, Michel. *The Order of Things: An Archaeology of the Human Sciences* [1966]. Translated by Alan M. Sheridan Smith. New York: Vintage Books, 1994.

Bibliography

Frankfort, Henri. *Kingship and the Gods: A Study of Ancient Near Eastern Religion as the Integration of Society and Nature*. Chicago, IL: University of Chicago Press, 1948.

Frazer, James G. *The Golden Bough: A Study in Magic and Religion*, abridged edition. London: Macmillan, 1941.

Frazer, James G. *Lectures on the Early History of the Kingship*. London: Macmillan, 1905.

Frazer, James G. *The Scapegoat*. London: Macmillan, 1913.

Galli, Carlo. 'Carl Schmitt and the Global Age', *The New Centennial Review* 10, no. 2 (2010): 1–26.

Galli, Carlo. *Genealogia della politica: Carl Schmitt e la crisi del pensiero politico moderno*. Bologna: il Mulino, 1996.

Galli, Carlo. *Lo sguardo di Giano: Saggi su Carl Schmitt*. Bologna: il Mulino, 2008.

Galli, Carlo., ed. *Multiculturalismo: Ideologie e sfide*. Bologna: il Mulino, 2006.

Galli, Carlo. *Political Spaces and Global War*. Translated by Elisabeth Fay. Minneapolis: University of Minnesota Press, 2010.

Gerth, Hans H. 'Max Weber's Politics: A Rejoinder', *Politics* 3, no. 4 (1945): 119–20.

Giesey, Ralph E. *The Royal Funeral Ceremony in Renaissance France*. Geneve: Droz, 1960.

Ginzburg, Carlo. *Clues, Myths and the Historical Method*. Translated by John and Anne C. Tedeschi. Baltimore, MD: Johns Hopkins University Press, 1989.

Ginzburg, Carlo. *Wooden Eyes: Nine Reflections on Distance*. Translated by Martin Ryle and Kate Soper. New York: Columbia University Press, 2001.

Girard, René. *A Theatre of Envy: William Shakespeare*. New York: Oxford University Press, 1991.

Girard, René. *Battling to the End: Conversations with Benoît Chantre*. Translated by Mary Baker. East Lansing, MI: Michigan State University Press, 2010.

Girard, René. *Deceit, Desire and the Novel. Self and Other in Literary Structure*. Translated by Yvonne Freccero. Baltimore and London: Johns Hopkins University Press, 1966.

Girard, René. 'The Goodness of Mimetic Desire'. In *The Girard Reader*. Edited by James G. Williams, 62–5. New York: Crossroad Publishing Company, 1996.

Girard, René. *I See Satan Fall Like Lightning*. Translated by James G. Williams. Maryknoll, NY: Orbis Books, 2001.

Girard, René. 'Mimesis and Violence'. In *The Girard Reader*. Edited by James G. Williams, 9–19. New York: Crossroad Publishing Company, 1996.

Girard, René. *Quand ces choses commenceront… Entretiens avec Michel Treguer*. Paris: Arléa, 1994.

Bibliography

Girard, René. *Things Hidden since the Foundation of the World*. Translated by Stephen Bann and Michael Metteer. Stanford, CA: Stanford University Press, 1987.

Girard, René. *Violence and the Sacred*. Translated by Patrick Gregory. Baltimore, MD: Johns Hopkins University Press, 1977.

Girard, René, Pierpaolo Antonello, and João Cezar de Castro Rocha. *Evolution and Conversion: Dialogues on the Origins of Culture*. London: Continuum, 2008.

Gluck, Mary. *Georg Lukács and His Generation, 1900–1918*. Cambridge, MA: Harvard University Press, 1985.

Gombrich, Ernst H. *Art and Illusion: A Study in the Psychology of Pictorial Representation*. London: Phaidon, 1960.

Habermas, Jürgen. 'Discussion on Value Freedom and Objectivity'. In *Max Weber and Sociology Today*. Edited by Otto Stammer, 59–66. Oxford: Basil Blackwell, 1971.

Habermas, Jürgen. 'Notes on Post-Secular Society', *New Perspectives Quarterly* 25, no. 4 (2008): 16–29.

Habermas, Jürgen. 'On the Relations between the Secular Liberal State and Religion'. In *Political Theologies: Public Religion in a Post-Secular World*. Edited by Hent de Vries and Lawrence E. Sullivan, 251–60. New York: Fordham University Press, 2006.

Habermas, Jürgen. 'Remarks on Dieter Grimm's "Does Europe Need a Constitution"?'. *European Law Journal* 1, no. 3 (1995): 303–7.

Habermas, Jürgen, and Joseph Ratzinger. *The Dialectics of Secularization: On Reason and Religion*. San Francisco, CA: Ignatius Press, 2006.

Hartmann, Nicolai. *Ethics. Volume II. Moral Values* [1929]. Translated by Stanton Coit. London: Allen and Unwin, 1932.

Hehir, Aidan. *The Responsibility to Protect: Rhetoric, Reality and the Future of Humanitarian Intervention*. Basingstoke: Palgrave Macmillan, 2012.

Heidegger, Martin. *Being and Time* [1929]. Translated by John Macquarrie and Edward Robinson. Oxford: Blackwell, 1962.

Heidegger, Martin. *Bemerkungen zu Kunst—Plastik—Raum*. St. Gallen: Erker Verlag, 1996.

Heidegger, Martin. *Contributions to Philosophy (Of the Event)* [1989]. Translated by Richard Rojcewicz and Daniela Vallega-Neu. Bloomington and Indianapolis: Indiana University Press, 2012.

Heidegger, Martin. *Off the Beaten Track* [1950]. Translated by Julian Young and Kenneth Haynes. Cambridge: Cambridge University Press, 2002.

Heidegger, Martin. *Philosophical and Political Writings*. Edited by Manfred Stassen. New York and London: Continuum, 2003.

Heidegger, Martin. *The Question of Being*. Translated by William Kluback and Jean T. Wilde. New York: Twayne Publishers, 1958.

Bibliography

Heidegger, Martin. *Wegmarken* (GA9). Edited by Friedrich-Wilhelm von Herrmann. Frankfurt am Main: Vittorio Klostermann, 1976.

Hempel, Carl Gustav. *Aspects of Scientific Explanation and Other Essays in the Philosophy of Science*. New York: Free Press, 1965.

Hempel, Carl Gustav, and Paul Oppenheim. 'Studies in the Logic of Explanation'. *Philosophy of Science* 15, no. 2 (April 1948): 135–75.

Hirschman, Albert O. *Exit, Voice and Loyalty*. Cambridge, MA: Harvard University Press, 1970.

Hobbes, Thomas. *Behemoth* [1681]. Edited by Paul Seaward. Oxford: Clarendon Press, 2010.

Hobbes, Thomas. *De cive* [1642]. Oxford: Oxford University Press, 1983.

Hobbes, Thomas. *The Elements of Law: Natural and Politic* [1640]. London: Routledge, 2013.

Hobbes, Thomas. *English Works, Volume I*. Edited by Sir William Molesworth. London: John Bohn, 1839.

Hobbes, Thomas. *English Works, Volume II*. Edited by Sir William Molesworth. London: John Bohn, 1841.

Hobbes, Thomas. *Leviathan: A Critical Edition*. 2 vols. Edited by. G.A.J. Rogers and Karl Schuhmann. London and New York: Continuum, 2005.

Hobbes, Thomas. *Leviathan. Sive de materia, forma, et postestate civitatis ecclesiasticæ et civilis* [1668]. Aalen: Scientia, 1961.

Hobbes, Thomas. *The Leviathan or, the Matter, Form, and Power of a Common-Wealth Ecclesiastical and Civil*. London: Andrew Crooke, 1651.

Hocart, Arthur M. *Kingship*. London: Watts & Co., 1941.

Hope, William H. St John. 'On the Funeral Effigies of the Kings and Queens of England, with Special Reference to Those in the Abbey Church of Westminster', *Archeologia* 60 (1907): 526–8.

Huxley, Aldous. *The Perennial Philosophy* [1946]. London: Fontana Books, 1961.

Illich, Ivan. *The Rivers North of the Future: The Testament of Ivan Illich as Told to David Cayley*. Toronto: Anansi Press, 2005.

Jacobi a Voragine. *Legenda aurea. Vulgo historia lombardica dicta*. Lipsiae: Impensis Librariae Arnoldianae, 1850.

Jaspers, Karl. *The Perennial Scope of Philosophy*. Translated by Ralph Manheim. Hamden, CT: Archon Books, 1968.

Jay, Martin. 'Scopic Regimes of Modernity'. In *Vision and Visuality*. Edited by Hal Foster, 3–23. Seattle: Bay Press, 1988.

Joannides, Paul. *Masaccio and Masolino: A Complete Catalogue*. London: Phaidon, 1993.

248 Bibliography

Jung, Carl Gustav. *The Collected Works of C.G. Jung, Volume 1: Psychiatric Studies*. Edited by Herbert Read, Michael Fordham and Gerhard Adler. New York: Routledge, 1970.

Kant, Immanuel. *The Metaphysics of Morals* [1797]. Translated by Mary Gregor. Cambridge: Cambridge University Press, 1996.

Kantorowicz, Ernst H. *The King's Two Bodies: A Study in Medieval Political Theology* [1957]. Princeton, NJ: Princeton University Press, 1997.

Kantorowicz, Ernst H. 'Pro Patria Mori in Medieval Political Thought'. *The American Historical Review* 56, no. 3 (April 1951): 472–92.

Kelsen, Hans. *Pure Theory of Law*. Translated by Max Knight. Clark, NJ: The Lawbook Exchange, 2005.

King, Russell, and Daniela DeBono. 'Irregular Migration and the "Southern European Model" of Migration'. *Journal of Mediterranean Studies* 22, no. 1 (2013): 1–31.

Kojève, Alexandre. *Introduction to the Reading of Hegel*. Translated by James H. Nichols, Jr. Ithaca and London: Cornell University Press, 1969.

Koptev, Aleksandr. 'The Five-Day Interregnum in the Roman Republic'. *The Classical Quarterly* 66, no. 1 (2016): 205–21.

Koyré, Alexandre. *From the Closed World to the Infinite Universe*. Baltimore, MD: Johns Hopkins University Press, 1957.

Krautheimer, Richard. 'Le tavole di Urbino, Berlino e Baltimora riesaminate'. In *Rinascimento: da Brunelleschi a Michelangelo. La rappresentazione dell'architettura*. Edited by Henry A. Millon and Vittorio Magnago Lampugnani, 233–57. Milan: Bompiani, 1994.

Labat, René. *Le caractère religieux de la royauté assyro-babylonienne*. Paris: Adrien-Maisonneuve, 1939.

Le Goff, Jacques. *À la recherche du temps sacré: Jacques de Voragine et la Légende dorée*. Paris: Perrin, 2011.

Leibholz, Gerhard. *Das Wesen der Repräsentation unter besonderer Berücksichtigung des Repräsentativsystems* [1928]. Berlin: de Gruyter, 1973.

Lévi-Strauss, Claude. *Structural Anthropology*. Translated by Claire Jacobson and Brooke Grundfest Schoepf. New York: Basic Books, 1963.

Lévi-Strauss, Claude. *Totemism*. Translated by Rodney Needham. Harmondsworth: Penguin Books, 1969.

Lewis, Bernard, and Buntzie Ellis Churchill. *Islam: The Religion and the People*. Upper Saddle River, NJ: Prentice Hall, 2009.

Litten, Julian. 'The Funeral Effigy: Its Function and Purpose'. In *The Funeral Effigies of Westminster Abbey*. Edited by Anthony Harvery and Richard Mortimer, 3–19. Woodbridge: The Boydell Press, 2003.

Bibliography

Longhi, Roberto. 'Masolino and Masaccio'. In *Three Studies*. Translated by David Tabbat and David Jacobson, 1–91. New York: Stanley Moss-Sheep Meadow Book, 1995.

Löwith, Karl. 'Die Entzauberung der Welt durch Wissenschaft'. *Merkur* 18 (1964): 501–19.

Löwith, Karl. *Heidegger and European Nihilism*. Edited by Richard Wolin and translated by Gary Steiner. New York: Columbia University Press, 1998.

Löwith, Karl. *Meaning in History*. Chicago and London: University of Chicago Press, 1949.

Lukács, György. *The Destruction of Reason*. Translated by Peter R. Palmer. London: Merlin Press: 1980.

Magdelain, André. *Jus imperium auctoritas: Études de droit romain*. Rome: École française de Rome, 2015.

Magdelain, André. *Recherches sur l'"imperium": la loi curate et les auspices d'investiture*. Paris: Presses Universitaires de France, 1968.

Marder, Michael. *Groundless Existence: The Political Ontology of Carl Schmitt*. New York: Continuum, 2010.

McCormick, John P. *Carl Schmitt's Critique of Liberalism*. Cambridge: Cambridge University Press, 1997.

McCormick, John P. 'Transcending Weber's Categories of Modernity? The Early Lukács and Schmitt on the Rationalization Thesis'. *New German Critique* 75 (1998): 133–77.

Meier, Heinrich. *Carl Schmitt and Leo Strauss: The Hidden Dialogue*. Translated by J. Harvey Lomax. Chicago and London: University of Chicago Press, 2006.

Merrill, Elmer T. 'The Roman Calendar and the *Regifugium*'. *Classical Philology* 19, no. 1 (1924): 20–39.

Mezzadra, Sandro, and Bret Neilson. *Border as Method, or, the Multiplication of Labor*. Durham and London: Duke University Press, 2013.

Milbank, John, Catherine Pickstock and Graham Ward, eds. *Radical Orthodoxy*. London and New York: Routledge, 1999.

Momigliano, Arnaldo. *Quarto contributo alla storia degli studi classici e del mondo antico*. Rome: Edizioni di Storia e Letteratura, 1969.

Mommsen, Theodor. *The History of Rome*, I [1862]. Translated by William P. Dickson. Cambridge: Cambridge University Press, 2009.

Mommsen, Theodor. *Römisches Staatsrecht*, II. Leipzig: Verlag von S. Hirzel, 1874.

Mommsen, Wolfgang J. *Max Weber and German Politics, 1890–1920*. Translated by Michael S. Steinberg. Chicago, IL: University of Chicago Press, 1984.

Morgenthau, Hans J. *Scientific Man vs. Power Politics*. London: Latimer House Limited, 1947.

Mouffe, Chantal. 'Carl Schmitt and the Paradox of Liberal Democracy'. In *The Challenge of Carl Schmitt*. Edited by Chantal Mouffe, 38–53. London: Verso, 1999.

Mumford, Lewis. *The City in History*. New York: Harcourt, 1961.

Mußgnug, Dorothee, Reinhard Mußgnug, and Angela Reinthal, eds. *Ernst Forsthoff – Carl Schmitt. Briefwechsel 1926–1974*. Berlin: Akademie Verlag, 2007.

Niebuhr, Reinhold. *Christianity and Power Politics*. New York: Charles Scribner's Sons, 1940.

Nietzsche, Friedrich. *Beyond Good and Evil* [1886]. Translated by Judith Norman. Cambridge: Cambridge University Press, 2002.

Nietzsche, Friedrich. *On the Genealogy of Morality* [1887]. Translated by Carol Diethe. Cambridge: Cambridge University Press, 2007.

Nietzsche, Friedrich. *Untimely Meditations* [1873–76]. Translated by R.J. Hollingdale. Cambridge: Cambridge University Press, 2007.

Nietzsche, Friedrich. *The Will to Power*. Translated by Walter Kaufmann and R.J. Hollingdale. New York: Vintage, 1968.

Oakes, Guy. *Weber and Rickert: Concept Formation in the Cultural Sciences*. Cambridge, MA: MIT Press, 1988.

Ojakangas, Mika. '*Potentia absoluta et potentia ordinata Dei*: On the Theological Origins of Carl Schmitt's Theory of Constitution'. *Continental Philosophy Review* 45, no. 4 (2012): 505–17.

Ortega Y Gasset, José. *Introducción a una estimative: Que son los valores?* [1923]. Madrid: Ediciones Encuentro, 2004.

Palaver, Wolfgang. *René Girard's Mimetic Theory*. Translated by Gabriel Borrud. East Lansing, MI: Michigan State University Press, 2013.

Panofsky, Erwin. *Perspective as Symbolic Form* [1927]. Translated by Christopher S. Wood. New York: Zone Books, 1991.

Pattison, James. *Humanitarian Intervention and the Responsibility to Protect. Who Should Intervene?* Oxford: Oxford University Press, 2012.

Peirce, Charles S. *Collected Papers of Charles Sanders Peirce: Elements of Logic*. Edited by Charles Hartshorne and Paul Weiss. Cambridge, MA: The Belknap Press of Harvard University Press, 1960.

Pessoa, Fernando. *Livro do desassossego*. São Paulo: Montecristo Editora, 2012.

Pickles, John. *A History of Spaces: Cartographic Reason, Mapping, and the Geo-Coded World*. New York: Routledge, 2004.

Pitkin, Hanna Fenichel. *The Concept of Representation*. Berkeley and Los Angeles: University of California Press, 1972.

Plato. *The Republic*. Translated by Tom Griffith. Cambridge: Cambridge University Press, 2009.

Bibliography

Plato. *The Republic of Plato*. Edited by James Adam. Cambridge: Cambridge University Press, 1902.

Plotinus. *The Enneads*. Translated by Stephen MacKenna. London: Faber and Faber, 1956.

Prodi, Paolo. *Una storia della giustizia: Dal pluralismo dei fori al moderno dualismo tra coscienza e diritto*. Bologna: il Mulino, 2000.

Pulgram, Ernst. 'Proto-Indo-European Reality and Reconstruction'. *Language* 35, no. 3 (1959): 421–6.

Rahola, Federico. *Zone definitivamente temporanee: I luoghi dell'umanità in eccesso*. Verona: Ombre Corte, 2003.

Reder, Michael. 'How Far Can Reason and Faith Be Distinguished?'. In *An Awareness of What Is Missing. Faith and Reason in a Post-Secular Age*. Edited by Jürgen Habermas et al., 36–50. Cambridge: Polity Press, 2010.

Rickert, Heinrich. *The Limits of Concept Formation in Natural Science* [1902]. Translated by Guy Oakes. Cambridge: Cambridge University Press, 1986.

Richard, Jean-Claude. 'Enée, Romulus, César et les funérailles impériales (Dion Cassius, 56, 34, 2; Tacite, *Annales*, 4, 9, 3)'. *Mélanges de l'école française de Rome* 78, no. 1 (1966): 67–78.

Roth, Guenther. 'Max Weber's Ethics and the Peace Movement Today'. *Theory and Society* 13, no. 4 (1984): 491–511.

Rousseau, Jean-Jacques. 'Lettre a Monsieur le Marquis de Mirabeau'. In *Collection complète des oeuvres de J.J. Rousseau*, vol. XXIV, 110–17. Genève, 1782.

Ruggie, John G. 'Territoriality and Beyond: Problematizing Modernity in International Relations'. *International Organization* 47, no. 1 (1993): 139–74.

Ruinart, Thierry, ed. *Acta martyrum: opera ac studio collecta, selecta atque illustrata*. Ratisbonae: Josephi Manz, 1859.

Salzani, Stefano. 'La città dei martiri: *bios* e *zoe aionios*'. *Teologia politica* 3 (2007): 177–205.

Schapiro, Meyer. 'A Note on Max Weber's Politics'. *Politics* 2, no. 2 (1945): 44–8.

Schele, Linda, and David Freidel. *A Forest of Kings: The Untold History of Ancient Maya*. New York: Morrow, 1990.

Scheler, Max. *Formalism in Ethics and Non-Formal Ethics of Values: A New Attempt toward the Foundation of an Ethical Personalism* [1913–16]. Translated by Manfred S. Frings and Roger L. Funk. Evanston, IL: Northwestern University Press, 1973.

Schmarsow, August. *Masaccio Studien*. Kassel: T.G. Fisher, 1895.

Schmitt, Carl. 'The Age of Neutralizations and Depoliticizations' [1929]. In *The Concept of the Political*. Edited by George Schwab and translated by Matthias Konzett and John P. McCormick, 80–96. Chicago, IL: University of Chicago Press, 2007.

252 *Bibliography*

Schmitt, Carl. 'The Changing Structure of International Law' [1943]. Translated by Antonio Cerella and Andrea Salvatore. *Journal for Cultural Research* 20, no. 3 (2016): 310–28.

Schmitt, Carl. *The Concept of the Political* [1932]. Translated by George Schwab. Chicago, IL: University of Chicago Press, 2007.

Schmitt, Carl. *Constitutional Theory* [1928]. Translated by Jeffrey Seitzer. Durham and London: Duke University Press, 2008.

Schmitt, Carl. *The Crisis of Parliamentary Democracy* [1923]. Translated by Ellen Kennedy. Cambridge and London: MIT Press, 1988.

Schmitt, Carl. *Der Begriff des Politischen. Text von 1932 mit einem Vorwort und drei Corollarien* [1932]. Berlin: Duncker & Humblot, 1963.

Schmitt, Carl. *Der Nomos der Erde im Völkerrecht des Jus Publicum Europaeum* [1950]. Berlin: Duncker & Humblot, 1974.

Schmitt, Carl. *Der Wert des Staates und die Bedeutung des Einzelnen*. Tübingen: Mohr, 1914.

Schmitt, Carl. 'Die Einheit der Welt' [1952]. In *Staat, Großraum, Nomos: Arbeiten aus den Jahren 1916–1969*. Edited by Günter Maschke, 496–512. Berlin: Duncker & Humblot, 1995.

Schmitt, Carl. *Die Tyrannei der Werte* [1967]. Dritte, korrigierte Auflage. Berlin: Duncker & Humblot, 2011.

Schmitt, Carl. 'Die vollendete Reformation. Bemerkungen und Hinweise zu neuen Leviathan-Interpretationen'. *Der Staat. Zeitschrift fur Staatslehre, öffentliches Recht und Verfassungsgeschichte* 4, no. 1 (1965): 51–69.

Schmitt, Carl. 'Ethic of State and Pluralistic State' [1930]. In *The Challenge of Carl Schmitt*. Edited by Chantal Mouffe and translated by David Dizenhaus, 195–208. London: Verso, 1999.

Schmitt, Carl. *Ex Captivitate Salus. Erfahrungen der Zeit 1945/47*. Köln: Greven, 1950.

Schmitt, Carl. *Glossarium. Aufzeichnungen der Jahre 1947–1951*. Berlin: Duncker & Humblot, 1991.

Schmitt, Carl. *Land and Sea* [1954]. Translated by Simona Draghici. Washington, DC: Plutarch Press, 1997.

Schmitt, Carl. *The Leviathan in the State Theory of Thomas Hobbes: Meaning and Failure of a Political Symbol* [1938]. Translated by George Schwab and Herna Hilfstein. Chicago, IL: University of Chicago Press, 1996.

Schmitt, Carl. *The Nomos of the Earth in the International Law of the Jus Publicum Europaeum* [1950]. Translated by Gary L. Ulmen. New York: Telos Press, 2003.

Schmitt, Carl. *Political Romanticism* [1919]. Translated by Guy Oakes. Cambridge, MA: MIT Press, 1985.

Bibliography

Schmitt, Carl. *Political Theology: Four Chapters on the Concept of Sovereignty* [1922]. Translated by George Schwab. Cambridge, MA: MIT Press, 1985.

Schmitt, Carl. *Political Theology II. The Myth of the Closure of Any Political Theology* [1970]. Translated by Michael Hoelzl and Graham Ward. Cambridge: Polity Press, 2010.

Schmitt, Carl. *Roman Catholicism and Political Form* [1923]. Translated by Gary L. Ulmen. Westport, CT: Greenwood Press, 1996.

Schmitt, Carl. *State, Movement, People. The Triadic Structure of the Political Unity* [1933]. Translated by Simona Draghici. Corvellis, OR: Plutarch Press, 2001.

Schmitt, Carl. *Theodor Däublers 'Nordlicht': Drei Studien über die Elemente, den Geist und die aktualität des Werkes* [1916]. Berlin: Duncker & Humblot, 1991.

Schmitt, Carl. *Theorie des Partisanen. Zwischenbemerkung zum Begriff des Politischen* [1963]. Berlin: Duncker & Humblot, 1975.

Schmitt, Carl. 'Three Possibilities for a Christian Conception of History' [1950]. Translated by Mario Wenning. *Telos* 147 (2009): 167–70.

Schmitt, Carl. *Un giurista davanti a se stesso. Saggi e interviste*. Vicenza: Neri Pozza, 2005.

Shakespeare, William. *Henry IV, Part 1*. Oxford: Oxford University Press, 1987.

Simon, Herbert. *Reason in Human Affairs*. Stanford, CA: Stanford University Press, 1983.

Springborg, Patricia, ed. *The Cambridge Companion to Hobbes's Leviathan*. Cambridge: Cambridge University Press, 2007.

Strauss, Leo. *Natural Right and History*. Chicago, IL: University of Chicago Press, 1953.

Taubes, Jacob. *The Political Theology of Paul*. Translated by Dana Hollander. Stanford, CA: Stanford University Press, 2004.

Taylor, Charles et al. *Multiculturalism: Examining the Politics of Recognition*. Princeton, NJ: Princeton University Press, 1994.

Tertullian. *De pudicitia*. Paris: Alphonse Picard, 1906.

Thomas, Yan. *La Mort du père. Sur le crime de parricide à Rome*. Paris: Albin Michel, 2017.

Thucydides. *The Peloponnesian War*. Translated by Martin Hammond. New York: Oxford University Press, 2009.

Toesca, Pietro. *Masolino da Panicale*. Bergamo: Istituto italiano d'arti grafiche, 1908.

Topitsch, Ernst. 'Max Weber and Sociology Today'. In *Max Weber and Sociology Today*. Edited by Otto Stammer, 8–25. Oxford: Basil Blackwell, 1971.

Ulmen, Gary L. *Politischer Mehrwert: Eine Studie über Max Weber und Carl Schmitt*. Weinheim: VCH Acta humaniora, 1991.

Ulmen, Gary L. 'The Sociology of the State: Carl Schmitt and Max Weber'. *State, Culture, and Society* 1 (1985): 3–57.

Usener, Hermann. *Kleine Schriften. Vierter Band. Arbeiten zur Religionsgeschichte*. Leipzig und Berlin: B.G. Teubner, 1913.

Vasari, Giorgio. *The Lives of the Artists* [1568]. Translated by Julia Conaway Bondanella and Peter Bondanella. New York: Oxford University Press, 1998.

Voegelin, Eric. *The New Science of Politics: An Introduction* [1952]. Chicago and London: University of Chicago Press, 1987.

Waltz, Kenneth. *Man, the State and War: A Theoretical Analysis* [1959]. New York: Columbia University Press, 2001.

Weber, Marianne. *Max Weber: A Biography*. Translated by Harry Zohn. New Brunswick, NJ: Transaction, 1988.

Weber, Max. *Collected Methodological Writings*. Edited by Hans Henrik Bruun and Sam Whimster and translated by Hans Henrik Bruun. New York: Routledge, 2012.

Weber, Max. *Gesammelte Aufsätze zur Wissenschaftslehre*. Tübingen: J.C.B. Mohr/Paul Siebeck, 1922.

Weber, Max. *The Methodology of the Social Sciences*. Edited and translated by Edward A. Shils and Henry A. Finch. Glencoe, IL: Free Press, 1949.

Weber, Max. *Political Writings*. Edited by Peter Lassman and Ronald Speirs. Cambridge: Cambridge University Press, 2007.

Weber, Max. 'Science as a Vocation'. In *From Max Weber: Essays in Sociology*. Edited and translated by Hans H. Gerth and Charles Wright Mills, 129–56. New York: Oxford University Press, 1946.

Weber, Samuel. *Benjamin's –abilities*. Cambridge, MA and London: Harvard University Press, 2008.

Weiss, Johannes. 'On the Irreversibility of Western Rationalization and Max Weber's Alleged Fatalism'. In *Max Weber, Rationality and Modernity*. Edited by Sam Whimster and Scott Lash, 154–63. London: Allen & Unwin, 1987.

Windelband, Wilhelm. *An Introduction to Philosophy* [1914]. Translated by Joseph McCabe. London: T. Fisher Unwin, 1921.

Wittgenstein, Ludwig. *Tractatus Logico-Philosophicus* [1921]. London: Routledge, 2001.

Wolin, Sheldon S. 'Max Weber: Legitimation, Method, and the Politics of Theory'. *Political Theory* 9, no. 3 (1981): 401–24.

Name Index

Agamben, Giorgio 5, 11, 18–19, 27–8, 148–72, 183, 187, 190, 193 n.8, 234 n.56, 236 n.20
Alberti, Leon Battista 61, 207 n.26, 208 n.43
Antoninus Pius (*Titus Aurelius Fulvus Boionius Arrius Antoninus Pius*) 29
Aquinas, Thomas 77
Arendt, Hannah 8, 170
Aristotle 19, 77, 139, 148, 165, 167
Aron, Raymond 74
Artaud, Antonin 45
Augustine of Hippo 95, 99–101, 123, 183, 222 n.32, 222 n.39, 223 n.43, 239 n.43

Benjamin, Walter 17–19, 193 n.2
Bentham, Jeremy 162
Berenson, Bernard 207–8 n.41
Bergson, Henri-Louis 148
Berlin, Isaiah 87
Bickerman, Elias 26
Böckenförde, Ernst-Wolfgang 134–5, 212 n.8
Brown, Peter 175
Brunelleschi, Filippo (Filippo di ser Brunellesco Lapi) 48, 61, 207 n.26
Buonarroti, Michelangelo 54

Caligula (*Gaius Iulius Caesar Augustus Germanicus*) 29
Cardi, Lodovico 173–4
Cassirer, Ernst 6, 8
Cavalcaselle, Giovanni Battista 50
Cavendish, William (2nd Earl of Devonshire) 59
Cittinus (Christian martyr) 178
Coke, Edward 31
Colliot-Thélène, Catherine 72, 212 n.7
Commodus (*Lucius Aelius Aurelius Commodus*) 29

Conan Doyle, Arthur 159
Croce, Benedetto 6
Cusanus, Nicolaus (Nicolas of Cusa) 64, 197 n.27

Danto, Arthur C. 7
Darwin, Charles 5
Däubler, Theodor 92
Delanty, Gerard 133
Dionysius of Halicarnassus 41, 199 n.56, 204 n.93
Donata (Christian martyr) 178
Donatello (Donato di Niccolò di Betto Bardi) 48, 207 n.26
Dumézil, Georges 200 n.64
Durkheim, Émile 22, 80, 145–8, 195 n.20

Edward II (of England) 25
Eliade, Mircea 8, 36–7, 146–8, 182
Euclid of Alexandria 59

Factor, Regis A. 80
Festus, Sextus Pompeius 35, 200 n.68, 203 n.83
Florensky, Pavel 47, 56–7, 65, 233 n.45
Forsthoff, Ernst 212 n.8
Foucault, Michel 5, 7, 45–7, 148–9, 158, 186, 188
Frankfort, Henri 39, 203 n.82
Frazer, James G. 37–8, 41, 202 n.79, 203 n.83
Freund, Julien 212 n.8

Galilei, Galileo 59
Gehlen, Arnold 212 n.8
Gentili, Alberico 124
Giesey, Ralph E. 27, 30, 198 n.35
Ginzburg, Carlo 26–8, 159–60, 162, 198 n.35
Girard, René 10, 11, 94, 96–100, 102–11, 114–15, 148–54, 156–64, 167–8, 224 n.56–7, 234 n.56, 237 n.24

256 Name Index

Habermas, Jürgen 10–11, 73, 118–21, 131–6, 138, 140, 228 n.34, 229 n.61
Hartmann, Nicolai 212 n.8
Hegel, Georg Wilhelm Friedrich 98, 148
Heidegger, Martin 1, 6–7, 9, 60, 66–8, 78, 113–14, 167, 185–6, 215 n.36, 218 n.69
Hempel, Carl G. 163
Henry II (Holy Roman Emperor) 31
Henry VII (of England) 25
Hertz, Robert 26
Hobbes, Thomas 10, 20–3, 32, 43, 47–8, 59–65, 67, 77, 91, 95, 97, 126, 184–5, 189–90, 194–5 n.15, 195 n.19, 209 n.67, 209 n.70, 216 n.42, 228 n.36
Hobhouse, Leonard 80
Hocart, Arthur M. 40
Horace (*Quintus Horatius Flaccus*) 180

Illich, Ivan 190–1

Jacobus da Varagine (Jacopo De Fazio) 173
Jaspers, Karl 137–8
Joannides, Paul 51, 206 n.12
John Paul II (Pope) 213 n.8
Jung, Carl Gustav 8, 48

Kant, Immanuel 78, 86, 214 n.23
Kantorowicz, Ernst H. 26–7, 29–30, 180–1, 184, 193–4 n.8, 226 n.12
Kelsen, Hans 22, 126, 135, 196 n.25
Kojève, Alexandre 98, 221 n.22
Koselleck, Reinhart 212 n.8

Le Goff, Jacques 176
Lenin, Vladimir (Vladimir Ilyich Ulyanov) 95
Lévi-Strauss, Claude 23, 146–8, 197 n.26, 231 n.14
Liberius (Pope) 54
Livy (*Titus Livius*) 35, 199 n.56, 200 n.69, 201 n.70
Löwith, Karl 75, 82, 89
Lukács, György 73

Machiavelli, Niccolò 87
Macrobius (*Ambrosius Theodosius Macrobius*) 203 n.83
Magdelain, André 33–6, 199 n.55, 200 n.62, 202 n.73

Martin V (Pope, born Otto or Oddone Colonna) 50, 207 n.39
Masaccio (Tommaso di ser Giovanni di Mone Cassai) 10, 48–52, 56–7, 205–6 n.11, 207 n.26
Masolino da Panicale (Tommaso di Cristoforo Fini) 48–57, 206 n.12, 207 n.26
McCormick, John 74
Merrill, Elmer T. 37–9, 201 n.72
Mill, John Stuart 80
Momigliano, Arnaldo 35, 200 n.66
Mommsen, Theodor 201 n.70
Mommsen, Wolfgang 73–4, 214 n.20
Monet, Claude 9
Morgenthau, Hans J. 98, 100
Mouffe, Chantal 132, 139
Mumford, Lewis 238 n.29

Nicéron, Jean-François 209 n.70
Niebuhr, Reinhold 100
Nietzsche, Friedrich 2–6, 78–9, 81, 158

Oppenheim, Paul 163
Ovid (*Publius Ovidius Naso*) 36, 201 n.72

Paul the Apostle 123
Peirce, Charles S. 111
Pessoa, Fernando 1
Peterson, Erik 222 n.39
Plato 77, 90, 122
Plotinus 77
Plutarch (*Lucius Mestrius Plutarchus*) 36, 200–1 n.69
Polycarp (bishop of Smyrna) 237 n.25
Proudhon, Pierre-Joseph 134
Pulgram, Ernst 13

Ratzinger, Joseph 118
Rée, Paul 2–3, 5
Ricardo, David 77
Rickert, Heinrich 79–80, 83–4, 215 n.35, 216–17 n.57
Ritter, Joachim 212 n.8
Roth, Guenther 73
Rousseau, Jean-Jacques 22, 196 n.22

Saturninus, Publius Vigellius (Roman proconsul) 178

Name Index

Scheler, Max 85–6, 213 n.8
Schmitt, Carl 5, 7, 10, 19, 20–1, 23–5, 43,
58–9, 64, 71–6, 78, 80–1, 84, 85–92,
93–9, 101–3, 105–8, 111–15, 120–1,
123–31, 133–6, 139, 141, 150, 172,
183, 187–8, 194 n.11, 197 n.27,
209–10 n.74, 212 n.7, 212–13 n.8,
215 n.36, 222–3 n.39, 223 n.41,
226–7 n.21, 227 n.31, 228 n.36
Scotus, John Duns 47
Shakespeare, William 105, 224 n.56
Sieyès, Emmanuel Joseph 23
Simon, Herbert A. 81
Smith, Adam 77
Socrates 77, 122
Speratus (Christian martyr) 178
Strauss, Leo 73, 82, 97, 218 n.69, 221 n.16

Tarquinius Superbus 35–6
Taubes, Jacob 91
Taylor, Brook 62
Taylor, Charles 118
Tertullian (*Quintus Septimius Florens
Tertullianus*) 179
Thomas, Yan 240 n.49

Thucydides 95–6
Toesca, Pietro 49, 206 n.12
Turner, Stephen P. 80

Usener, Hermann Karl 203 n.83

van Gogh, Vincent 45
Varro, Marcus Terentius 34, 199 n.61
Vasari, Giorgio 49–51, 54, 205–6 n.11, 206
n.19
Vattel, Emmerich de 198 n.34
Velázquez, Diego 45, 67
Voegelin, Eric 204 n.92, 226 n.12

Waltz, Kenneth 95–6
Weber, Max 8, 10, 71–6, 80–90, 92, 110,
129, 168, 185, 212 n.7, 216–17 n.57,
220 n.10, 226 n.12, 229 n.51
Wilbrandt, Robert 80
Windelband, Wilhelm 79, 83
Wittgenstein, Ludwig 151

Yeh, Emily T. 181

Subject Index

abandonment of being (*Seinsverlassenheit*):
    Heidegger's concept of 167
abolition: of monarchy 35, 41; of time 37–8
absolutism 21, 84, 137, 159
actualization of law (*Rechtsverwirklichung*):
    Schmitt's concept of 126
adaptation 4–5
animal symbolicum: Cassirer's concept of 8
animus dominandi 98
annual cycle 36, 176, 202 n.73
anthropogenesis 19, 149, 155–7, 163–6,
    193 n.8
apotheosis 27–9
apriorism 84–5
arbor vitae ('tree of life') 12
arcanum 5, 24, 27–8, 32, 118, 154
archaeology: Agamben's conception of
    149–50, 154, 158–9, 164–6, 168;
    Foucault's conception of 45–7;
    Girard's conception of 150–5,
    158–64, 167–8; as method 11, 47
archē: Agamben's notion of 5, 18–19, 149,
    151, 158, 193 n.8
archetype 8, 77, 150, 182, 187
archōn basileus 35, 201 n.70
Atharva Veda 12
auctoritas 33, 125, 181, 195 n.19
authenticity: Benjamin's notion of 18
axiology (*Wertphilosophie*) 79–80, 85–6

biologism 8
biopower 171–2, 186

carnality 189
causality 96, 220 n.10
christianitas 12, 127, 162
civitas Dei 123, 181
civitas terrena 123, 183
complexio oppositorum 111, 114, 125
conditions of possibility 3, 5, 9, 13, 162,
    178; *see also* genealogy

consecratio 27–8
Copernican revolution 123
corporeity: modern conception of 20–3,
    43, 59–62, 189, 198 n.34
corpus mysticum 180–1, 184
cosmogony 37, 39–40
crown: as symbol of immortality 175, 237
    n.25
cuius regio, eius religio 112, 117, 124

damnatio memoriae 28
Darwinism 3
decisionism: Schmitt's theory of 73, 75,
    89–90, 106–7, 126, 228 n.37; Weber's
    theory of 90
deterritorialization 113, 189
dichotomies: cognitive 146; modern 74,
    120, 124, 130, 150
dignitas 26, 198 n.34
disenchantment: Weber's conception of 72,
    82–4, 89–90, 212 n.7
double transference: Girard's notion of 96,
    104
duality: ancient's conception of 182;
    Augustine's conception of 183;
    medieval conception of 30; Plato's
    conception of 122

ego cogitans 149
emanationism 11, 110–11, 167–8
ens repraesentans 7, 168
epagomenal days 34, 36
episteme: Foucault's notion of 45–7
essentialism 111
evidential method 159–60, 162
extensio 60

flamines maiores 35, 200 n.66
friend-enemy opposition 97–8, 101, 106,
    124, 136
Fugalia, *see* Regifugium

Subject Index

functional explanation 163–4
funeral effigies, *see* royal doubles
funus imaginarium 27–8

genealogy: as method 6, 9–10, 12–13,
76, 94, 153, 157–9; Nietzsche's
conception of 2–5
gigantic: Heidegger's concept of the 1–2
globalization 1–2, 9–11, 94, 112–14,
119–21, 130–2, 138, 140–1, 187–190
Großräume: Schmitt's theory of 106
Grundnorm 23, 135, 196 n.25

hierophany: Eliade's concept of 8, 146–7
Historia Augusta 29, 198 n.43
historical a priori 163–8
historicity 5, 138
homo artificialis 32, 64
homo desiderans 110
homo sacer: Agamben's notion of 28,
153–4, 161
humanism: modern conception of 48, 65–6
humanitarian intervention 236 n.13
human rights: Agamben's critique of 171–2

imperium 33, 41, 178
individualism, *see* subjectivity
infinity: Hobbes's conception of 63
intentionality 160–1, 166, 233 n.45
interregnum 30–6, 199 n.56

Kallipolis 122
Kantian ethics 78, 84–5
katechon: Schmitt's concept of 71, 112–13,
127

legal positivism 126
legitimacy: Böckenförde's conception of
134–5; Habermas's conception of
135; Schmitt's theory of 24, 112,
128–9; Weber's theory of 74, 87–8
life: modern conception of 3–6, 43, 90–1,
184, 186, 188–9, 240 n.49
linear perspective 9–10, 48–51, 54–6, 65–6,
208 n.43
logos 19, 67, 155–6

makros anthrōpos 43
Mamuralia 203 n.83

martyrdom 11–12, 173–83, 237 n.22, 237
n.24; *see also* sacrifice
metaphysical anchorage (*metaphysische
Veränkerung*): Windelband's notion
of 83
methodological individualism 87–8, 161
mimesis: Girard's notion of 94–8, 100,
103–4, 110, 151–3
mimetic rivalry: Girard's notion of 96–7,
151–2
modernity: crisis of 2, 10, 21–2, 71–3, 76,
108, 211 n.2
morphology 13, 147, 162
mundus imaginalis 71, 168

negative anthropology 97, 184, 221 n.16
nihilism 76–7, 79, 82, 86, 97, 101, 126, 218
n.69
nomos: Schmitt's concept of 93, 106–7,
130–1, 172

ontogeny 7, 164, 236 n.20
ontological dispositive 18–19, 159–61,
165–8
origin: Agamben's view of 149–58, 193 n.8;
Benjamin's view of 17–19; Girard's
view of 103–8, 149–58; Nietzsche's
view of 3–6

panopticism 162
parousia 106
pharmakon 153
philosophia perennis 140
phylogeny 164, 236 n.20
place: Aristotelian doctrine of 60
pluralism 11, 74, 117–18, 120–1, 128–32,
137, 140–1
polis 18, 122
politeia 122
pontifex maximus 35, 200 n.68, 200 n.69
post-secularity 10, 118–21, 131–4, 140–1,
228 n.34
potestas 24, 33, 126, 178, 181
principium rationis 157
pro patria mori 180–1, 187
Protestant Reformation 111, 123–4, 228 n.36

rationalization: process of 10, 68, 71–2,
76–7, 82–3, 95, 130, 212 n.7, 218 n.69

260   *Subject Index*

refugee camps 169–70

Regifugium ('the flight of the king') 34, 36–8, 201 n.72, 203 n.83

renovatio auspiciorum 33

representation: artistic 55–6, 61, 207 n.41; 208 n.43; Durkheim's view of 196 n.24; historiographic 6–9, 168; Hobbes's doctrine of 21–2, 59–60, 63–5, 194 n.15, 195 n.19, 209 n.70; of martyrdom 173–7; political 25–7, 30–2, 39–43, 67, 114, 204 n.92; Schmitt's doctrine of 20–1, 23–5, 58, 108, 111, 125, 135–6, 194 n.11, 197 n.27, 210 n.74, 227 n.31; *see also* royal doubles

res publica Christiana 117, 123

return of religion 11, 119

reverse perspective 55–6

rex nunquam moritur 30

rex sacrorum 35–6, 38–9, 42, 200 n.69, 201 n.70, 203 n.83

Roman law 180

romanitas 162

royal doubles 9, 25–8, 30–1, 41–2, 198 n.35

sacertas 28, 153

sacred: dialectic of the 145–9; Durkheim's view of the 145–6 Girard's view of the 103–11, 152–3, 158–9; and profane 122, 125, 140, 145, 154

sacrifice 12, 178–181, 201 n.69; Girard's view of 103–5, 107–9, 152–5, 158; of the king 37–42; political 11, 43, 90, 185–6, 189

sacrificial economy 9, 39–43

Salii 203 n.83

scapegoats 39, 202 n.79, 203 n.83; in Girard's mimetic theory 103–5, 152–5

secularization: process of 10, 57, 67, 71, 76–8, 89, 94, 109–12, 121, 125, 137, 163, 225 n.2, 228 n.34; *see also* razionalization

self-transcendence 22–3, 115, 190, 196 n.23

sin: Augustine's conception of 100–2

sovereign power 26, 30–2, 91, 157, 188–91; Agamben's notion of 18–19, 159, 170, 181; Foucault's notion of 186; Hobbes's notion of 32, 184

sovereignty 2, 18–19, 26–8, 39–43, 67–8, 170–2, 188, 190, 203 n.83; Girard's

view of 105; Hobbes's doctrine of 22, 59; and sacrifice 180–1, 238 n.40; Schmitt's doctrine of 23–4, 64, 197 n.27; *see also* sovereign power

space: Hobbes's definition of 60

Special Interrogation Plans (SIPs) 171

stasis 32, 195 n.19, 223 n.41

state of exception: Agamben's concept of 170–1

subjectivity: modern conception of 66–7, 109, 112, 127–8

subjectum 1, 155

supernumerary time 34, 36, 202 n.73; *see also* epagomenal days

symbol 8; political 64–5; sacrificial 152, 154–5; and social unity 22–3

teleology 3, 5, 73, 99, 160–1, 212 n.7, 233 n.46

Terminalia 34, 37, 199 n.61, 202 n.73

Terminus 200 n.62

territoriality 188–9

thanatopolitics 172

theodicy 10, 71, 94, 99–102, 153, 223 n.39

totem 22–3, 145–6, 197 n.26

transcendental signifier 64, 121, 128, 136, 152, 164, 166

transvaluation of all values (*Umwertung aller Werte*): Nietzsche's notion of 78–9

universalism 133, 136–7, 140–1; *see also* Western rationalism

value relation (*Wertbeziehung*): Rickert's notion of 80

wacah chan ('the world tree') 12

Wars of Religion 111, 123–4, 128, 195 n.19

Western rationalism 71, 133, 135, 137, 140–1

will to power 2, 4–5, 68

Wittgenstein's critique of Newtonian mechanics 151

Yggdrasil 12

Zentralgebiet ('central domain'): Schmitt's concept of 7, 113, 150

Zohar 12

CPSIA information can be obtained
at www.ICGtesting.com
Printed in the USA
LVHW081059081021
699915LV00013B/549